PHILIP JONES GRIFFITHS · NAOMI JAMES
MILES KINGTON · WILLIAM SHAWCROSS
NORMAN STONE · COLIN THUBRON
HUGO WILLIAMS

GREAT JOURNEYS

Photographs by
TOM OWEN EDMUNDS

A Touchstone Book
Published by Simon & Schuster Inc.
New York   London   Toronto   Sydney   Tokyo   Singapore

Endpapers: The Western Highlands of Guatemala

Frontispiece: Jiayuguan fort in the Gobi Desert, China

SIMON AND SCHUSTER/TOUCHSTONE
Simon & Schuster Building
Rockefeller Center
1230 Avenue of the Americas
New York, New York 10020

Copyright © 1990 by The Contributors and
BBC Enterprises Limited

Maps by Line & Line

First published in Great Britain in 1989
by BBC Books, a division of BBC Enterprises Limited
Woodlands, 80 Wood Lane, London W12 0TT

Set in 12 pt Monophoto Bembo
Printed and bound in England by Butler & Tanner Limited
Frome and London
Color separations by Technik Limited, Berkhamsted
Jacket printed by Belmont Press, Northampton

1   3   5   7   9   10   8   6   4   2
1   3   5   7   9   10   8   6   4   2   Pbk.

Library of Congress Cataloging in Publication Data
available upon request

ISBN: 0–671–70835–X
        0–671–70834–1   Pbk.

CONTENTS

THE SILK ROAD

Colin Thubron

Nothing prepares you for the place where China ends. For 2000 miles the Great Wall has lumbered westward from the Pacific and seems set to go on into eternity. Then, where the Qilian Mountains descend to the Gobi Desert, the Wall stumbles into a ruined cross-section between distant ranges. Beyond its last watch-tower a grey-blue chasm opens like a mantrap, and you gaze down 300 feet into an ice-grey river. And in the centre of the wide, blank pass which it spans – where the Gobi drifts northward in a violet stone-scattered plain – the Ming fortress of Jiayuguan puts a full stop to the traditional Chinese world.

It is an arid, glittering pile of a fortress. Above its battlements the gate-towers erupt in flurries of colour: vermilion pillars and upturned eaves. Its architects named it the 'Impregnable Pass under Heaven', and for two thousand years, under most dynasties, it marked the westernmost reach of China's Celestial Kingdom.

Even now it signalled a frontier in the Chinese mind – and in my own. I walked its ramparts with the feeling of patrolling an ineradicable divide. Within the Great Wall the Chinese located all known civilization – the harmony of a sacred empire ruled by the Son of Heaven. But the wastes beyond it were obscured in ignorance. Those who died there would be tormented by demons, and Buddhists were condemned to a cycle of repulsive reincarnations. Even now, when China's political frontier extends 1000 miles to the west, these lands are distrusted. They are near-empty. I had never been there. My memories were all of a China to the east – a land of deep homogeneity (despite surface diversity), steeped in its own order, hierarchical, self-sufficient.

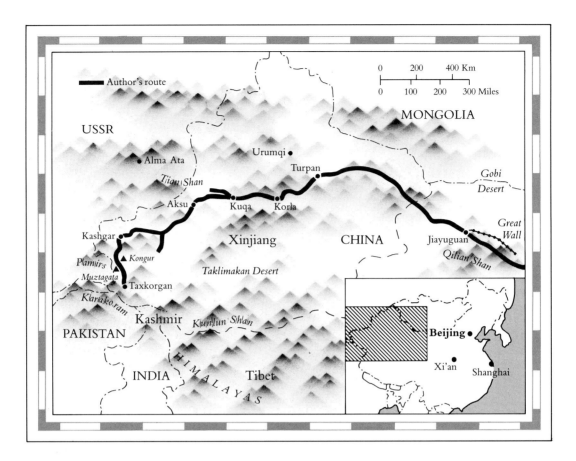

In the fort's tunnelled gateway, which opens out on the desert, the bricks were once covered with inscriptions: poems and laments in the elegant, mannered hand of exiled officials. Before passing out into the unknown, they had left their despair there. For this was China's 'mouth'. Those whom it vomited out did not return. People still describe those living beyond it as 'outside the mouth' – exiled, in some deep sense, beyond the pale of civilization.

Now I found the tunnel half blocked. It was lined with the bunks of workmen restoring the fort. The inscribed bricks had gone. I never discovered when or how. In the plain behind me the community of Jiayuguan – once a wretched garrison post – had mushroomed into a bungaloid steel-town. In front, the Gobi spread to faded hills and emptiness.

I was going where the Silk Road crossed into the unknown – 1500 miles through these formless backlands of China to the edge of the Russian Pamirs. It had moved north-west from the old imperial capital of Xi'an on the Yellow River, a cosmopolis of two million people at the height of the Tang dynasty in the seventh century. The railway from Xi'an (which I had taken) followed the ancient road up the harshly beautiful Gansu corridor – a road once crowded with the caravans of Central Asia: Persians, Indians, Sogdians, Arabs.

Looking west from Jiayuguan, I felt the childlike excitement of crossing a historical divide. Beyond the Wall lay somewhere not truly Chinese, but a vast, unwatered hinterland of Asia, the province of Xinjiang, huger than France, Spain and Germany combined. Its population was a sparse fourteen million, and more than half of these were not native Chinese at all, but Uighurs and Kazakhs – Turkic peoples who had not united since the death of Tamerlane.

I emerged from the gateway to face a falling sun. I should have been staring over desert; but in fact I was standing 2 feet in front of a camera crew. The real outer gate was unfilmable, closed by concrete blocks and the workers' dormitory; and we were shooting my exit from an (identical) inner gateway. So I gazed in spurious heroism over a desert which was not there.

Filming is haunted by these little infidelities. A travel documentary may have the appearance of randomness; but such is the expense of keeping a camera crew in the field, that we had arranged our journey months in advance, ordered Range Rovers, booked accommodation, hired cranes for overviews, camels, buses, guides. The film of our fantasies, we hoped, would move painlessly forward (as travel itself never does), by a seamless flow of premeditated locations.

In fact this was a pipe-dream. China broke rudely in. Officials at key points proved ignorant of us. Hotel rooms were unbooked. Drivers mutinied, camels ran amok, crane-arms shuddered to an unplanned stop.

A travel film, I began to realize, was different from a travel book in ways not always obvious. A book records a journey. A film creates it as it goes along. A book selectively mirrors and expresses something that has already happened. A film premeditatedly makes it happen, in a context which is imaginary. And the film journey, of course, is haunted by another journey – by the battle with angles and light, tripods and permits and officials. Over this unseen voyage preside the director and his crew; yet on screen only the presenter officially exists. A book's journey, by contrast, is best carried out alone. Solitude invites the fiercer excitement and exposure, the vulnerability to others, the chance intimacies. But a film is a group endeavour, in which the presenter is encased by his own people, his own world.

With forty-five pieces of luggage we piled into the train going west. These diluvian steam-engines – China is the last nation in the world to manufacture them – grumble along the desert's fringe 600 miles to the provincial capital of Urumqi, and there stop. Ours reeked of unequal privilege. High officials and officers sat in luxury, their seats covered with lace antimacassars. Potted plants wilted on their tables, and a deferential attendant periodically replenished the hot water thermos beneath. We sat in the lesser comfort of 'hard berth', while the poorest inhabited 'hard seat' in stoical, close-knit ranks. By night our dim-lit sleeping-carriage became a phantasmal aisle of projecting feet and snoring heads; by day it was companionable with minor officials and intelligentsia. Outside spread a country of red earth and sun-blackened stone, wrenched into miniature hills and canyons. Sometimes shallow gulleys split it end to end, where vanished floods had poured across our track.

I sat beside an army officer returning to Kashgar. For ten months of the year he lived separated from his wife and child, garrisoned in a city whose Turkic inhabitants were mutely hostile. The train was full of such people: soldiers and civilians transferred westward to this bitter province for a few years or a lifetime. They have been migrating west for the past four decades. Some, especially in the idealistic fifties, had

Above: Dawn t'ai chi exercise in Xi'an, ancient capital of China.

Right: Girl behind the bamboo curtain.

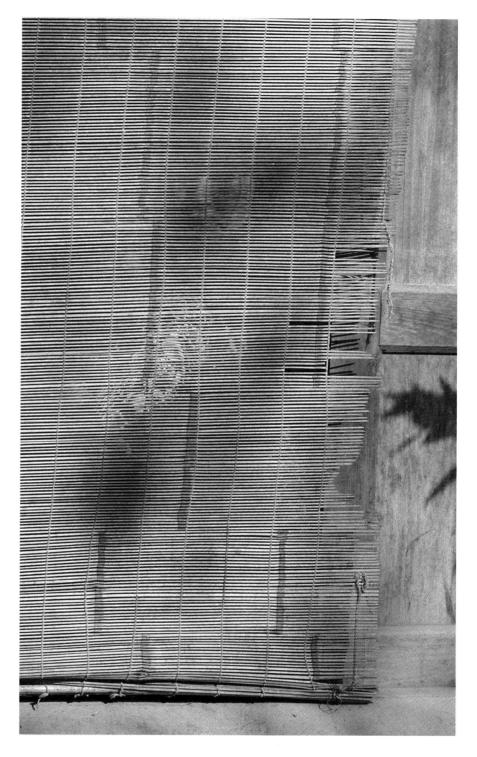

volunteered to come. But most were ordered from the overpopulated coastal cities and settled without choice 'outside the mouth', where millions of Red Guards – who had rampaged through the onset of the Cultural Revolution – were forcibly settled in 1967. Now, in more lenient times, the more enterprising exiles were finding ways to return, but a greater flow continued inexorably westward, sent without redress by their government. Fifty years ago the Turcomen comprised a vast majority in this province; but with the Chinese population close to six million they were already almost outnumbered. For two thousand years Chinese rule here has alternated with periods of independence, when the Silk Road oases flowered into miniature kingdoms or lapsed into stagnation. For forty years before the Communist victory in 1949, Xinjiang was governed by warlords. Only now, for the first time, does the Chinese presence threaten to overwhelm by sheer numbers.

It was the Turkic peoples who made the Silk Road work – the subjects of oasis cities strung through the core of Asia. The route went on for nearly 5000 miles, linking successive Chinese capitals to the Mediterranean, periodically adapting to the fall of an empire or a nomad upsurge. For more than two thousand years the trade continued, in spices, metals, cloth, horses, jade. Above all, to the West, came the silks whose manufacture was a long-kept secret (the Romans thought it grew on trees like floss) together with ceramics, lacquer and the art of paper-making; while eastward went Roman gold and glass, Indian spices and cotton, and a miasma of products from lands in between.

In times of unrest the caravans would plod south through the sparse oases along the foot of the Kunlun Mountains, protected from bandits by uninhabitable desert. But more often, when the nomads in the Tian Shan grasslands were quiescent, merchants would thread the larger cities of the great northern route – Turpan, Korla, Kuqa, Aksu – and at last come to Kashgar.

Turpan lies where the Tian Shan, the 'Heaven Mountains', overlook deepening wilderness. In July it is so hot that an egg buried in the sand will be soft-boiled within minutes. In winter it is the coldest region in China. The train dropped me at a run-down station, and I approached the town over a gravel-strewn plain. The divide between sand and green, desert and sown, lay precise as a crayon-stroke across the flats. Backed by ranges of glaring mountains, the oasis descended to the deepest waterless region on earth. But as I wandered its suburbs, they were filled by the inexplicable glitter and splash of water. The irrigation channels brimmed, the pools shone. The trellised walks sagged with vines, and an autumn glut of melons and apricots was about. In the perforated brick huts along the fields dangled tiers of harvested grapes which were drying into raisins.

This sense of relaxed plenitude was echoed in the people. They were Muslim Uighurs. They were burlier than the true Chinese, but moved with an easy grace and ebullience. Their eyes glittered wider in more heavy-featured faces. Some were startlingly pale. Compared to the muted greys and blues of Chinese clothes, the women were flamboyant in scarlet headscarves and velvet dresses. Their ears dropped pendants of imitation rubies, and their eyebrows were often thick with kohl.

Now, in September, half the families were camped out in their courtyards (in the fiercest heat they retreat to underground rooms). Their children bathed naked and shouting in the pools, and an old nomad habit attached these people to their carts and horses. In the bazaars they showed an opportunistic cunning, and they still sang and danced in a sensuous overflow from ordinary life.

The Uighur and the Chinese are deeply unlike. Steeped in the legacy of Confucius (who thought dancing absurd), Chinese life is conventional, practical, collective; whereas the Uighur, whose people grew up in the flux of trade and wandering, are mercurial, easy-going, individualistic. They are culturally inferior – the officer on the train had said – because of their remoteness from the centre, Beijing. But Beijing was only *his* centre, not theirs, and I watched them with the perverse sympathy of an Englishman for the colonized underdog. Their antagonism to the Chinese had erupted in periodic riots: the worst reputedly left several hundred dead in 1981.

Whereas the Chinese universe is a network of outer and internal constraints – they fear disorder, want to impose system – the Uighur seem to live in a random hedonism. Compared to the Chinese, they are free. Theirs seems a Middle Eastern world, at once instinctual and canny. To the Chinese esteem for security, they oppose an anarchic opportunism: less admirable, perhaps, and more lovable.

The Uighur have inherited complex traditions. A Turkic people, they moved south from Outer Mongolia and allied themselves with the Tang dynasty Chinese in the seventh century. Their script is Arabic, borrowed from Persian peoples whom they absorbed along the Silk Road soon afterwards. By the twelfth century they had converted to Islam, and were settled, and for centuries their language was the merchant's lingua franca throughout Central Asia. In Turpan even the *karez* irrigation system – an arterial mass of tunnels pouring down from the mountains – was learnt from lands to the west.

These *karez*, although dug only a few centuries ago, were probably copied from a Persian system three thousand years old. In Turpan alone there were more than four hundred of them. They resembled horizontal wells. All along their length they were betrayed by a series of mounds, like the run of some monstrous mole, where the shafts for digging and cleaning them had left their detritus on the surface. At their head, near the base of foothills, they locate water more than 200 feet underground, and channel it for as long as 10 miles downhill on a slow gradient to the oasis.

I descended by a wooden pulley which farmers dragged to a well opening. An ox, heaving at the windlass ropes, lowered me through its gloom. The shaft's sides were crumbling and flecked with stones. My feet landed in water still running fast and cold. One of the farmers followed me: a slight man with an open, boyish face. 'I was working in these places with my father, as soon as I was born. . . .'

The ceiling dropped so low that I went crouched like a hunchback. Our torch-light wavered over walls soft as putty. Once or twice a shoal of tiny, blind fish flickered in front of us. Otherwise there was nothing, only the subterranean river – the snow-melt from unimaginable mountains – curling icy round our ankles and disappearing beyond the ripples in our torch-beams. Here and there the makers of this labyrinth had altered course or joined some other channel, and sometimes the

In its progress westward the Silk Road soon leaves the Chinese
heartland, entering the barbarian wastelands of the Gobi Desert at the
Ming dynasty fortress at Jiayuguan, the last outpost of China's
Celestial Kingdom.

Left: In backstreet Xi'an a taste of old Han China still survives.

corridor closed in so tightly that it was impossible to turn. Our light wobbled over walls of coagulated stones which dropped into the water at a touch. They were weirdly impressive. The water's rustle echoed ahead of us. We might have been wading down the arteries of some organism half alive. How old was it?

'Two thousand years,' the man said, not knowing.

'And whose invention was it? The Chinese?'

'I'm not sure,' said his voice out of darkness. 'Only the old people know. My father would know.' Then a Uighur pride surfaced. 'But no . . . not the Chinese. No. Some older people here. Perhaps it came from Iraq, or maybe Iran. Or perhaps it was the Uighur made it. I don't know. . . .'

The channel bed came soft underfoot. It lifted momentarily as we passed the vacant eye of each shaft above us. Only near its end the walls became matted in white roots, which flowed like hair in the current under our feet, and toads appeared, and a whining gauze of flies.

Once I asked him: did he know that the water from the mountains was gradually failing? Were the farmers worried? But he had not heard of it.

In fact the climate of all this region has fluctuated violently. Towns which were flourishing around AD 300 – a period of Chinese recession, when the Silk Road had broken up into city-states – now lie ruined 80 miles into the desert. Their heyday was followed by a time of drastic aridity, which eased again after the ninth century. Then, from the sixteenth century onward, the process reversed. The rainfall faded. The mountain glaciers which fed the oasis rivers decreased by almost half. And now the drought is accelerating.

On the edge of Turpan, the ruins of Gaochang drastically illustrate this flux, and the tides of conquest too. I found a stoneless city, ringed by 4 miles of ramparts. Its palaces and temples had compacted into wind-smoothed stubs and cones, like plasticine reductions of themselves, with scarcely a detail or coherent shape remaining. They were pale and colourless as the earth from which they sprang. They seemed, in fact, to be little more than the earth reared upright, half formed, then forgotten.

But two thousand years ago Gaochang was laid out by the conquering Chinese, and their classic pattern of grid streets, inner and outer city, still showed faintly through the rubble of fifteen later centuries. The corpses of a Tang dynasty couple lay unnervingly complete in a nearby grave. Their limbs were indecently splayed, their heads thrown back and their dried clothes stuck to their bones. Now Uighur villagers propped their hovels against the city's ramparts, which had split into hunks and foundered to the ground.

By the tenth century the city was the Uighur capital: head of an independent kingdom, half settled, half nomad. At this time, before their conversion to Islam in the next two centuries, they oversaw a state of vigorously contending cultures, and the town was still scattered with the remains of Buddhist stupas, Persian-style tombs and the monasteries of Nestorian Christians. Earlier this century the villagers used to unearth fragments of statuary – figures shaped through the Hellenism imported to Central Asia by Alexander the Great: their Buddhas' features touched by those of Apollo. But at last the Muslims invaded, the wells ran dry, and the city began to die.

I discovered an old merchant, Yol Dashe, near the bazaar in Turpan. He was rumoured to be a hundred years old and had travelled the Silk Road more than seventy years before, leading a train of donkeys to Kashgar in the spring. But he could remember almost nothing. In the courtyard of his home, hung with vines and stray electric wires, he sat between a haggard wife and a younger brother. His tongue stuck swollen and inarticulate between his lips, and his eyes seemed to be looking at nothing any more. Sometimes he would begin a sentence which would fade away instantly with his memory. And often his brother would answer for him, or his wife intrude with hectic versions of her own. In the viewfinder of our camera these three faces seemed to make a triptych of timeless dignity. But the ramble of their Uighur speech grew untranslatable, and only when we returned with the recordings to London did we discover that they were all cantankerously contradicting the old man, or speaking in his place, aided by a flowery interpreter. Our dialogue went, in part, thus:

THUBRON Do you still remember what you did when you were young?

YOL DASHE I travelled ... travelled....

UIGHUR INTERPRETER He looks as if he'll remember.

WIFE When he was twenty years old he travelled from Kashgar and lost all his possessions, which were stolen by robbers on the way to Turpan. He wept and suffered a lot. At last he managed to reach Turpan and was lucky enough to meet and marry me....

THUBRON (to Yol Dashe) How was your journey? The desert is said to be very stormy? Is that true?

INTERPRETER We have been told that the desert is a very horrifying, frightening and treacherous place, a hub of barbarous robbery and thieves. Is that so? Did you meet any danger like that?

YOL DASHE No.

WIFE If he were healthy and feeling well enough he would talk without stopping. But today his brain is not working.... Why don't you ask him if he wants to have dinner?

YOL DASHE I'll tell what I can recall.

WIFE Why don't you tell them that in the past travelling was very hard and dangerous, but as a result of the leadership of the Communist Party it is now very easy and very comfortable to go by bus? Why are you mumbling and can't say anything?

YOL DASHE I'm trying to organize what I want to say. Don't pester me.

WIFE Go on then, don't mumble.

YOL DASHE The Silk Road was very sandy and barren. No plants, no trees or grass.

WIFE But as a result of the leadership of the Party, everything is now changed to green.... He used to speak quite well in the past but now his brain is exhausted.

BROTHER He is too old to talk as we expected.

WIFE Yes. He is now very old. Ah, our most gracious Allah, Allah....

Top: Gobi Desert dunes near Dunhuang. Above: Buzghashi, *a mounted tug-of-war over a decapitated sheep carcass.*

Top: The oasis town of Kashgar. Above: A man and his wife going to market.

Westward from Turpan the ancient route runs 800 miles to Kashgar along the foot of the Heaven Mountains. There is no rail, only a road under intermittent repair, travelled by a few buses and lorries carrying coal or timber. On one side, on a clear day, snow-peaks litter the sky; on the other the Taklimakan Desert drifts from gravelly plains into the sand dunes of a storm-haunted wilderness. It is a schizophrenic landscape. Our bus jolted and roared, partaking of neither country. The road dribbled between a wintry privacy of mountains and a naked horizon of sand. Until the lure of both became unbearable.

We defected north into the Tian Shan for a few days, on another bus. Of the twin dangers between which the Silk Road went – desert and mountains – the mountains were the less predictable. Beyond their barren foothills, split by gulleys where flash-floods poured, rose intermittent grasslands and belts of pine: the old terrain of nomads.

Here are the summer grasslands of the Kazakhs, a Turkic people who assimilated Mongol and other blood during centuries of nomad wars. In the lower valleys their winter homes were bright with carpets and felt rugs, but half deserted. Their flocks and herds had gone up into the pastures above us, and we found their summer yurts pitched in a camp of halcyon solitude. Horses and cattle drifted over the grasslands, with a few camels.

This was the semi-nomadic life – winter houses, summer tents – which the Uighur had finally abandoned eight hundred years before. Its trade and pleasure centred on the horse. Where a long valley formed a natural stadium under the mountains, two teams of riders plunged into a barbaric game of *buzghashi* – a mounted tug-of-war over the carcass of a freshly-killed sheep. They ripped it off the ground, tore it from one another's hands, coalesced into a wrestling mob of backs and fetlocks until somebody broke away with it. Then they circled the valley in a whooping steeplechase, before it was flung down again where they had begun.

At evening they were robustly hospitable. They regaled us with mare's milk, batter fried in sheep's fat, improvised songs. Under their shabby caps or scarves the moon faces showed burnished Mongol cheekbones, and grinned fiercely. Outside, the mares loitered by their tethered foals, and a few men were smoking in the dying light. A cart was being loaded for the descent to winter valleys.

This mobility continues from deep habit. When their way of life was threatened twenty-five years ago, sixty thousand Kazakhs simply moved across the border into the Soviet Union and settled among their kinsmen in Kazakhstan. Their people's lives, I imagined, were the ultimate celebration of individualism – the least Chinese existence in China. But that evening in his yurt – a womb of red willow and carpeted walls – the herdsman I questioned fidgeted anxiously, slopping milk from a ladle into a bowl, over and over. Their lives were hard, he said. In summer they wandered; in winter they just survived, hibernating with their herds as best they could.

'But would you prefer city life?'

He said: 'We know nothing about working in the city. We've lived like this since childhood. So I prefer the nomad way.'

'And what of your children?'

The ladle went on fidgeting. 'I want them to go to the city and find jobs there. . . . Otherwise they will gain nothing here – and become the same as me.'

Was this, I wondered, the start of their end? Perhaps this was how the Uighur had felt eight centuries ago, drifting into the oases towns.

I said: 'Do most of your people feel the same as you do?'

He looked at me with an odd, wan emptiness, and said: 'The same.'

The road to Kashgar from Turpan, which had taken the old merchant Yol Dashe two months to complete, can be travelled in four days now – although we spent three weeks along it. The buses are filled by people plying small trade, or visiting relatives. They move between oases which span the way like giant stepping-stones – towns whose factories and offices, filled with Chinese workers, sit in a sprawling bed of wheat, rice and cotton fields, farmed by the Uighur and fed by melted snows from the mountains to the north. For centuries, in times of Chinese recession, these places took their freedom and stayed rich. A seventh-century pilgrim described the oasis-kingdom of Kuqa as a Buddhist paradise, its kings pious and peaceful, its orchards brimming. 'The ground is rich in minerals – gold, copper, iron, lead and tin. The air is soft and the people honest. . . . They excel other countries in playing the lute and pipe. They clothe themselves with ornamental garments of silk and embroidery.'

Some 50 miles to Kuqa's west, where the Muzart river went through empty hills, we reached a monastery complex which had flourished at this time: the cave-sanctuaries of Kyzil, the oldest Buddhist shrines in China. They hung secluded in a cliff of lustreless brown tufa – more than two hundred of them – suspended high and defensive like the pueblos of American Indians. Some were inaccessible. Others I could reach only by ropes or ladders.

I found myself in small, rectangular sanctuaries at whose end a sculptured or painted Buddha had once focused adoration. Now there remained only a niche or the trace of a mandorla faded in the stone, and a little ambulatory behind. Sometimes, still visible on its wall, a frescoed Buddha lay in his last sleep, watched by mourning disciples as he receded from them into paradise.

The shrines had been frescoed as early as the third century, and still arched above in haunting tints of green and blue. Across their vaulted ceilings the Buddha, in previous incarnations, sacrificed himself for animals and men. In the lunettes over the doors he presided with his followers in a senate of haloed heads and oxidized robes. Over the walls he passed through his earthly career, eerie with miracles. As I looked at them, they seemed to portray a world unimaginably remote. They appeared at once delicate and savage.

They came from centuries when a high Buddhist culture in all this region percolated along the Silk Road into the heart of China, and at last Japan, while Chinese pilgrims began to venture the other way into the holy land of India. The monasteries grew rich on the donations of local rulers and merchants, who – in attitudes of smug supplication – were painted into the murals they commissioned. The monks became landowners and money-lenders. They lived well; until, in the twelfth century, Islam arrived with the sword.

In north-west China the Silk Road passes through deserts and mountains dominated by Muslim peoples of Turkic origin. Kashgar, the main town, is populated mainly by Uighurs and mosques abound in the smallest back streets.

I found the scars of Muslim iconoclasm everywhere. The celestial army of Buddhas which sat along the ceilings – the same figures repeated, over and over – had been systematically defaced. The gold of their robes was hacked away. Later Red Guards, drunk with their own faith, had slashed the faces of others. And most flagrant of all, the German archaeologist Albert von Le Coq had sawn away whole panels for transport to Berlin in 1906, leaving behind brutal, empty rectangles.

An ancient force of belief survives. It was hard to look at the chapels, or at the Elysian valley beneath, without a creeping wonder. For seven centuries these corrupted monks had limned their faith on to the plaster, reproducing the same saints and Buddhas, the same icons of promise and transmigration, on and on, until they had turned the whole mountain into a pious echo-chamber. Perhaps they felt that the very repetition of a figure made it true. Yet in the end their frescoed certainties had been defaced as heresy or abducted as art, stranding in my imagination whole generations dedicated to entering a vanished paradise.

The way westward went through deepening wasteland. Sometimes the mountain foothills broke loose from their ranges, crossed the road and scattered the desert with solitary cones. More often the sands were pimpled by millions of tiny hillocks, where the roots of tamarisk or camel-thorn, isolated by the floods which had swirled between, sent up green spikes in a sea of piedmont gravel.

On our bus I sat beside a bitter-faced man who had been ordered west in the fifties, with thousands of others. He had been assigned work as a truck-driver, which bored him, and longed hopelessly to return. He found the Uighur incomprehensible and he could not speak a sentence of their tongue. They were still rebellious, he said. They would like to drive the Chinese back 'inside the mouth'; yet could not progress without them.

This gulf between the races stays unbridged. From time to time, in the villages we passed, the divide was flagrant between the drab cottage-rows of the Chinese and the flat-roofed Uighur dwellings with their brushwood stockades and rush of chickens. Even their cemeteries stood on opposite sides of the road. The Uighur tombs looked almost celebratory, gay with domes and balustrades. But the Chinese graves were mounded together in a peculiar pathos: piles of dust and improvised memorial stones.

The Chinese say that 'the falling leaf returns to the roots of the tree' – that it is good to die where you were born. But these people did not. They came from the eastern provinces – volunteer or forced, in the fifties and sixties – and perished here in exile while constructing roads and factories, laying telegraph lines, driving lorries. Their graves were desolately poor. Some, in homesickness, had been laid facing east, back to the motherland. Often their dead had been buried by their work unit because their families were far away to the east and they had nobody else to inter them.

Their inscriptions, as I wandered amongst them, seemed relentlessly practical – statistics of work and life span – as if these were the graves merely of molecules in the social body. (But the body had not sustained them.) 'Comrade Liu Menglu: died while here on duty at the age of 36. . . . Comrade Xu Huilin: born in Shanghai. Died in a work accident. . . . A driver of the 2nd Construction Company. . . . Xinjiang

Though fiercely independent in spirit the fair-skinned Uighur have absorbed some Chinese influences, including the use of chop-sticks and making noodles.

Pages 28 and 29: However, the omnipresent kebab stalls in Kashgar attest to a culture more Middle Eastern than oriental.

Production and Construction Corps.... Died 1974 at the age of 25 in the collapse of a flooded mine.... Ji Feng [this, the desecrated grave of a soldier] In defence of Chairman Mao's revolutionary line, gave up his life gloriously on 22 February 1969. ... Comrade.... Aged 22.... Duty.... Kashgar Anti-Revisionist Mine Unit.... Comrade.... Died....'

Our interpreter, usually the gentlest of women, was developing plans to strangle our Uighur guide. He was all that was worst in the Uighur: self-centred, disingenuous and bursting with surplus machismo. Above all he had contracted the Chinese preoccupation with food (a national obsession greater than in other famine-stricken countries) and ate at every halting-place. While we interviewed Uighur farmers, he would whisk away their grapes with a proprietory flourish; before we left the Kazakhs, he had commandeered half a sheep from them. His booty was enormous. But at every other site, where he had once promised arrangements – rooms, permits, transport – he became a Falstaff of evasiveness and incompetence.

We had to bring him to book one evening, in a room fidgeting with hostile camera crew. As he entered, secreting self-importance, our interpreter watched him with muted fury. He sat down opposite her. As the director, with studied restraint, outlined his shortcomings, she faithfully interpreted them.

But as he replied, a change came over him. His voice dwindled into melodious pathos. He looked flaccid and spent. His hands collapsed between his knees. 'It is so difficult,' he cried. 'When I telephone to make arrangements, I can't know if my wishes will be carried out. I haven't been able to oversee everything personally. You see, I'm having trouble in my home....'

He carried on like this for twenty minutes (he was once a professional actor), elaborating and ornamenting his distress. Our interpreter's eyes grew soft and round as she translated. 'And I know I am too fat,' he lamented, 'to follow you all about ... you are so active....'

By now her voice, as she interpreted, had melted into helpless solicitude. As his perorations and sorrows became longer, her translations grew shorter. She shrank away from him into private contrition. For the rest of our journey she never mentioned him at all.

Again the road, in its confinement, became unbearable, and the emptiness of the desert pulled us south for four days. All along the eastern Silk Route the desert is a pervasive presence. Looking south, you see nothing but a stone-littered plain and a level skyline, but know that beyond this the gravel recedes before a purer deadness of sand, one of the most dangerous voids on earth, which the Uighur call Taklimakan, 'You Enter and Never Return'. The early caravans never crossed this, and nor would we. We planned simply to enter the stoneless sands for a while, and momentarily experience the desolation so feared by early travellers.

But it was hard to reach. We took Range Rovers to a nearby town for the night, then blundered on next day to a village of wheat and straggling orchards, protected from the wilderness by a forest of desiccated willows. By the afternoon we were pushing through these ghostly woods – a haunt of wolves and wild boar – in a pall of fine sand. The forest seemed to age as we advanced. Its trees writhed in colourless confusion, their trunks withered under a shroud of etiolated leaves. By dusk we had reached our base camp where some twenty officials, labourers and herdsmen had assembled seven Bactrian camels and a water-truck.

Camels are the only beasts which can negotiate this wilderness. Horses' hooves scorch in the sands and donkeys founder. But the camel can march for two weeks without water, and only starts to sweat in a temperature at which a man would be dead. The stilt-like legs lift its body above the sand's surface heat, and its padded feet dissipate its weight as they strike the surface, as if it were shod in snow-shoes.

Ours were disparate animals. One was young and unbroken; another a natural leader, handsome and cream-coloured. But the rest made up a rabid and contemptuous gang. They kicked and bit in all directions; they spat gobs of yellow froth. Even in profile, they were majestically ridiculous. At one end was a short, absurd, twisted tail. At the other, above the curve of the shaggy neck, rose a head of feminine arrogance, with pale-lashed eyes and a punkish tuft of hair sprouting far back on the forehead.

Next morning saw the extravagant launching of twin journeys: the filmed and the real. The first was like the ghost of the second – calmer, stranger. In the camera's eye I marched through a wobbling heat-haze (redoubled by telephoto lens) with a Uighur guide and a trio of camels. We looked theatrically romantic. The willow forest disintegrated around us into a scatter of tamarisk. The earth was as fine as talcum powder. Even the camels' hooves left no sharp trace in it, only blurred furrows of dust. Within a few miles the last trees had died into mounds of roots and splintered bark, and we crossed the track of a dried river. Its reeds crackled and broke at our touch; our feet crunched through the pastry-crust of its bed. We were making for a horizon of pure sand – a film-maker's plaything – and now moved across the wastes with the cinematic splendour of Man in Wilderness.

But the real journey, of course, was different. I and my guide were not alone at all. We were vanguard to another, larger camel-train, complete with director, camera crew, Mandarin interpreter, Uighur interpreter and two cameleers. We had barely started filming our desert dream before reality broke boorishly in. Our camels were not true pack-animals at all, but herd camels, and they resented their loads. Suddenly they tore loose in bellowing terror, and ran amok. Their drivers lost control. First one beast then another thundered away across the sand, their leading ropes broken or trailing, scattering baggage and stores as they went. It was perfect *cinéma-vérité*. But we could not film it because our cameras were strapped to their backs.

So we plodded on stoically to the stark horizon of dunes, while our cameleers recaptured their charges far away, one by one. The desert purified itself round us. The shrubs vanished. The sand underfoot paled to gold, silvered with flecks of mica. Once a strange camel appeared out of nowhere and followed us pathetically. It looked close to exhaustion, its humps drained and flattened.

This desert has been named the harshest on earth. The explorer Aurel Stein, who travelled here early this century, thought Arabia tame by comparison. At its heart is

a wilderness utterly dead, 600 miles long by 250 miles wide. Its dunes can reach 300 feet. Sometimes freak hurricanes have churned whole ranges of them into a sky grown black as midnight, and overwhelmed caravans travelling too close, mummifying their bodies under sand. 'When these winds arise,' wrote a Chinese pilgrim in the seventh century, 'both man and beast become confused and forgetful, and there they remain perfectly disabled. At times, sad and plaintive notes are heard and piteous cries, so that between the sights and sounds of the desert, men get confused and know not whither they go. Hence there are so many who perish on the journey. But it is all the work of demons and evil spirits.'

On windless nights, in sharp temperature changes, the dunes shift with fantastical noises, as if invisible caravans were passing. So, wrote Marco Polo, 'the stray traveller will hear as it were the tramp and hum of a great cavalcade of people away from the real line of march, and taking this to be their own company they will follow the sound: and when day breaks they find that a cheat has been put upon them and that they are in an ill plight. Even in daytime one hears those spirits talking....'

The people most natural to this changeful country were not the Chinese, who fear or despise nomadism, but the Turkic Uighur. The Chinese try to impose system on the land, but the Uighur traditionally adapted to it, as my guide did, who raided its fringes to hunt hares.

By evening we were overlooking its heart: a petrified sea. It bled whitely into a whitened sky. I followed its dune-lips with my guide and camels while the camera tracked us. Occasionally we crossed some alkaline flat or descended a miniature valley-side of eerie smoothness. The lit shapes in this changeless sand became hypnotic: hard-edged domes and chiaroscuro curves. But the director, sensitive to bombast, watched us unhappily. Wherever he looked there was cliché: skyline camels, shimmering dunes, questing Englishman, even (by now) a sunset.

Then reality barged in again. As we ascended a long dune, the sands began to slither under us. We looked (I supposed) heroically purposeful. But the gradient was too steep. One by one, like dominoes, the camels foundered to their knees, lurched upright again, flailed the sand into commotion, collapsed. The guide heaved on the leading beast, while I blundered among the others, trying to beat them to their feet with a flimsy stick. One was defecating into the sand, but I only saw this as I struck it – an abuse recorded on camera. Another clambered to the summit, then lashed out with its forelegs and lacerated the guide's shin.

Darkness brought no respite from them. All night they fed on dried foliage which they had carried. For hours, as I lay under a makeshift shelter, the munch and crash of their gorging kept me awake, and the desert seemed filled with twin humps profiled against the sky as they sauntered back and forth. Near dawn one of the tent poles above us attracted the largest beast, and in another lost moment of *cinéma-vérité* it sank its teeth into the wood and brought the whole tent crashing over us.

All morning and afternoon, as we returned, the camels cemented their reputation. They rioted and bolted in a renewed litter of thrown-off baggage. The Uighur broke into surly cliques. My guide, limping from his damaged leg, needed to mount; but the camel-drivers refused. He was not from their village. If he let a camel strike him, it was no concern of theirs. Finally they mutinied, refused to await our filming, and rode back alone with their delinquent charges in a trail of rebellion and dust.

The epic remoteness of Kashgar suggests a place in the mind rather than on a map. Here, by late September, we had arrived at a city whose people were 90 per cent Muslim – Uighur, Kirgiz, Tajik – and whose heart resembled Isfahan or Herat more than any Chinese town. Its streets curved among porticoed and balconied houses, and were filled with the scarlet canopies of horse- and donkey-carts, whose harnesses shook with bells. The feel was all of a landlocked Islam. The men were hardy oasis farmers; their women went veiled in brown calico. On the gaunt cliffs where the inner city stood, the alleys twined about each other in a skein of clay and straw, crudely whitewashed, and doors left ajar disclosed courtyards of Damascene intimacy: flowering trees, gossipers, bicycles. It was in back streets like these that I would find myself searching for the city's heart, as if the lanes were arteries leading to some precise and all-explaining core. But of course they did not. Their diffused secrecy, the domestic labyrinth, was itself the heart.

Even before the Cultural Revolution, whose proselytizing atheism left bitter memories, the most powerful focus of Turkic unity was the mosque, and on Friday I watched resurgent believers fill up the huge enclosure of the Id Kah, the largest in China. They came by lorry and on foot – some two thousand of them: boys, young men, and sashed and booted ancients whose eyes stared bloodshot above scrappy beards. All across the poplar-sown courtyard, over the rush matting beneath the porticoes, inside the sanctuary under a ceiling of carved wood dangling microphones and old lamps, the bodies knelt in murmuring unison – stood, prostrated, stood again. As they bent, their coats eased up from lines of belts dangling decorated Uighur knives.

There could be no more powerful symbol of religious unity, I thought, yet something was disquieting too. Its fervour was sternly focused, masculine. Women were relegated to the gates. Some greeted the departure of the faithful by holding out loaves and plates of sugar. The older men made a show of spitting on these as they left, and the food was then carried back home to be eaten by the sick.

Yet for a decade after 1966 all religious activity and private trade had been suppressed. An imam, seated in the mosque after prayer, remembered the Cultural Revolution with fear. 'Some of our mosques were demolished,' he said, 'and all signs of Islam were extirpated. The Red Guards burnt our Korans. Only this mosque was saved from them by the intervention of the government.'

'And what happened to you and the other imams?'

'We just stayed in our homes. We prayed in secret.'

Above the main street one of the last public statues of Mao Tse-tung, 60 feet high and built of granite, lifts an avuncular hand over the city he desecrated. In this stronghold of devotion the statue is a double insult – an offence against the Muslim abhorrence of images and an insult to the Uighur sense of nationhood. But when the local authorities moved to blow it up they realized that detonations would threaten nearby buildings; and when they tried to saw it down they encountered a core of solid steel.

But the Maoist legacy has gone now – except in angered memory – and the slogans washed away. The communes have been disbanded, and a market economy revived. On Sundays more than fifty thousand Uighur stream into the bazaar for an orgy of free enterprise. The streets jam with carts pulled by tractors, horses and donkeys, where the women huddle laughing together, their veils thrown back. The market is subdivided into improvised streets like any Middle Eastern souk: spices, harnesses, rock salt, offal, poplar wood, cummin, wool, skins. But compared to any Arab bazaar, it is oddly quiet. People sit in the dust. The loudest sounds are not human but animal: the croaking of trussed hens, the bellowing of cattle. In this slow world, where time is less important than money, a girl wanders vacantly with a netted basket of pigeons, hoping she may sell two; and old men linger all day peddling a column of sesame-sprinkled bread or a handful of peppers.

At the horse and cattle market I found thousands of animals tethered by breed in a cloud of lowing, braying, roaring, whinneying. I could have bought a two-year-old horse for £200 or a handsome white camel (but I'd had enough of camels) for £140. Here was a chaotic reincarnation of the old Uighur mobility and nomadism. Down an improvised aisle between the crowds the horses were galloped by their vendors in a caracole of dust. They were small, stocky mounts from the Ili and Barkol regions near the Russian and Mongolian borders. The Ili were shapely and docile. But the Barkol horses were kin to those on which the Huns had overrun the Roman Empire. They could travel 100 miles a day, but 'the holes in their hearts are crooked', as the Chinese say. They were wily and vicious.

'The Ili is usually bigger,' an old horse-dealer told me, 'and it doesn't run so smoothly, because the Ili country is stony. But if you ride a Barkol you won't feel anything, its leg movements are so finely attuned – the Barkol earth is soft sand.'

This man acted as a go-between when traders could not agree a sale, completing his deals in a gale of bullying and cajoling, and charging each man 5 per cent. In this hard trade, he was respected. He filled people with a sense of urgency. 'This man is keen on your horse,' he would say, seizing the vendor's hand, 'even if it's uncontrollable when harnessed to a cart. Let Allah protect him from being eaten by your horse! Would you please accept 1100 kwai for it?'

'My horse is fine with carts,' the vendor would reply robustly. 'Just bring me your cart and I'll harness it up, by Allah. . . .'

Then the middleman would clasp the buyer's hand. 'Why not offer 1200 kwai? Let's reach agreement. Don't be stubborn. . . .'

And usually, effecting a compromise, he would touch the palms of both men's hands to the earth in ancient token of fidelity to their word.

Kashgar is the last great oasis within China. From here the ancient Silk Road rises into the ramparts of the Russian Pamirs, one path splitting off north to Samarkand, the other dipping south-west across northern Afghanistan, before they reunite at last near the frontiers of Iran, and run for another 2000 miles to the Mediterranean.

We found a truck carrying porcelain, cloth (and contraband pearls) to the Pakistani border. Pakistani merchants negotiate these in Kashgar and collect them from Chinese lorries which reach their own frontier along the Silk Road, metalled only a month before, where it levers itself west into the mountains. The Soviet and Afghan frontiers are closed here, and the trade with Pakistan is still small, the border only opened a few years ago. The Chinese export silks, porcelain and simple agricultural tools; while the Pakistanis bring their own fabrics in exchange, together with Uzbek silks from the Soviet Union.

As the road entered the first, treeless Pamir valley, I seemed to be alighting on another planet, and understood why the Chinese feared it. It is one of the bleakest regions on earth. Over the millennia the geological upthrust of the Himalayas – they are still rising more than 2 inches a year – has cut it off from the southern monsoons and shriven it into a searly beautiful wasteland. Its few nomads hibernate for half the year, and its animals have grown huge to counteract the cold – the colossal bear called *ursus torquatus,* the giant yak, the Marco Polo sheep, biggest in the world, whose horns measure 5 feet.

We climbed through steepening defiles – a mineral void of glittering schist and cracked boulders and dust. White crags dangled 300 feet above the road, or had crashed and slid across it in shaley floods to slop into the stone-coloured river on the far side. Behind its clefts loomed the flanks of mountains, dusted with early snows. It was a land only of stone – stone towering solid above, fragmented and pulverized below.

Then the 25,300-foot Mount Kongur appeared, piled on itself in white shelves above a glacial lake, and soon we were travelling beneath a glimmering dinosaur's back of peaks. Then the road turned beside an alluvial plain, part lake, part desert. The wind had smoothed its sand over the nearby mountains, turning them to ghosts. And beyond the snow-mass of Muztagata we entered the valley of Taxkorgan, the last town in the west.

It is the capital of a little Tajik province whose inhabitants number only 30,000. As long ago as the first century it was known to the Romans as a trade emporium. From its citadel – a blistered maze of rubble and mud – we gazed up a valley of sudden pastureland, which ran in a giant corridor between the mountains, and travelled on for a few hours southward. Once we passed a ruined caravanserai where the skeletons of unknown men – slaughtered in battle, the local people say – still nestled in their stone-filled graves.

At last we came to where the thin Wakan corridor linked China with Afghanistan 40 miles on. We saw no movement on its track. A river wound in sterile grandeur under the mountains. A single camel train followed it. Nothing blurred this stark clarity of land but a weft of yellowing grass. Here, where half the great Asian ranges converged in unearthly stillness, we made a halt. To our east the Tian Shan and Kunlun came circling out of China. In the south, just beyond the Pakistan frontier, the Karakoram lay adrift in thunder-clouds. And before us the Russian Pamirs – shining so clear that they seemed within hand-reach – pointed the ancient Silk Road through its chain of cities westward: Samarkand, Ctesiphon, Palmyra and Antioch, to the sea.

Above and right: Taxkorgan, one of the remotest outposts on earth.
Here the Tajiks eke out a lonely living, the exuberance of their dress
providing the only colour in a hostile landscape.

Pages 32 and 33: Beyond Kashgar the Silk Road rises sharply towards
the Pamirs, reaching the desolate plateau where China collides with
Russia, Afghanistan and Pakistan.

THE POLYNESIAN TRIANGLE

Naomi James

Five years ago, when my husband was killed in a sailing accident, I turned my back on the sea. I hadn't been brought up in a sailing environment but a lifetime (even one of nine months' duration) spent sailing around the world, with one's fate at the mercy of the ocean, cannot be dismissed so easily. In the following years, busy bringing up our small daughter, I found that I was drawn back to the sea – to write, talk and dream about it – though still sure that I would never involve myself again. Then, one day, a letter arrived through my door offering me an opportunity to go on a journey to the South Seas. I put the letter aside, but when I read it again some time later thoughts began surfacing.

I was brought up in New Zealand, part of Polynesia. Although New Zealand is a long way from tropical South Sea Polynesia, the Maori are Polynesian people who arrived in New Zealand after a very long (and probably accidental) canoe journey from one of the northern groups. My feelings about the native Maori were ambivalent. To a large extent the white majority (who run New Zealand) see the Maori as a lazy, good-for-nothing race who can't be bothered to work for a 'decent standard of living'. The gaols are full of Maori, they drink too much, few hold down 'good' jobs. The Tongans, Fijians and other Polynesians who emigrate to New Zealand are viewed by many whites as a different class of citizen and are accorded even less respect than the Maori.

It would be tempting to examine my views on the subject now, I thought. I got out an atlas and studied the Pacific Ocean. The Polynesian triangle is formed, roughly, by Hawaii in the north, New Zealand in the south and, a long way east, Easter Island.

A horse and cart on the remote island of Ha'ano, part of the Ha'apai group in Tonga which Captain Cook named the Friendly Islands after his arrival here in 1773.

The main street of Nuku'alofa, capital of Tonga, the last remaining monarchy in Polynesia and the only Pacific nation never to be colonized.

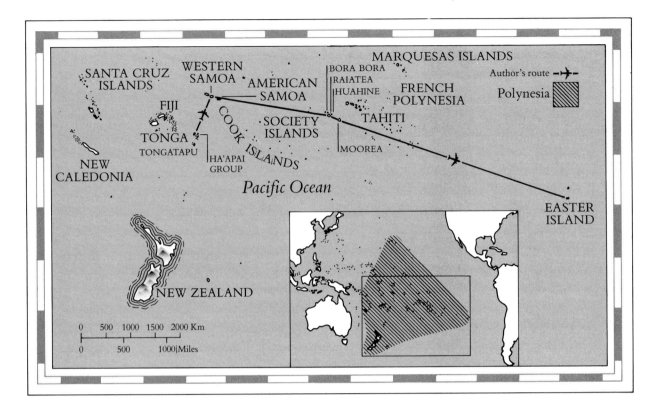

Since reading a book on Easter Island years ago I'd been fascinated by the isolation and mystery of the place – I'd even carved chesspiece copies of some of Easter Island's extraordinary stone statues. This might be my only chance of going there. After five years of marking time I felt I was ready for a new challenge – a new direction. Journeying was not exactly new for me, but this time it would mean involving myself with people, not something I'd done in the past. I was apprehensive at the thought, but attracted too. And, oddly enough, it seemed that having a good reason to go back to sea was sufficient to do away with my qualms.

One cool August morning we – the producer, the film crew and I – boarded a jet and began the long haul to the other side of the world. For the past few weeks I'd been asking myself the question: who are the Polynesians? Despite having grown up among them, I was aware that I knew very little about the Maori or the Polynesian race in general. How the first Polynesians actually got into the area they now occupy had been easy enough to discover by research. Migrations from Southeast Asia began about 50,000 years ago, moving first into new Guinea and Australia, then many centuries later into the western sector of the Pacific. A group called the Lapita people (named after their distinctive pottery) entered the Pacific by way of Indonesia and the Philippines and traded back and forth along a vast migratory route before settling the Polynesian island chains of Tonga and Samoa in about 1300 BC. There they remained until AD 300 when strife, perhaps caused by overpopulation, initiated further voyaging.

New Zealand was one of the last islands in the Polynesian domain to be discovered by humans, using an incredible means of travel developed over the centuries. According to legend, heroic warriors in huge double- or single-hulled canoes, guided by wind, wave patterns and stars, crossed vast distances of open ocean in search of new island homes to the east. They carried their women, food supplies and tools with them. Within a few centuries they had settled the thousands of islands in Polynesia. A number of these ocean-going canoes, constructed of wood planking and lashed together with rope, still existed in the eighteenth century when Captain James Cook arrived, a century after the first Europeans discovered the Pacific.

Polynesian voyaging still ranks as an extraordinary enigma, but I gathered from my reading that the traditions of the navigators had virtually died out. Why, I wondered? Had the explorers, the missionaries, the traders, and now the twentieth century destroyed not just the South Sea paradise as conceived by the West but the real thing as well? If that turned out to be so, what, I wondered, had the real Polynesia been?

The logical place, it seemed to me, to start looking for answers to these questions was Tonga, the oldest and last remaining monarchy in the region and the only Pacific nation never to come under foreign rule. Surely Tonga, with its proud traditions of voyaging, would have preserved much of the Polynesia of long ago: if it was not quite the South Sea paradise of Cook's time, it must still be a lot closer to it than modern New Zealand.

We landed some days later in Tongatapu. The Tongan group consists of three scattered clusters of islands occupying no more than 269 square miles in 20,000 square miles of ocean. Of Tonga's hundred and fifty islands – some flat coral outcrops unable to sustain life, some soaring volcanoes too steep to stand on – only thirty-six are suitable for habitation. The main island of Tongatapu is flat except for Mount Zion, 60 feet high. But to compensate, the surrounding ocean is 6 miles deep.

My first impression of paradise on the drive from the airport to the main town was discouraging. Corrugated iron and weatherboard seemed to have largely replaced native materials for housing. Pigs and half-naked children played or wandered about in dusty back yards where purple flowering trees added a touch of garish colour to an otherwise bland landscape. Closer to the town colourful buildings in haphazard rows propped up shacks on the verge of collapse, but others were surprisingly modern in design. We booked into the Dateline Hotel – the 'best' hotel on the island. After a dinner of indifferent Western cuisine we watched a show of Tongan dancing and singing. The girls in their native costumes looked surprisingly demure. Their hand and hip movements were conservative, nothing like I had imagined Polynesian dancing to be, but the men more than made up for the girl's sobriety in exuberant hallooing and leaping about. It was a tantalizing glimpse of the old Tonga I hoped to find outside the tourist environment.

The sea has always formed the natural route for voyagers in the Pacific, so it seemed right that we should go to as many islands as possible by sea. I was disappointed to discover the following day that there was no locally made native boat seaworthy

In Apia, the capital of Western Samoa, a woman shelters under a parasol.

Left: A Tongan aboard the inter-island ferry in Nuku'alofa harbour holds a traditional fan to keep the fierce heat at bay.

enough to take us the hundred-odd miles to the outer islands. Tongatapu could only offer a most unromantic form of transport: a ferry.

So the following afternoon I presented my ticket to a man on the quayside and boarded the ferry, alongside crates of protesting pigs, goats and domestic fowl and large numbers of good-humoured Polynesians. We were heading for the middle cluster of the Tongan islands, the Ha'apai group. Although geographically less remote from Tongatapu than some other islands, it had less to recommend it to the average tourist and economically it appeared cut off. There were no harbours, therefore little scope for exports or inter-island communication; however, the islands had gained a certain notoriety as a result of the visits of Captain Cook, who had made prolonged stops there between 1773 and 1777. He had been sent to the South Sea islands to observe the movements of heavenly bodies, so as to further the science of navigation, and to find out whether a large continent existed to the south. The island we were heading for, Lifuka, was where Cook coined the term 'Friendly Islands' because of the warm welcome he received there. We were also due to pass close to the spot where Captain Bligh was cast adrift from the *Bounty*.

I surfaced at midnight when we reached the first of the islands, and went up on deck for a look. Moving about the ferry was difficult as there were sleeping forms everywhere; but if one was inadvertently stepped on it would, rather than budging, just grunt and wrap itself tighter in its covering. The sight that greeted me on deck was extraordinary. We had anchored in the lee of a perfect castaway island. Black fingers of palms etched a vivid outline against an immense starry blackness. An army of little boats clustered around the stern of the ferry, sharply lit by spotlights, like a swarm of ragged moths attracted to a lamp. Dark shapes blundered about, throwing aboard all manner and shape of parcels and boxes, turtles, goats like walking kebabs and the odd bewildered-looking granny. I was told this rendezvous took place once a week – weather permitting. Among the paraphernalia I noticed drums of fuel being offloaded and became aware of an incongruous element in this otherwise primitive operation. Expensive American and Japanese outboard engines protruded from the stern of every small boat, disturbing the soft night air with their strident whining.

We reached Lifuka at 4.30 in the morning. Our guesthouse in the main village of Pangai was extremely basic – just a bed in each room, a cold shower and plenty of cockroaches. By 9 o'clock we had found a Japanese fishing boat to take us to Ha'ano, an island further north, with its only village one of the most remote in Tonga.

Ha'ano is a low-lying atoll, one of a broken ring around a large lagoon. It looked very picturesque with its graceful palm trees and white beaches. Suddenly my mouth went dry. Never had I imagined myself with a group of people – or alone for that matter – walking into a foreign village unannounced and trying to engage people in conversation. I felt they had every right to regard us as intruders and throw us out. We stepped ashore and walked towards a group of children gathering a little way up the beach. They stared at us and backed off as I approached. A question directed randomly at the group brought forth giggles and more wide-eyed stares, but one child eventually said, 'What's your name?'

I told him and asked him his.

There was no response, just the repeated question, 'What's your name?' That was the extent of their fluency, it seemed.

Nothing more was forthcoming from the children, so we began to walk away from the beach towards the village. The dwellings were sheets of rusty corrugated iron with tin, wooden or thatched roofs. There wasn't much greenery or flowers in the village itself – just large areas of bare dirt and a few bedraggled trees. Taking a deep mental breath I walked up to a woman standing at the door of a shack and asked her if she spoke English. She didn't, but a girl of about fifteen was summoned and somewhat uncertainly said that she would show us the village.

As we walked on the girl called out to someone in a neighbouring shack, another girl of the same age, who came too. The two girls – the one we'd met first was called Vienna – began to look quite animated as we walked along, peering into this and that. Pigs, goats, chickens and children were everywhere, scratching or playing in the dust. I asked the girls about school, because of the number of children running around. Vienna waved her hand vaguely in the direction of Pangai, but wasn't able to explain why they weren't there on this week day. We passed a woman sweeping her yard, shuffling leaves, sticks and some bits of litter to the sides where it was left for the next puff of wind to redistribute.

I could see only a few women about and asked Vienna where the men were, but she was confused at the question and didn't know how to answer. It was a little while before I realized that their understanding of English was very minimal: I thought at first that my difficulty in communication was coming from my inability to relate to them. We eventually came across four men putting up concrete blocks. They took no notice of us. Vienna drew my attention to what the men were doing. 'A kitchen,' she said proudly. It was being put up against a shack whose sheets of warped tin looked as though they might collapse at any minute like a house of cards.

Nearby was an ugly block construction, the beginnings of a church. Tongans are very devout Christians, as we'd discovered when we'd tried to get a few things done in Tongatapu on a Sunday: there is even a move to ban driving on the Sabbath. Village life revolves around the church, but this village didn't have one – so, somehow, the villagers were scraping money together to buy materials and build their own.

We asked permission of Vienna's mother to see inside her house, one of the few traditional oval houses with wooden walls. A woman sat cross-legged by the door doing basket work, while another laboured in the dark interior at an ancient treadle sewing machine. I still felt like an intruder but their faces were friendly, inviting us to come inside and film. Coconut matting was laid on a dirt floor where a couple of small children played: this must also have been where the family slept, for there was no other suitable room.

When my eyes had become accustomed to the gloom I noticed a bizarre thing: the interior walls were covered with pictures cut out of American glossy magazines. Pin-up girls smirked at me, suave men leaned on the bonnets of Rolls-Royces, and glitzy socialites shimmered in the dull light. The two girls beside me chewed gum incessantly, their expressions animated, believing that I would share their excitement

A Samoan pauses for reflection while washing in the freshwater Piula Cave pool outside Apia.

Left: Further round the island, a boy bathes in the sea near the idyllic village of Lalomanu.

Pages 52 and 53: At dusk in Lalomanu a fisherman sets out for the reef in an outrigger canoe.

in the pictures. Instead I found the Hollywood images, in that setting, very disturbing. I searched the faces of the older women; were they alarmed at their children's desire for Western possessions? I couldn't tell. I began to feel increasingly frustrated at my inability to ask more searching questions. These villagers obviously lived at subsistence level: how could they ever afford even vaguely to emulate the lifestyle portrayed in those pictures?

As we left the village I felt very annoyed at my lack of understanding of how the villagers really felt about their lives. I was depressed, too, about the failure of my first attempt at investigative journalism.

Next day we caught the ferry back to Tongatapu and I tried to sort out my impressions of the Tongan village. Had they really traded in all their proud traditions in favour of Western ways? What I'd found most upsetting was the aspirations of the teenagers towards the worst sort of Western trivia, but I knew these were judgements that I had no right to make. If that is what they want, who can say they shouldn't have it?

Later I did more research on Tonga which threw some light on village problems. Social changes brought about by the introduction of a cash economy with the coming of Europeans have caused stress and confusion, especially in the poor villages. Many traditional values and attitudes have been found to be incompatible with a cash economy. For instance, the property of an extended family used to be shared by every one of its members. Now, if an individual wants to keep his money to himself he has to alienate himself from the extended family. Young people are leaving in droves for the bigger towns to find paid work, but an exploding population and an educational system increasingly geared to white-collar jobs, of which there are few, are causing growing discontent. The constitution of 1875 created a new land tenure system guaranteeing the head of each family enough land for his needs, but now there is insufficient land to go around. Most Tongans seem to be aware that their benign monarchy works better than a political party, but if the avenues of escape to New Zealand and elsewhere should close, the economic strain on the country, and therefore on the monarchy, would be severe.

The next place I wanted to go to was Samoa, a country run along democratic tribal lines which, apart from a century of disruption from squabbling colonialists, had been serving the Samoans well for a thousand years. Samoa was split in two in 1870 when the USA appropriated Pago Pago harbour for merchant shipping and later as a naval base. America has since poured huge amounts of money into American Samoa, while Western Samoa, having achieved independence from New Zealand in 1962, battles with the desperate problems of many Third World countries – high birth rate, an agricultural economy and little industry.

We flew the 600 miles north-east to Western Samoa and landed in Apia, the capital. Our woman bus driver drove in unseemly haste through the night towards the town, allowing us only fleeting glimpses of the Samoan *fale*, the traditional open house. A few poles and a thatched roof above a raised stone platform are all that separate Samoan families from the tropical weather – and their neighbours. Hurricane lamps cast pools of light on groups eating, talking or sleeping. I caught sight of the odd cooker standing alone in a corner, or double bed or chest of drawers, but more common was a bundle of rolled up sleeping mats and a large trunk.

We arrived in time to see a captivating performance of Samoan singing and dancing at the most famous hotel in the Pacific, Aggie Grey's. The Samoans were so obviously enjoying themselves, and the action songs and traditional dancing were performed with so much skill and expression, that I forgot the hotel surroundings for a while and got caught up in the spectacle of Polynesians doing what came most naturally to them. The men had an animal masculinity, and the women a femininity that was very beguiling.

When the dancing was over and the Samoans had left the stage the tones of American and Japanese tourists rose from the surrounding tables. Someone had said to me before I started this journey that these traditions would have naturally died out if it weren't for the tourists. It can't be true, I thought, that they didn't dance for themselves any more. Their chief mode of communication had always been through dance and oral expression: the written word didn't exist in Polynesia before the coming of Europeans. Abandoning their traditional form of expression, it seemed to me, would be as unlikely as the Africans giving up their drums.

Early next morning I set out for the centre of Apia. I didn't want to repeat the mistakes I'd made in Tonga. Rather than going cold into a village where I couldn't communicate, this time I wanted to find a Samoan who spoke English to help me get to the heart of the Polynesian people. By midday, after some fruitless hours searching tourist offices, airline offices and various shops, I was suffering from heat, dust, traffic fumes and my inability to think of what to do next. By chance I was passing another tourist office so I walked in, desperate to sit down. To my surprise I was greeted by a thirty-five-year-old Samoan called Uelesa, not on the staff but obviously on the look-out for lost souls requiring guidance. I explained why I was there and he rose to the occasion.

Uelesa first suggested a visit to the market, so that he could introduce me to an aspect of Samoan life that had hardly changed at all. Apia market is the best and most colourful in this part of the Pacific. Besides those who come daily to sell their goods, many people live in the marketplace for a week at a time, coming from afar and staying until their produce is sold. They sleep on mats on the ground, as they would at home. The place has more the feel of a village than that of a market. You could wander along after midnight and people would still be sitting around, talking and drinking *kava*, an alcoholic beverage extracted from the *kava* root that has a similar taste and the same lethal kick as schnapps. Uelesa led me past mounds of *taro, kava*, breadfruit and a vast assortment of tropical fruits into the fish market, where he waved me towards a bench. From a cabinet he chose a large fish head dressed in boiled green bananas and put it in front of me. Unfortunately I don't like bananas and the fish head looked rather revolting, so I was at a loss to know what to do.

'Surely you don't expect me to eat this?' I said, trying not to look disgusted.

'Why, of course,' said Uelesa. 'The most honoured guest gets the biggest fish head. There are some good things inside there, especially the brain. It has special properties to give you wisdom.'

I hastily diverted Uelesa's attention off the fish and on to Samoa. He told me that he had lived abroad for some years (one of the thousands of Samoans who emigrate to New Zealand) until he got fed up with the stresses of the Western world and returned home, as he said, to the sanity of Samoa. Nevertheless, having acquired Western needs he was not keen to get back to basic Samoan ways, although he was keen to show me just what remained of those ways.

I told him about my depressing debut as a reporter in Ha'ano and was amused to discover that my new guide ran a local newspaper. Uelesa thought over my dilemma for a moment and came up with another suggestion. He knew a village on the coast where he could arrange for the people to welcome me in their own way, entertain me, accommodate me, and show me how they spent their time. He would come with me to act as guide and interpreter. His confidence that what I would find at Lalomanu would be very different from Ha'ano was encouraging. This was exactly the chance I had been hoping for.

Several days later we were up at dawn and driving through heavy bush country along a very bumpy road. After a two-and-a-half-hour drive and two flat tyres we were near the village. Uelesa took me into a friend's house to rest while he organized a fishing boat so that we could approach the village from the seaward side. He had alerted the people to the arrival of a seafaring guest, and to make the most of this traditional welcome, he felt, I should come in from the sea. Uelesa had hinted at certain procedures of protocol with the village chiefs, the *matai*, which included speeches: the thought of making speeches makes my stomach turn over. I began to wish that I could be a witness to this ceremony and not on the receiving end.

We headed out in the fishing boat through the coral outcrops. As we turned the corner in sight of the village I could see people gathered on the beach, backed by tall palms and native huts. Half a dozen dugout canoes were paddling out through the surf to meet us. Although the setting was vastly different I was suddenly reminded of another welcome, returning from my circumnavigation of the world twelve years earlier.

Before the fishing boat reached the beach Uelesa grabbed one of the dugouts, put me in and gave it a great shove towards the shore. I fetched up on the sand, my skirt tucked up inelegantly above my knees, shoes in hand. Uelesa introduced me first to the chiefs' wives, who, wreathed in smiles, placed long strings of flowers around my neck, murmuring '*Talofa*', the Samoan greeting. Then I was led up the beach to the line of chiefs, five large, affable gentlemen. We solemnly shook hands (I had half expected to rub noses as the Maoris do, but that obviously wasn't the form here).

At the invitation of the head chief Uelesa shepherded me further away from the water to a *fale*, beautifully decorated with flowers and plaited coconut fronds. I sat down cross-legged with Uelesa beside me and the chiefs arranged on either side of us. The head *matai* then gave a welcoming speech, which Uelesa translated. Feeling as though I was treading a minefield of *faux pas* and potential embarrassments, I returned what I hoped was an appropriate response, relying on Uelesa to edit if necessary. My words were received with nods, grunts and a polite clap. Then the feast started.

Women came out from a nearby *fale* in a long line carrying food on woven coconut mats. They put it down on the floor in front of us, then sat down in the middle of our circle and fanned away the flies with coconut fronds. I asked Uelesa why the women weren't eating with us. Custom forbids it, he answered prosaically. He later hinted that a woman's role was not quite the passive one that this situation suggested. The Women's Committee gets together the day before a meeting of the chiefs to decide village policy; then they work on their menfolk to get across the ideas they particularly favour.

I looked in alarm at the quantity of food spread out before us – boiled *taro,* breadfruit, yams and several other boiled things I didn't recognize, fish, crabs – and more boiled bananas! Alas, my appetite had forsaken me days earlier after picking up a stomach bug. To judge by appearances these villagers were not much better off materially than the people of Ha'ano, so gathering all this food together must have represented some hardship for them. As Uelesa and the chiefs tucked in I became acutely embarrassed at the slight my lack of appetite might be causing. I was very thankful when the crew finished filming and sat down with us to help out. One of them asked Uelesa why there was no *kava* to drink, being under the impression that this ritual was the most important part of the feast. Uelesa said that if women were present no drinking was allowed. Not the way to make myself popular, I thought.

The feast came to an end, the women took the debris away and the chiefs retired to the shady veranda of a nearby house. I could see bottles of beer being surreptitiously passed round. I wandered around the village for a while, followed closely by a knot of children who had learnt my name and practised it on me non-stop.

The Women's Committee was responsible for entertainment that evening and the ladies were busy decorating a large *fale* with flowers, singing to themselves. Two men were preparing an *umu*, a sort of underground oven, filling a hole with stones heated on a fire. On top of the stones went yams, *taro* and breadfruit for our supper. A woman roasted cocoa beans in a tin pan over a open fire, and the smoke drifted lazily up into the canopy of palm leaves above. Another woman, breasts exposed, sat in an open washhouse with water pouring from a tap over her head while she pummelled clothes and hung them to drip over the tin sides of the building.

Smoke wreathed the children playing on the ground, crying out in shrill voices in the languid sunshine. Everyone was absorbed, happy. I had the impression that little had changed here for a hundred years. The poet Rupert Brooke said of Samoa:

You lie on a mat in a cool Samoan hut, and look out on the white sand under the high palms, and a gentle sea, and the black line of the reef a mile out, and moonlight over everything.... And then among it all are the loveliest people in the world, moving and dancing like gods and goddesses, very quietly and mysteriously, and utterly content. It is sheer beauty, so pure that it's difficult to breathe it in.

The men threw a last layer of coconut branches over the smoking *umu* and drifted off to snooze the rest of the afternoon away.

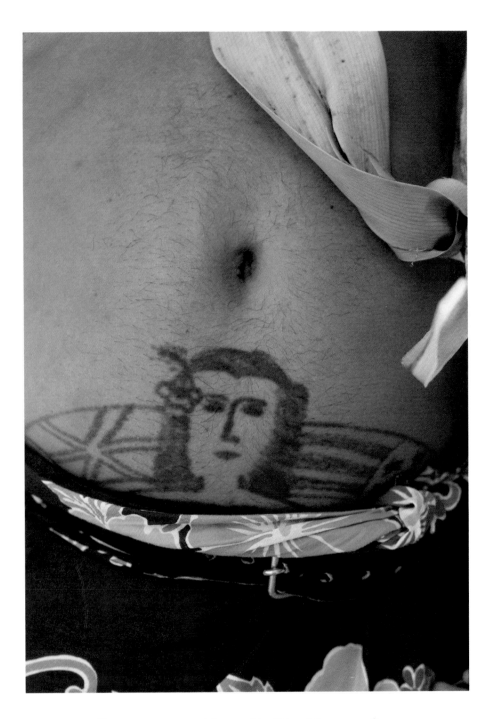

*Tattoos are an essential part of traditional Samoan culture.
Stretching from waist to knees they are the symbols, and proof,
of a man's courage.*

Right: The matai, *or village chiefs, dressed for a ceremonial welcome,
sit in a* fale *decorated with flowers and twisted coconut fronds.*

I went back to our *fale*, puzzling over the difference between Lalomanu and Ha'ano. These villagers seemed so much more positive than the Tongan ones, although I couldn't help wondering what would have happened if we had asked Ha'ano to perform a welcome ceremony for us. The way society and politics are structured in Samoa is very different from Tonga. The family here is everything, and village life is paramount: everything is shared and everyone has somewhere to sleep and a feeling of belonging. Each extended Samoan family elects from among its members a representative, a *matai*, who looks after the assets and lands of the clan. He settles disputes, makes sure that no one is in dire need and sees to the family's social obligations (the Samoans have a high regard for rank and etiquette). This family control of individuals extends all the way to Parliament. The *matai* form a council to run village affairs: from each council a representative is chosen for a district, and a number of *matai* from all districts form the Parliament of the country.

Towards dusk the village stirred and stretched. More food and coconut milk were brought out. I chatted to Uelesa and he translated any enquiries anyone had, but there were few. Their initial curiosity had been satisfied when a chief asked Uelesa who I was and why I merited special attention. Uelesa replied that I had sailed around the world on my own. There was silence while the chief digested this piece of information, a baffled look on his face. His response sent Uelesa spluttering into his coconut milk. What a stupid thing to do! There were no further questions on that subject.

As night fell, lanterns were hung in the roof of the *fale*. Uelesa and I sat ourselves down at one end and waited. Soon, girls dressed in *lava lavas* – colourful wrap-around skirts – drifted in and arranged themselves self-consciously at the other end. When about ten had assembled they began to sing. It was immediately apparent that these girls lacked the polish of those who performed for tourists, but they more than made up for it in enthusiasm. Then, to my horror, I was invited to dance. Uelesa's expression when I glanced pleadingly at him convinced me that I couldn't refuse. Blushing wildly for my reserve and complete lack of grace, I tried to imitate their dancing. Uelesa leaped to his feet, instantly losing the appearance of a Westernized Samoan with the casting off of his shirt (he was only wearing a shirt and *lava lava*), and became a virile native enacting the ancient rituals of the courting dance. Several women made me jump when they beat on the floor close to me with large palm fronds, part of the ritual of emphasizing the beauty and eligibility of the maiden being courted.

I was flattered, but very thankful when the dance came to an end and I could sit down. After a while the crew put away their cameras and the fun really began. Obviously thinking the women were making a poor job of it (except for our crew and Uelesa, no men had been invited to this party) the head chief detached himself from his veranda, where he had spent the whole afternoon supping beer, and entertained us with his own *siva*, the traditional dance performed by the girls, much to the delight of the women. His very large circumference bounced up and down, a glistening brown expanse of sweaty mobility. Screams of laughter came from the horde of children crammed into the *fale*, and deeper guffaws could be heard from men lounging under the trees in the darkness. The children were convulsed because his *lava lava* had almost fallen off, but the others were laughing at his gestures: some of them might have been traditional, but others were definitely designed to make a young girl blush.

After a few minutes he melted exhausted into the shadows and the women carried on, determined not to to be outdone. The hurricane lamps hissed and swayed gently in the breeze coming off the sea which one could hear, above the general noise, collapsing on to the reef. The party looked set to last all night, but eventually the chief reappeared and suggested that it was time to stop. The women sang one more song and then fetched mats which were rolled out on to the floor of the *fale* for us to sleep on. We settled down for the night, virtually under the stars, the soothing sound of the ocean close by.

Breakfast appeared shortly after 6 o'clock, and consisted of hot paw-paw and coconut milk. We then joined one of the *matai* for a trip into the interior to see how land was cultivated. Lush green palms enveloped us as we pushed further and further along a dirt track into the steaming jungle. Uelesa explained how land was distributed. Eighty per cent of it is owned communally by the *aiga*, the family group. The *matai* distribute parcels of land to family members for their personal needs and to those who want to farm for profit.

We stopped at a large area being cultivated for *taro* and coconut crops by half a dozen young men who were members of a large family. There was no shortage of land to go round, Uelesa told me. But not very many young men were prepared to put in the amount of work needed to extract a good income from it. Unfortunately for many modern Samoans who aspire to riches, Uelesa explained, working hard does not come easily to them. There has never been any necessity to do so. The islanders' needs have never been great: they were, and still are, able to subsist on what they grow for themselves, producing crops all the year round with the minimum of effort. Their non-materialistic approach to life inclined them to simple housing and a habit of giving things away rather than acquiring them. Sadly but inevitably, in Uelesa's view, children are now being taught in school to achieve and acquire on a more individual, Western basis. Educated Samoans prefer to work in offices in town, and if they can't find work there they emigrate; going back to traditional ways is considered retrogressive and inferior.

As Uelesa talked, I thought about the impressions of the Polynesians I had gained during my childhood in New Zealand. Answers to some of my questions were unfolding here. The slow, easy rhythm of the South Sea islands is deeply ingrained in the character of the Polynesian. When it comes to competing in a materialistic, European world, he is at a disadvantage. One aspect of white prejudice against the Polynesian, the 'lazy and good-for-nothing' label, was now clear to me – and the cruel injustice of it also. Europeans were drawn here in the first place by the simple, unsullied ideology of the islanders, and now, having polluted them with our standards, we deride them for their inability to adapt.

Tahiti, capital of French Polynesia, has been all but subsumed by Coca-Cola culture.

Sunset over Moorea, the model for Bali Hai in the musical South
Pacific, *affords a brief glimpse of Gauguin's paradise islands.*

We returned to the village for lunch and a short leaving ceremony. The people of Lalomanu had treated us to every hospitality and friendliness, yet I sensed, through their easy courtesy and good manners, a lack of comprehension of us and what we were doing there. I still felt, as I had in the Tongan village, that I had no very good reason for being there – and, indeed, that I was a part of the disruptive influence that would undoubtedly change the peaceful, timeless tenor of their lives. As we drove away, they quickly became engrossed again in their usual occupations.

On the drive back to Apia I tried to analyse the sense of sadness that I felt about Samoa. Was it because, having found a strong, traditional culture that refuted all those ingrained New Zealand prejudices I once had, I now found it impossible to imagine how that strength could endure?

After Tonga and Samoa I felt pretty apprehensive for the natives of the next group of islands I wanted to see. We moved on eastwards towards the South Sea paradise that initiated the fantasy in Europe: Tahiti and the Society Islands.

The scene, at least, from the plane window as we approached Tahiti promised everything that had enthralled Captain Cook, Captain Bligh and the French painter Paul Gauguin. Bligh's crew of the *Bounty*, visiting the island for breadfruit plants, developed a passion for Tahiti and her women that led to the most famous mutiny of all time. Less than a hundred years later Gauguin's fascination with the people, which resulted in the powerful visual images that can be seen today in art galleries all over the world, was tinged with sadness. Not one of his Tahitian women smiles.

A lagoon of indescribable blue rushed beneath the wheels and coconut palms stretched out their leafy fronds towards us as the plane swept on to the runway. The airport was modern and bustling. We jumped aboard a bus heading down town and were disgorged, blinking, into the noise, fumes and chaos of a Paris boulevard. On one side stretched boutiques and pavement cafés. On the other traffic snarled away from the lights, revealing lines of foreign yachts tied up to the quay. Beyond lay the lagoon and beyond that the romantic outline of Moorea, the mysterious island of Bali Hai in the musical *South Pacific*.

In 1842 a French admiral sailed into Papeete, the main harbour in Tahiti, and informed the Tahitians that their islands (the Windward group – not to be confused with the Windward and Leeward Islands in the Caribbean) had become a protectorate of France. Huahine and the other Leeward Islands to the west of Tahiti resisted the invasion fiercely, but they too were forced to give way in 1897. Now, at a time when other colonial powers are retreating from the Pacific, France is tightening her strategic grip on eastern Polynesia. Although I was no longer surprised at the presence of outsiders in the Pacific islands, the sight of French warships tied up to the quay and gendarmes on the streets was disconcerting. Already I wanted to get away from Tahiti, which I felt had nothing to do with the Polynesians any more, and sail to the Leeward Islands. Because of their history of resistance, they sounded to me more likely to have retained some of their original character.

Enquiries next day produced pleasing results – a 70-foot, turn-of-the-century Baltic trader, owned and skippered by an American with a Tahitian wife. She was a strange sort of boat to find in these waters, but an ideal vessel on which to explore some of the islands in much the same way as Captain Samuel Wallis, who had discovered Tahiti in 1767, had done. We took a ferry to Moorea, where the boat was based, made contact with the owner and discovered that the vessel was free to charter. Two days later we joined *Erika* and set sail for the Leeward Islands.

A fresh, warm wind blew towards Bora Bora. *Erika* ploughed forward in the ponderous way that old wooden ships have in a seaway, rigging and blocks creaking, faded red sails swaying against a deep blue sky. The sea rose and fell, rolling and tumbling across the coral reefs. Their nearness brought forth a familiar thrill of excitement. I felt content, even happy, at being on board a sailing boat again. The motion of the deck enveloped me pleasantly; my only slight worry was the thought of disgracing myself by being seasick, a complaint I've never managed to overcome – unless I stay at sea. But I had taken the precaution of swallowing a couple of seasickness tablets.

I sat by the wheel with Joel House, our skipper, a self-confessed American drop-out. With his skinny frame, sun-streaked hair and face, he bore an uncanny resemblance to the writer Robert Louis Stevenson. The resemblance was one of spirit as well as looks. Joel had been lured to the Pacific by Stevenson's stories of the South Seas. Finding his own Tahitian girl and marrying her, he had had a family and now, seventeen years later, seemed more Tahitian than the Tahitians. He talked of the people with a mixture of affection and exasperation, extolling the generosity and good humour of his Tahitian crew while regretting their resistance to anything that smacked of hard work. In explaining his views on the Polynesian attitude to generosity and how it worked against them in the modern world, Joel confirmed what I had discovered for myself in Samoa.

Bora Bora hardened up in the distance. From the lush vegetation sprouting around its base, black pinnacles of volcanic rock soared into the clouds. The island looked utterly beautiful and serene. It was easy to imagine what Cook's seamen must have felt on seeing these islands, particularly Tahiti, for the first time, and their reaction to the behaviour of the women. In the words of Joseph Banks, the naturalist who accompanied Cook, '. . . on the island of Otaheite where love is the chief occupation, the favourite, nay, the sole luxury of the inhabitants, both the bodies and souls of the women are moulded into the utmost perfection. . . .'

Nothing in the education of the average seaman could have prepared him for the indolence and generous attitude to love and life that was the way of the Tahitians. Whether or not the women really were as free with their favours as myth suggests depends on whose experiences one reads, but Captain Cook, after having spent some time on the island of Tahiti, had this to say: 'Upon the whole these people seem to enjoy liberty in its fullest extent, every man seems to be the sole judge of his actions and to know no punishment but death. . . .' Cook, a tolerant and broad-minded man for his time, had grave doubts about the morality of upsetting this sublimely simple and guilt-free outlook on life. Having witnessed what effect the luxuries and conveniences were having on the natives, how they had given up making their traditional tools in favour of those obtained from the Europeans, and how their freedom of

*The sheer, jungled hillsides of Raiatea, second largest of the
Society Islands.*

*Right: The Erika sails past Raiatea, believed to have been the starting
point for the great Polynesian voyages to Hawaii and New Zealand.*

expression was being savagely curtailed by missionary fervour, he himself was plagued with a sense of guilt for the rest of his life.

Joel anchored off the beach and we all went ashore to eat. The French food was very mediocre, and grudgingly served by Polynesian girls who did not make happy waitresses. Below decks on *Erika* the heat was suffocating. Everyone slept on deck that night, under a large canvas canopy that gave good protection in anything but driving rain. At least one shower of driving rain occurred every night for the next nine days.

Whatever else it may have become, Polynesia is still a paradise for divers – or so we thought. I had listened to a tirade of bitter condemnation from Joel and his wife Moea on the French government's policy of nuclear testing in the Pacific and the effect that it had had on marine life and on the island inhabitants. I'm not a keen swimmer – on the contrary, the idea of diving into that dark, creepy underworld I have so often studied from the safety of a deck has never appealed to me. Still, there was an alarming issue in this part of the world which impelled me to put personal reservations aside, don breathing apparatus and go down to see how paradise looked underwater.

The anxiety I felt as I sat on the edge of the boat, plucking up the nerve to roll in backwards, went as soon as I was on the bottom of the sea looking round. Brilliantly coloured fish flitted here and there among outcrops of blue, yellow and black coral. There was certainly not the quantity of coral that one would expect to find on the Great Barrier Reef, say, but there was no shortage of wildlife. Small reef sharks swam in and out of our vision, keeping a respectful distance, while a few yards away a giant manta ray glided past on a 10-foot wingspan, looking like a spaceship. Moray eels peered bad-temperedly out of many holes: some came out to grab bits of dead fish that a French diver waved under their noses. We surfaced after twenty minutes and I asked the Frenchman why there was so little coral about. The last hurricane destroyed it, he said simply.

My reading hinted at more ominous possibilities. Since 1966, more than a hundred underground and atmospheric explosions have rocked the Tuamotus, Gambia islands and Mururoa atoll, causing fissures to open up underwater and allowing radioactive poisons to escape into the ocean where they slowly accumulate in sea foods. Tagged tuna caught as far away as Australia have shown signs of radioactivity. Thousands of Polynesians employed by the French army on Mururoa atoll are warned not to eat fish, crabs or squid, but many ignore the warning because they are totally ignorant of the dangers of radiation. Gruesome stories are told of children playing with what they thought was snow but turned out to be nuclear fall-out, of women miscarrying, of infant deaths and cancer-related diseases. The French government has failed to publish health reports on French Polynesia since starting their nuclear testing programme on the Pacific atolls. Of a thousand deaths in French Polynesia in 1985, only ninety-five people had death certificates issued, and official statistics state that two hundred died from 'no specific cause'.

The environmental problems in the Pacific were overwhelming and immediate, but, having delved into this twentieth-century phenomenon, I still felt that I wasn't much closer to understanding the Polynesians themselves, how they felt about their lives now, or what their lives had been like before any contact with Europeans. Oddly enough it is on these islands, where the culture has been virtually annihilated, that the most powerful reminders of ancient Polynesia can be found. We decided to visit some archaeological sites: I wanted to get an idea of how substantial this civilization had once been.

We set sail again with Joel for the island of Raiatea, the second largest of the Society Islands and once the religious and cultural centre of the group. An important ancient *marae* (temple), called Taputapuatea, is situated on its eastern shore, directly opposite a pass through the reef from which migrations to Hawaii and New Zealand are said to have departed. We approached the pass late in the afternoon and anchored close to the shore. As they had never been to Taputapuatea I took Joel and Moea with me; I wanted to see what Moea made of it.

An air of eerie stillness and silence lay about the place. On this site high chiefs had performed elaborate ceremonies, including gruesome human sacrifices to Oro, the god of war. Religious systems in the Society Islands had been extremely complex. The highest chiefs claimed direct descent from the gods, and were so sacred that they had to be carried everywhere to prevent the ground under their feet becoming *tabu*. An infringement of a chief's *tabu* could be punishable by death.

Moea suddenly informed me that her grandmother was buried somewhere near there. She looked around at the silent conconut trees as though she thought her grandmother's remains might be under their roots. 'I ought to come back and find out more about her,' she said wistfully.

Moea and Joel had tried to convince me that Tahitian culture was still alive, and that given half a chance the Tahitians would get back to their roots, but I felt they were being romantic. There is a very strong lobby by the Tahitians towards independence, to which the French may eventually have to accede, but in some respects it will be too late. The native language was banned in schools forty years ago – the curriculum, including culture, history and geography, is entirely French, to the exclusion of everything Tahitian. An added dilemma for these islanders, along with the Hawaiians and the American Samoans, is that they have mixed blood and ancestry and have been swamped by French and American culture. When they talk of getting back to their roots, what do they want to get back to? I asked Moea if she would like to return to an old settlement such as this and eke out a subsistence living fishing; she replied, 'No.' She was half French.

I left the *marae* feeling the perplexity of irreconcilable contrasts: the ancient culture versus the new; the granite of a ceremonial altar versus the shifting ground of present values. It seemed to me that the ancients believed that what they had was enduring. Taputapuatea looked untouched, as though the priests had just walked out. They meant their civilization to last, yet nothing remains of the old god worship; Christianity and the West have crushed it completely.

*Like most Polynesian islands the pace of life is slow in Raiatea.
In Uturoa, the main town, people rest in the shade of a shop.*

Right: A woman sells water-melons outside the market.

There was still a last island in the group left to visit. Huahine had gained the reputation – which it still holds – of being the stronghold of resistance to the French invasion. In Papeete we had heard that a Japanese archaeologist, who had devoted the past twenty-five years to uncovering one of the most significant dwelling sites in Polynesia, was on the island. We sailed to Huahine and found Dr Yoshi Sinoto about to lead an expedition up a mountain covered in jungle, where the remains of a large settlement lay. We were invited to join the trek.

Sinoto was not at all as I imagined an archaeologist should be. In his enthusiasm for his subject he almost skipped from one slab of stone to the next, explaining and hypothesizing. We were preceded by three Polynesian youths with machetes who slashed a path through the overgrown tracks: six months after a site has been cleared in this area it is swamped again by the jungle. To the inexperienced eye the jumble of rocks and tangled undergrowth looked exactly like rocks and undergrowth, but with Sinoto's help I picked out corners of houses or large stones that had once formed irrigation systems or fortification walls. Sinoto explained that if an attack came from the sea and couldn't be contained, the local population fled up the mountainside and counter-attacked from behind these walls.

We climbed on and up, over layer upon layer of terraces massively reinforced by huge coral slabs brought up from the seashore – by goodness knows what means – gradually realizing the scale and importance of this settlement and the sophistication of the race who built it. Near the top, under the tangled aerial roots of a huge banyan tree, Sinoto had found a burial ground unique to this island. After the corpses had been left to rot, bundles of long bones were tied together and buried. Among one pile of bones a piece of English porcelain had been found. It is difficult to carbon-date sites where most of the organic material has disintegrated, but Sinoto placed the settlement between the fourteenth and seventeenth centuries AD. Was this one of the first places where the petty chieftains slogged it out against Western intruders?

Sinoto maintained that even before European invasions Polynesian culture had begun to decline. Like all archaeologists he disliked speculation, but when I pressed him for an opinion as to why these sites had been abandoned he came up with a surprising theory. Besides the obvious possibility that they had had to move on due to overcrowding and dwindling resources, he wondered if there existed in the Polynesian character a spirit of adventure for its own sake. He likened the Polynesians to migrating birds, perhaps compelled by the need to press ever onwards, searching.

Was there a clue here, I wondered, to understanding the Polynesians of today? I thought about the difference between the Maori, who have given up their own culture and adjusted with some success to a Western way of life, and the Australian Aborigine, who haven't been able to adapt to modern Australia at all. The Aborigines share the same origin as Europeans, but isolation at a very early stage of man's evolution, combined with their harsh Australian environment, meant that further development had been arrested. At about the same time that the Aborigines arrived in Australia, the Polynesians were also en route to the Pacific, but unlike the Aborigines, they had the benefit of thousands of years of development from other cultures on their way to the eastern Pacific.

But having got here, some fifty thousand years later, did they find little in their environment to advance that incredible spirit that had brought them this far? Was their development, compared to modern Europeans, arrested at that point? It would help to explain why the Polynesians, though a thousand times better off in these modern times than the Aborigines, still find it difficult to cope with the materialistic and selfish attitude of Westerners.

We made our way wearily back down the mountain. My knees were weak, I'd been ill a lot of the day – food poisoning turned out to be the culprit, but I also felt a deepening sense of sadness and resignation. On this mountain I felt as though I'd reached a landmark of the journey. Like the Taputapuatea *marae*, once the heart of a powerful society, this settlement was witness to the end of an era.

There was one island left that I had to go to. Easter Island has presented a paradox to archaeologists and travellers since it was first discovered by Europeans almost three hundred years ago. There, I felt sure, I would find more answers to my quest for understanding old and new Polynesia.

We left Papeete at the unsociable hour of 2 a.m. and flew 1500 miles eastwards over an empty ocean. I woke at dawn to see Easter Island taking shape beneath the plane wing, dark and sombre in the half light. Anything less like a tropical island you could not imagine. Rolling, treeless yellow hills stretch away from a rugged shoreline against which the Pacific surge collides, unbroken by reef or lagoon.

We were delayed for some while at the airport until the Chilean officials decided we posed no threat to their plebiscite vote, due the following week. Easter Island is administered directly from Chile, 2300 miles to the east, which annexed the island in 1888, intending to build a naval base there. However, since there was no suitable site for a harbour, it was never built.

Our guesthouse was run by two friendly local women who spoke Spanish and Rapanui (the local Polynesian dialect), neither of which I knew. But an American called Mel, married to a local, was found to show us around. As it was only mid-morning we climbed into Mel's battered Land Rover for a tour of the island.

The entire island population lives in the town of Hanga Roa on a small hill close to the sheltered west coast. We drove down the main street to the sea, where the road turns sharply to the right. Our teeth rattled as we bumped over ruts and stones, following the coast which ran in a jagged line ahead of us. A few clumps of eucalyptus trees represent the only attempt at replanting the jungle of palms that once existed.

Mel pointed to something a few miles ahead on the hill side. 'Standing Moais,' he announced. At this distance they looked like a few fingers of rock pointing skywards, making little impression on the dramatic landscape. Closer up, they became giant statues carved out of stone. They stand in a row, staring mutely inland. Gazing at the stone figures, I was struck by an odd thought. In the faces of the Moais I detected a strange anomaly which seemed to hint at the fallibility of the Polynesians. Round-shouldered, pot-bellied, with lips compressed into an expression of faint disapproval, these images are thought to be not gods, but man: Polynesian ancestors. Was this the way they saw themselves?

A local boy riding on the back of a small reef shark off Bora Bora.

Bora Bora, the quintessential South Pacific island.

*Pages 76 and 77: A lone Moai on Easter Island – remote, desolate
and enigmatic.*

We drove to the other side of the island, to an extinct volcano where the statues were quarried. High up in the quarry hawks circle, crying shrilly over the heads of dozens of statues. There are over six hundred on the island, all carved from the same great mound of yellow rock. As each Moai was finished it was 'walked' with the help of wooden levers – the reason why the palms were all cut down, across rough terrain to its designated *ahu* (altar). Eyes were then inserted, eyes which gave it *mana*, power to protect its people. I thought it was strange that they faced inland and not out to sea. What did the people fear there?

The building began in the eighth century AD and continued until about 1700, when it suddenly and mysteriously stopped, leaving unfinished statues lying on their backs across the cliff face. At that time the culture started to decline rapidly. The exhaustion of slender resources by overcrowding led to civil war, and over the next hundred years starvation and cannibalism reduced the original population of twelve thousand to a third of that number. By the time Captain Cook arrived in 1774, the islanders' faith in the power of the stone statues had been destroyed and most had been toppled off their *ahus*. They lay in disarray, necks broken, eyes gouged out.

In 1862 a fleet of Peruvian slavers captured about a thousand Rapanui, uncluding the last king and the entire educated class, and took them off to work sugar plantations in South America. The fifteen who eventually returned brought with them tuberculosis and smallpox. By 1870 the total population of the island had been reduced to a mere one hundred and ten.

It now totals some two thousand. It's rare to see a face that looks Polynesian; a century of interbreeding with visitors, mostly from Chile, has resulted in a South American-looking people, but a Polynesian dialect is still spoken. The Rapanui are resentful of Chile's governorship of their island, but without it they would have nothing in the way of Western conveniences – which they don't want to do without. They garden the same staple crops grown in other parts of Polynesia – *taro*, pineapple, bananas and so on – and supplement their diet with what they can afford from supply ships, which call infrequently. All services on the island are heavily subsidized, and most people in work are employed by the government. Others earn a meagre living from tourists. As the Rapanui are Chilean citizens they can, and do, emigrate to the Chilean mainland.

I felt there was a dispirited air among the people we met. Isolated island communities are always plagued by irritations caused by the absence of outside stimulation, but these people seemed lost – at least that's how they struck me. They seemed to be a forsaken people stranded, like their crumbling stone statues, in the biggest museum in the world.

After the fall of the Maoi a remnant of Polynesian culture was carried on in the new cult of the birdman of Orongo. On the day before our departure I went up to this famous village, built on top of the crater rim of Rano Kau. The greatest god of Easter Island was Make-make, the god of creation, who became increasingly venerated as the old traditions declined. Members of tribal groups gathered once a year at Orongo to await the arrival of the sooty tern. While they waited, they carved petroglyphs of Make-make and birdmen into the cliff faces overlooking the sea. In a bizarre ritual, the first servant to secure a tern's egg from the off-lying island and bring it to his chief assured his tribe military success for the coming year.

It was a windy climb up the grassy, rock-strewn slope to the edge of the crater. Three hundred feet below my feet lay a dark, primeval swamp. Making my way along the path towards Orongo, I passed a line of caves where the chiefs had waited for their servants to achieve the near impossible. In one of the dark grottoes, with their 2-foot-high entrances, a carved wooden figure of an emaciated naked man was found by the first archaeologists to visit the site. Also discovered were some peculiar wooden tablets inscribed with hieroglyphic characters, now assumed to be mnemonic devices to aid the recitation of chants and royal genealogies. This pictorial script, the only example in the whole of Oceania, is the climax of Easter Island culture. The meaning and origin of the script have been lost.

I edged carefully past the petroglyphs of birdmen and round-eyed god faces staring out of the wet rocks, and slid out on to a promontory overhanging the crater. A squall of wind pulled jerkily at my jacket, then rushed down the steep sides of the crater and flattened the reeds in the lake below. It was a breathtaking view. The loneliness of the place intensified the melancholy train of my thoughts.

This was the end of the journey. I had come to Polynesia to search for authentic, original culture, but had discovered that it was all in the past. I had also come to try to understand modern Polynesia, and had seen a society disintegrating in the changing, strife-ridden South Sea islands of today. Struggling for identity, unwilling to hold on to the past and ill equipped to cope with the future, Polynesia is to me a fallen paradise, blighted by the very hand that conceived it in Europe.

As for me, besides learning something about Polynesia, I've gained a better insight into myself, although I'm not very happy with what I've found. It would be easy to blame my prejudice on the fact that I was brought up in New Zealand, a country which, while staunchly attacking the South African policy of apartheid, does little to change the attitude of the white majority towards its own native people – but it's not as simple as that. I've come to the depressing conclusion that I am prejudiced because I am part of the West.

Countries such as New Zealand, Australia and America were taken over by outsiders, Europeans, who swept aside those who were already there, and it still goes on today across the Pacific. The USA continues to dominate Pacific islands for strategic defence purposes against the wishes of the islanders, and the French continue to pollute the Pacific with the greatest evil the earth has ever known – all in the name of what? Progress? The salvation of our race?

There's nothing new in the concept of avarice; countless cultures have waxed and waned in this way. But I should have thought that Europe, in this 'civilized' age, might have risen above such greed. On the most basic level I think it's a matter of personal prejudice. If I see myself as better than those who lack Western drive and ambition, or our assumed superiority, then such gentle people as the Polynesians will continue to fall by the wayside. But one day, who knows, we might be on the receiving end ourselves.

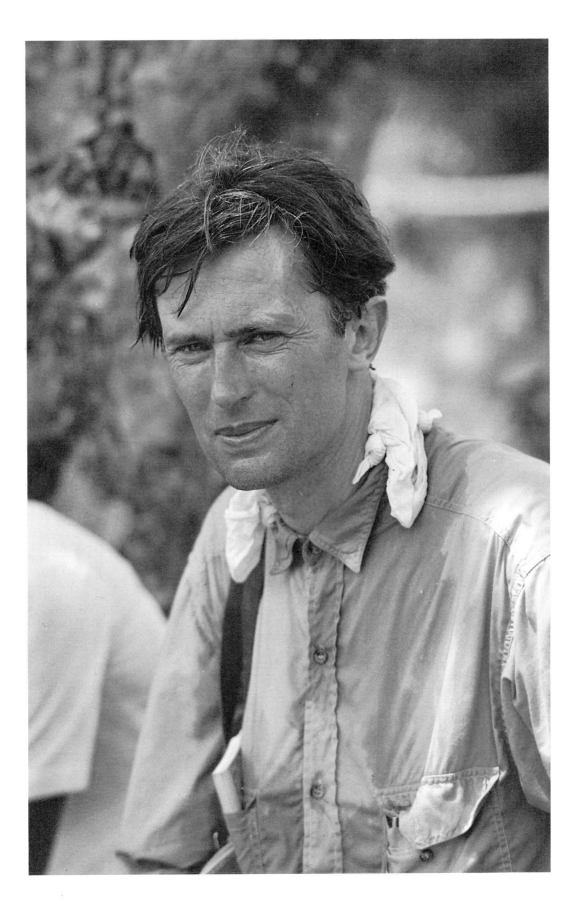

THE PAN AMERICAN HIGHWAY

Hugo Williams

Don't panic. Everything's going to be all right. Auntie will take care of you. . . . I imagine the map of North America as a funnel, with some kind of sugary substance – foreign aid perhaps, or Coca-Cola – pouring down from the benevolent First World into the open mouth of the Third. You can see at a glance why there's a blockage in places like Nicaragua and El Salvador: it's a bottleneck.

The first thing director Peter Dale and I see in the States is a Sex 'n Weight chat show on the TV above the bar in Houston Airport. One balloon woman says her husband doesn't wash or brush his teeth any more. The host says maybe he is trying to tell her something. Two others say they can't cross their legs they are putting on weight so fast. They try, and they are right – they can't. A leering newscaster informs overweight America that multiple child sex murderer Terry Bundy was electric-chaired this morning.

America is so *visible* compared to England. It wears its guts on the outside, like the Pompidou Centre – everything laid out like a map of itself. Conspicuous desire! Conspicuous satisfaction! The announcements of success in business stand on 40-foot-high poles and slowly revolve like muezzins calling the faithful to prayer. Mr Donut! Wottaburger! 'You're part of US. We're part of YOU. First National Bank.' The poverty is conspicuous, too.

I hadn't realized that half the United States used to belong to Mexico. What is now the American West and South was once the Mexican North. The tide from Spain rolled across the land in the sixteenth century, and when it rolled back three hundred years later it left behind its culture and its blood. The land changed hands

In Mexico City a female security guard brandishes a sub-machine gun.

Left: A Mexican telephones under the shadow of La Mafia in Nuevo Laredo, while just across the border an old Texan plays dominoes in the main square of Laredo.

Pages 84 and 85: Dawn over Lake Atitlán and Sololá village, Guatemala.

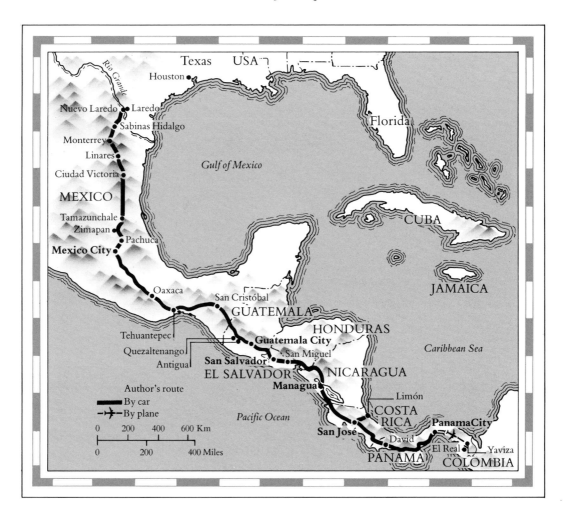

over a century ago, but Spanish-surnamed Southwesterners continue to see present-day California, Texas, Nevada, Utah, Arizona, New Mexico, Colorado and parts of Oklahoma, Wyoming and Kansas as a lost homeland, 'The Lost Land', occupied by Anglos.

When you realize this, it sheds a different light on America's great problem of 'illegal immigrants', more commonly known as 'wetbacks': these people view themselves as foreigners in their native land, more Spanish than truly Mexican. 'My father was a wetback,' goes the quip. 'I am an illegal alien, but my son will be an undocumented national.' The thousands of refugees from Nicaragua and El Salvador who pour across the border, only to find that the true frontier is at the checkpoints further north, are referred to by the Border Control as 'OTMs' – other than Mexicans. Many are now reduced to living in plastic bags, begging door-to-door in the trailer parks.

'Central America is a measured speculation,' says Othal Brand, self-made millionaire mayor of McAllen, Texas, and fruiterer to the Free World. 'It's a challenge and I've always been a gambler....' He warns us about earthquakes in these unstable areas. 'I always stay in small hotels down in San Salvador.... If you have an accident across the river you'll be immediately thrown in prison. It's Roman law down there.

You're guilty until you're proven innocent. The Thirty Years' War was the watershed. The northern half of Europe went Protestant, the southern half went Catholic. It's the same in the Americas. By the end of my time down there I was spending more time defending my interests than creating anything new. The Mexicans would get the New York prices index and tell me what I owed them for my own strawberries! I went to Russia last year. I was looking for my counterpart over there. Doesn't exist. That's their problem. See, you've got to allow the dominant in society to flower, otherwise your industry can't develop for the next generation....' He fetches us glasses of water and says he is about to have a Bible class in his home.

At this time of year (January) the warm border country, so unlike either Texas or Mexico, is full of 'Winter Texans' or 'Snowbirds' – frisky senior citizens from the freezing farm states up north, crowding dismal trailer parks with their hulking RVs (recreational vehicles). Recreation is their occupation, and they spend their time wandering around socializing or looking at colourful bits of border: Roma, where *Viva Zapata* was shot; Martha, where *Giant* was made; Fort Ringgold where Ulysses S. Grant and Robert E. Lee were cadets together – now a Mexican high school swarming with brown-skinned adolescents.

Los Ebanos is a two hundred-year-old *colonia* of shacks and bungalows with the only ferryboat crossing on any US border. Most of the passengers today are Snow-birds waiting to cross over to San Miguel de Camargo to have a look at Mexico. We stand and watch the little ferry being hand-hauled across the fast-flowing Rio Grande. The current takes care of the US-Mexican crossing, but eight seasoned Mexicans have to strain to make the uphill journey to the Land of the Free.

This is Starr County, where fortunes are made from illegal immigration and drugs. Fine drug-money houses perch on the choicest elevations. Rio Grande City, voted the meanest town in America, is the perfect location for border barons with something to hide. Due to a natural allergy to politics, the town has successfully avoided all attempts at incorporation. This means it has no municipal government; the town is run privately with the help of just four strong, silent and corruptible police commissioners.

'Something falls off you when you cross the border into Mexico'.
William Burroughs, *The Naked Lunch*

'Oh, life, that begins on the other side.'
Graham Greene, *Across the Bridge*

The bridge in question is the bridge from Laredo into Nuevo Laredo, from First World into Third, from credit into debt, from day into night. And it is true that life is mostly on the other side.

Laredo, Texas, where we pick up the Pan American Highway, is one vast retail outlet for mass smuggling enterprises. Outside the consumer emporiums the smugglers are openly taking things out of cardboard cartons and packing them away in old suitcases. Women are putting on layer after layer of new clothes. Lowlier beings collect the flattened cartons and load them on to cycle-carts. These will be

exported to Mexico at $5 a load, to be turned into papier mâché skeletons and devils for tourists. The two towns are two sides of an equation: supply and demand, capital and labour, hunger and greed. Politics goes south, as the saying goes, while people come north.

At dusk the bridge is jammed with cars and trucks and cycle-carts and crowds of tired workers pushing home through the turnstiles: 15 cents to go south, 20 cents to come back to America. You can't win. Dust and flies hang in the fume-saturated air, engines and bodies boiling over.

Is it an illusion that night falls as you cross the bridge into Nuevo Laredo? You imagine certain questions being asked at Mexican immigration, like what are you looking for in Mexico that the might of America can't provide? Desire mixes with guilt as daylight slips from your clothes. Fantastic animals glare from shop-front grottoes. '*Religiosos artículos* . . . if you do not find what you are looking for in this shop. . . .' The rest of the sentence blocked by a broken air conditioning unit hanging by a thread. Flayed goats display the inside of their rib-cages to the faint-hearted. Boy's Town beckons with its grown-up tummy upsets. Night sneaks up behind you in Nuevo Laredo, like a pickpocket. You tighten your money-belt.

The blue light area, known to gringos as 'Boy's Town', lies down a potholed track on the outskirts of Nuevo Laredo. It is a compound, like a Western fort, with a main gate and a dozen joints of every description set around a circular dirt road.

We choose The Marabu, a plush dance-hall with eight or so girls twirling on bar stools. One immense-hipped black girl comes over and starts telling us, parrot fashion, what she can do for us. She goes to work squeezing the hotel key in my pocket, which she compliments me on. Massage is offered for my tiredness. Or would I prefer to massage Alicia? When I ask her if she sings or dances she says, 'No, what you see is what I do for a living', and sticks out her tongue. She is twenty-seven, with two children of eleven and thirteen. She herself was married at fourteen, divorced six years ago. Does he pay anything? No, not in Mexico, nothing.

She sticks around for the statutory $2 drink, then leaves us to it. Waiters hustle drinks every four minutes, removing half-empty bottles and swabbing dry tables with wet cloths. This place is a money machine, a smooth-running containment area where the girls get a check-up and penicillin jabs every week. We drink more strong little Coroneto beers and decide to try one more dive.

The Dallas Cowboy is pure Wild West cantina: a circular dance floor with ten or so girls perched on the staircase to a gallery above. Letitia comes over and starts squeezing my hotel key. She is very outrageous and very cheap, $25. After a short dance, I ask her where the *baño* is and she shows me a room ankle deep in urine. 'No clean, no nice, why not you don't use my room?'

I have had so many Coronetos I have no choice, but instead of leaving me to it, she stands in the doorway, waiting, I can't begin to get started and give up in desperation. When I turn round she is standing between me and the door with nothing on. This might seem like the moment to have admitted defeat, but you don't feel like it in that heat. I give her $5 and scarper.

I wake next morning hungover and hot and look incredulously at an obscene picture she has drawn on my left palm, showing the various possibilities that were on offer. I suppose there are worse things to wake up with.

The Pan American Highway is really a series of highways that extends from the US-Mexican border to southern Chile, with a 500-mile missing section in southern Panama known as the Darien Gap. The idea to link North and South America was first proposed from the 1880s, but the organization of the system didn't start until the late 1920s.

The modern Pan American Movement dates from the First International Conference of American States in 1889, but the real spirit of Pan Americanism flowered after Franklin D. Roosevelt's 'Good Neighbor' policy in the 1930s. During the Second World War the American republics co-operated to fight the Axis nations and afterwards took steps to improve their communications. By 1950 most of the Highway between the United States and Panama had been completed, though you had to put your car on a train for a few hundred miles in south Mexico.

Each South American country financed the building of the Highway within its own borders, but in 1930 the United States began giving financial support to speed the building of the Highway between Texas and Panama. Only Mexico has not used US financial aid in building the system. The Highway is sometimes described as running through the western United States and Canada and up into Alaska, but neither country has officially recognized any highway as part of the Pan American system.

Dan Sanborn, who has wrapped up all the motor insurance for visitors to Mexico, also provides a detailed log of your itinerary to keep you out of trouble and save himself money. 'Drive offensively,' he suggests. 'If you see a stop sign, "*Alto*", it doesn't necessarily mean stop if you *feel* you should go on. Use your intuition. If you get lost, remember the most important word in the Spanish language is the first letter of the alphabet. In Spanish it's pronounced "Ah", as in "Ah, sweet mystery of life!" and it means "to". When you're driving in Mexico and aren't exactly sure where you're going, just stop and ask any Mexican, "Ah Monterrey?" or "Ah Motel Santa Fe?" and with your forefinger sort of point down the road and at the same time nod your head in the general direction you are going. If you're on the right track, the Mexican will say "*Si!*". If he says "*No*", then turn around, head the other way, and ask somebody else "Ah Monterrey?". Above all, always remember to smile when you get to Mexico and keep on smiling. Shake hands *every* chance you get. Those nice folks will *love* you if you only shake their hand. Wave at everyone along the way, especially kiddies. Don't poke fun at them, or their language, or their money. For instance, don't say, "How much is that in real money?"'

If ever there was a case for asking this last question it is in Mexico, but we pin smiles on our faces, stick our heads out the window and wave at everything that moves. 'Ah Mexico?'

Trucks and mud and urban sprawl. Hamburgesas!!! El Gladiator Social Club is a roadside café. Café La Paz is a lean-to hovel. The Vallecillo Motel looks like a

A small mountain village in the Western Highlands of Guatemala.

Left: The grand colonial architecture of Antigua, the old capital

deserted pigsty. Mile upon mile of little motor-part services – mud, junk and rain. Long before we pick up the Pan American Highway outside Nuevo Laredo our windscreen is smeared thick with mud. Fields of container trailers. Miles of car dumps. Bronco Autoparts. Chaos under grey skies with a vague sense of altitude. 'Remember altitude is more important to temperature than season,' Dan Sanborn reminds us. 'Just as attitude is more important than amplitude.' Thank you, Dan.

A barber shop, a tyre shop, a bar, all like dog kennels, separated by clapboard bungalows, all with some kind of grandiose lettering on. Taller Mecanico. Deposito Plaza. Carta Blanca. Transportes del Norte. At last we hit the open road and turn up the Hank Williams.

The first landscape is distinguished by short, cactus-like palm trees with bad haircuts, called joshua trees, like coconut-heads sticking up to see over the surrounding scrub. Hump-back cattle remind us once more that this is at least the Third World we have entered. There goes a Volkswagen plant where they still make Beetles.

First night at the Alamo Hotel in shacky Sabinas Hidalgo, where a weird little scene is developing in the Gato Negro bar. Ignacio is a handsome old gent in an overcoat, scarf and dark glasses, who wants us to guess how old he is – that old game. I subtract ten years and guess right. Ignacio spent forty years driving a cab in Chicago and gets $390 a month from his US pension. He is nothing if not honest about his finances, but it is we who buy. 'You work to eat to drink to fuck to die,' he tells us three times. He stands behind the bar the better to talk to us in his incomprehensible English, emphasizing his remarks in chalk on the bar-top. He writes the figure '$390' on the bar and adjusts his shades. His wife and four children are in California picking grapes: 'I can live like a king here. This is my town.' He smooths his fine overcoat. 'I fuck two times a week. Is enough. Any more and I might die, he ha ha!' We all bust a gut at this. Ignacio is a smooth old fake mafioso hypochondriac pimp, but we buy him lots of Coronas and he expands still further. 'You wanna go with me two three miles outta town have a few drinks meet a few girls OK, we go to Nick's Place. You wanna fuck, fuck!'

Except for this set piece his speech is no better than that of the other drunks he is trying to impress. They communicate with us in more-drink signs and broad winks, but Ignacio wants his friends to think he is talking English. One sad case, long past talking, can still do a trimphone whistle, which interests Peter. The drunk has got a small cane liquor bottle which he tops himself up with. I turn round and there they are, trimphone whistling to each other. We buy another round and find that metropolitan prices have been applied to us, despite the bonhomie. After Boy's Town last night, we pass up on Nick's Place. 'Next time round maybe.'

Next day, we negotiate the endless recycling suburbs of polluted Monterrey. The little shacky establishments each have there own bewildering dignity of hand-lettering. The run-down, one-man, one-storey commercial fantasy with dream ambition and grinning unshaven proprietor beloved of bleached out, bled-off colour supplement layouts is hardly exotic in Mexico. It *is* Mexico.

At the army checkpoint at the State border south of Monterrey a boy soldier asks me where I am going and gets the one answer he isn't expecting: 'Linares.'

'Linares!' he echoes. 'Linares?' He cannot make this out as he knows we have just come through Linares. But it is a good gimmick as the laughs mean we do not have to bribe anyone.

Fear of the Spanish world is traditional in the USA, like fear of poverty, failure and darkness, which it symbolizes for them. Most people down here live in not much more than mud huts surrounded by mud, chickens, oil cans, tyres, goats, washing, dogs and children. Their menfolk wait endlessly beside roads in straw stetsons, waiting for a gang boss to pick them up. No matter where you go, the little Coca-Cola flags proclaim an outpost of civilization. It is more like Africa than I expected. The Pan American Highway is an insult to such poverty. It's not even a bad road! It just shoots through to somewhere else, benefiting only the livestock which graze its verges all the way from Texas to the Darien Gap: horses, cows, mules, pigs and goats – even, outside Yaviza, an exhausted-looking sloth.

Spain built one hundred thousand religious buildings in its American empire, but they are rarely seen from the road. Only the occasional big house from another universe, usually deserted, converted, or burnt out by terrorists. It's all so much nearer the ground than I imagined: a scraped, visceral existence from which you keep catching a glimpse of yourself, with some disquiet. Taking endless failed photographs of majestic mountain views is a kind of displacement activity for looking squarely at it all. Then suddenly you're in a town again and a middle class is trying to emerge.

After air-conditioned burgers at Charley's in Ciudad Victoria we pass the Tropic of Cancer and the sugar cane starts.

Moving up into cloud, forest and mist now, on the other side of Tamazunchale (pronounced 'Thomas 'n Charlie'), the little 'African' villages with their rows of striped beehives lost in a jungle of big leaves and purple flowers lush as Tahiti. Poor soaked Indians in ponchos and head-loads walking to work with long knives. A thatched Coke outpost called El Sacrificio, piles of dirty oranges beside the road, starched children crocodiling to the prefab school.

After Zimapan we leave the tropical highlands for drier stone hills with organ cacti down reddish ravines, range upon range of mountains getting bluer and bluer in the distance, sun shading one's face now, taunting our cameras. The Greyhounds I rode in the seventies have arrived in Mexico to pass a delinquent senility belching round mountain hairpins, their two outside wheels scuffling for purchase on 1000-foot precipices as they overtake us, tooting wildly. I got stuck behind one in a cloud just now and started to doze on its gaudy backside. The little wayside crosses, indicating fatal accidents, remind one not to push one's luck hereabouts.

At the highest point of the Highway, north of Pachuca, the American colony in Mexico erected a platitudinous bilingual tablet to commemorate the opening of the road by some forgotten general in 1936: 'May it serve always as a path of mutual respect and an indissoluble bond ... etc'. But the well-meaning monument has been defaced by the words: 'Fascismo Salinas Fascista' and upstaged by a drive-in-sized Coke hoarding which looks down on it from a slight hill. Coke, of course, have every reason to be grateful for this good road through a thirsty country.

Guatemala has a higher percentage of Indians than any other Central American country. The weekly market in the village of Zunil attracts large crowds from the surrounding hillsides.

All along the 5-mile triumphal entry to the boom steel town of Pachuca, relics of the area's mining past have been mounted on pedestals: tip-trucks, drilling rigs, smelting gear and an old delivery lorry of a kind I'm sure we saw in working operation in the country earlier today. The little flower-decked shrine marooned on the central reservation of the six-lane highway to Mexico City reminds us again of our catchphrase: Mexico, land of contrasts! As the big cars jockey for position I remember the bare-footed *campesinos* squatting beside the road a few miles back. Being without capital they have no choice but to invest what they do have plenty of – their time, their lives, their bodies. They are their own only advertisement. In a sense, they *are* what they sell. God protect them from the mile after mile of one-storey windowless block-houses joined together like walls beside the road as we broach the Mexico City struggle.

They say the definition of a split second in Mexico City is the time between the lights turning green and the first person tooting. But despite what its inhabitants like to think, the pace of the city is nothing like that of a European city, due perhaps to its rarified atmosphere. Mexico's central upland plateau – 7500 feet at Mexico City – is the biggest in the world. There are only two higher plateaux of comparable size, those of Tibet and Bolivia. It isn't as polluted as they tell you, either.

We check into the Geneva Hotel on Calle Londres and I drink hungrily from the bad T V. You see the same pushy armpit work from powerfully-built ladies on Mexican variety shows as in their Social Realist sculpture and the murals of Diego Rivera. In Mexico the comic and the tragic amalgamate casually in the grotesque. In official handicraft shops you can buy weird non-existent animals, red devil lamps, skull boxes, little plaster tableaux of skeleton surgeons operating on blood-soaked women.

The Mexican enthusiasm for the macabre knows no limit. The artist Frida Kahlo, who was unable to bear children, was comforted by the gift of a human foetus in a bottle. She called it 'My little boy'. When she went to New York in 1930 with her husband Diego Rivera, she looked around her and felt an easy superiority: 'I don't particularly like the gringo people. They are boring and they all have faces like unbaked rolls.' She christened America Gringolandia and longed to return to Mexican civilization. I tried to imagine the city in the 1930s when art, revolution and free love were in the air.

Mexico is an old country. In 1575 its books were printed in Spanish and in twelve Indian languages. Its first printing press was set up a hundred years before the first press appeared in the British colonies to the north. Under Spanish rule, Mexico for a time led northern Europe in art and science. Today the ruins of that glory lie on all sides. . . .

In the centre of the Zócolo, the massive central square, the national flag of Mexico flies. It is the same size as a tennis court and is suspended from a pole as high as a television mast. At 6 p.m. they haul it down. A door opens in the National Palace and a military band goose-steps across the square. The bugle call rings out and the vast flag is folded and laid in its plastic cradle.

What an incredible privilege to go sailing over the top of it all, as if one were performing some useful function in the world! There go Popocatepetl and Ixtac-cihuatl, snow-topped at 8.30 a.m. All is peaceful on the road until outside Pueblo I ram a stationary pig wagon and go into shock. 'I recommend you don't stop,' says our guide as I disengage, leaving bits of Suburban embedded in the wagon. 'Foreigners are automatically guilty here. They merely throw you in prison until your case comes up.' I force myself to drive on.

When we next stop I eagerly take up smoking and Coca-Cola again. The idea of me being anyone's first choice as driver in a road movie is one of life's jollier ironies. 'And to think, he did all that big journey on his own!' I put on a Dr Feelgood tape to steady my nerves, and closely observe the strange practice in these parts of drying corn husks in trees. If the scenery goes on improving, we should be in Heaven by about lunchtime.

In *Under the Volcano*, Malcolm Lowry calls Oaxaca the saddest sound in the world, a nonsense until you learn how it is pronounced – 'Wa-hah-ka'. This is the beautiful Spanish capital of Oaxaca province, laid out on a grid in a fold of the southern Sierra Madre. It is cool and I am taking the lemon sunshine under the two hundred-year-old willow trees of the main square. A blind guitarist is led by a boy between the tables. White shirts and straw hats criss-cross during a morning's work. Indian children come again and again to sell chewing gum, baskets, combs. The price of a lump of yellow plastic gives rise to some 'amberguity'. They buy back my English-language newspaper and sell it again at a profit. These are the little girls in pink dresses I dream about running over. They have bare feet and dusty plaits and they are waiting for me outside my hotel in the morning so I can apologize for running them over by buying some bubble gum or a paper knife. A shoe-shine kneels at my feet. I spend my time admiring the view and shaking my head. I have on suede shoes.

The incredible scenery somehow manages to go up one more notch south of Oaxaca. San José trees with the sun shining through their ten or twenty brilliant yellow blooms. The red-flowering jojoba tree that sends its oil into fashionable bathrooms. Some cactuses with white furry bits on top which we say must mean they're on heat. Highly subjective that. Having timed it, I know for a fact that you think about sex every eight minutes while travelling. Peter says it's supposed to be every seven. We stop at the mountain village of La Reforma to drink the milk from ice-cold coconuts.

The Hotel Oasis, Tehuantepec. We eat chicken in chocolate sauce in the Café Colonial where the local vamp, wearing enormous skintight jeans, takes the chairs off the tables. She returns my hangdog looks with friendly contempt and repeats '*Dos Bohemias por favor*' in gringospeak.

The town has something of an independent, friendly, faded aura, but the heat is coming on strong. I change my shirt by putting on a different dirty one and we drink more and more Bohemias in a hot dark arcade that might be in Bengal. Beggars and children are everywhere late at night. I wonder what it feels like to fall in love in such a place, and whether there is any liberation in it.

In the middle of the night a train howls down the main street, waking the dogs

A woman sells flowers on the steps of the church at Chichicastenango.

Left: Clouds of incense obscure the church entrance.

and cockerels all over town and the two parrots downstairs who imitate them. Live things of all kinds pop and squeak and moan. Why is it that one can do without sleep while the travelling lasts? Breakfast of the inevitable hotcakes and honey to cushion my handfuls of pills.

Popping along to San Cristóbal now. 'What had appeared to be a small route on the map was an enormous distance to be traversed in reality. Was not this too symbolical – how simple our journey seemed and yet how long, how dangerous it was – or would it be better to say, in our blindness, our dumb unawakened lives, how mean our journey seemed, how great in reality?' Thus Malcolm Lowry in *Dark as the Grave Wherein My Friend Is Laid*, which I am taking to my friend Michael Hofmann, who was supposed to be in Oaxaca. Perhaps he has gone to the cooler climate of San Cristóbal.

We pass Zinacanteca, where the male Indians are said to have the most beautiful legs in the world. To show them off they wear pink shorts and breeches, complemented with wide-brimmed hats trimmed with ribbons – tied for married men, loose for bachelors. No equivocating in Zinacanteca!

Hurrah! Michael is here in San C. and will come to Guatemala with us. He takes us to see the Indian village of Chamula, a semi-pagan community which is preparing for Lent with fireworks, banners, trumpets and cane liquor. Groups of costumed men, religious brotherhoods, make little trotting excursions here and there among the blue-clothed orange sellers in the marketplace, while the town's elders watch from the balcony with their authority sticks.

We enter the church and are struck dumb by the sights and sounds and smells. It is empty of furniture, but the blue-tiled floor is scattered with pine needles and clusters of candles among the groups of sitting or standing people, the men on little stools, the women on the floor, all drinking, talking or bowing down in prayer. Children run round us, playing. There is no priest, but a homely atmosphere of celebration and familiarity is borne to us on the smell of incense and the sound of harp, accordion, guitar and drums playing a beautiful bluesy little tune over and over again. Just in front of me a large family of Indians, their women standing just behind them, are being offered Coca-Cola by another Indian, who seems to be playing the priest. He refills their glasses with clear liquor, they pray together, then shuffle out, their kids tagging after.

Chamula is a religious community. The land is fertile and there is time for ritual and philosophy. Like everywhere else, it is the centre of the universe. Chamulans are 'The Real People'. Chamulan time is spatial as well as temporal. Faraway places are longer ago and are developing cyclically towards the ideal Chamulan way of life. Faraway people are primitive savages, the further away the more so, although England does figure on their map next to the United States. We meet a Chamulan selling soft drinks, who asks how much it will cost for us to get home. He says he will go with us wherever we are going, so long as we pay his passage. We think this is highly amusing until we remember we have been offered the same sort of deal ourselves.

Sadly, the meddlesome Evangelists have been making headway in Chamula by offering salvation from the endemic alcoholism. Converts are cast out of Chamulan society and have to exist in a limbo outside the village or on the fringes of San Cristóbal in a growing slum area. The town was originally set up by the Spanish to dominate the surrounding tribes, and until as late as the 1940s the Indians weren't allowed to walk on the pavements and were banned from the town after dark. It is hardly surprising that outsiders are unpopular and their scavenging cameras banned from Chamulan ritual. Recently two *National Geographic* photographers were stripped and paraded half-naked through the streets. A hundred and fifty years ago, a boy was famously crucified in Chamula.

We go for dinner to a restaurant where the owner says he may be able to get us permission to film in Chamula at Easter. I notice with some alarm that he employs Indians as waiters, wearing their native costume. He says he will talk to his friend the *principal municipal*, but I remember reading that the religious leaders are more important than the political ones in Chamulan society.

At Cuauhtémoc on the Guatemalan border we stand around eating the last of our banned tangerines while the car is fumigated. Each country has at least two border controls, not including customs, so it takes time – and money. 'Tourist cards are not issued to people from Communist countries or to black people unless they are citizens of the USA' says the bare-faced immigration leaflet.

At the Vegas Roadhouse there is a marimba band – three or four depressed old gentlemen playing chirpy little cover versions of things like 'Stranger in Paradise' on one big xylophone. The marimba, or xylophone, is the national instrument of Guatemala, and muzak is the national music. The less admired 'tropical' sounds of soca, salsa and reggae come from the Atlantic coast, where the black, English-speaking Caribs keep mostly to themselves.

The national bird of Guatemala (and also the unit of currency) is the fabulous but elusive quezal. Tonight we sleep in Quezaltenango, where the Indian leader Tecun Yman fell down, leaving feathers from his quezal head-dress on the ground after he had been killed by Pedro Alvarado, conqueror of Guatemala.

In our sterile hotel at Q. I drink ignominiously from the tawdry 'Movie Channel' – rubbishy films and did-you-knows about the stars, 'dished' out to a grateful Third World by satellite.

Two recurring contradictions: one, the beauty of pre-industrial landscape – the perfection of mountains and valleys – suddenly yielding to the jaded clichés of twentieth-century sprawl, and two, the impossibility of reconciling a subdued, shambolic people with the blazing eyes and piles of bodies of newspaper headlines.

Quezaltenango is distinctly down-at-heel and moody compared to the up-beat boom towns of Mexico. The electricity current is weak. A ghostly nineteenth-century atmosphere not unlike that of certain Iron Curtain towns, the stately colonial architecture now colonized in its turn by shabby, short-haul fast food outlets and jeans emporiums. The sign above a door says 'Correos y Telecomunicación', but a provisional-looking disco is flashing its lights inside.

A soft, dark main street leads us to a candle-and-gas-lit fair with families camping under sheets of polythene, women selling indecipherable goodies off charcoal fires

*In the Western Highlands of Guatemala two Indian children dress in
the clothes unique to their village, a custom that is dying out as
development spreads into the hills from Guatemala City (right).*

fanned by banana leaves. A little hand-hauled big wheel contains two rapturous couples.

A drunken Salvadoran gravitates towards the gringos, holding out his passport as if from habit. He was born in San Francisco of all places, in 1962, and is walking back there – '*Muchas problemas, muchas problemas*' – fleeing both the Salvadoran army *and* the FMLN (the left-wing guerrilla movement, supported by Nicaragua) as far as I can make out.

'You like Indian women?' he asks.

'Yes – you got one?'

'No.' His hopelessness and confusion reflect my own instinctive reaction to political analyses here and at home: that they too strongly resemble statistics. Having shown a little interest in his plight, I have trouble shaking off the poor bastard.

Next morning our guide takes us to the Indian village of Zunil – down an alley to an open door giving on to a windowless earth-floored room, a short of chapel. Inside is a short, grey-faced idol in a dark business suit and stetson. He has on circular sunglasses and there is a lit cheroot between his clay lips. This is Maximon, Indian wide boy and spy to the white man's Heaven. He has been around since the sixteenth century when the Indians decided, reasonably enough, that if Judas Iscariot had betrayed the Spanish god, he must be on their side and duly made a cult of him. The Spaniards tried to suppress the cult of 'Maximon' or 'San Simon', to no avail. They finally gave up destroying the clay figures and allowed the idol to appear for one week every year, in his own little temple. For the rest of the year he is looked after here by a keeper, called a tillinil, with his brotherhood of attendants.

When our gormless white faces appear in the doorway of this amazing shrine the tillinil is in the process of marrying a little Indian couple. A cluster of candles stands on the floor. Incense. Flowers and coloured polythene hang from the low ceiling. People sitting round drinking out of beer bottles. Maximon too likes a drink, and is said to be stuffed with old liquor-soaked newspapers. To one side lies the recumbent form of Jesus in a glass coffin, for he too is worshipped in this hybrid religion.

When he sees us, the tillinil drops his voice and starts whispering in Maximon's ear. He throws a yellow Mickey Mouse towel round the shoulders of the bride. Across a vast gulf of embarrassment I catch the bridegroom's eye and feel ashamed, but cannot drag myself away. Later, in Antigua, we would see an imitation of this touchingly decadent shrine, set up in a museum, already culturized.

It's sad, but from the comfort of your car you quickly get used to seeing cloud-topped volcanoes plunging to patterned valleys thousands of feet below, a handful of bright-clothed Indians posed picturesquely in the foreground with their obligatory bundle of faggots. Our guide tells us of the deforestation problem, of soil erosion, flooding and landslides, how every year the Indians must go higher and higher up the hillsides to glean their only source of fuel, while every year the tourists dig deeper into traditional Indian country, tempting them to forsake their culture for the illusory world of *Rocky* and *Rambo*, which play eternally in tiny village 'Video Palaces'. A five-minute telephone call home from Chichicastenango costs me the equivalent of five hand-made shirts. You cannot blame the Indians for falling drunkenly asleep, often in the middle of the road. Inevitably, the evangelical branch of Alcoholics Anonymous has a high profile in these villages. Whichever way they turn, the Indians cannot win.

No one in the team has been looking forward to El Salvador. Joan Didion's book and Oliver Stone's film, both called starkly *Salvador*, have led us to expect darkness and death squads.... We see demonstrations against the imminent arrival of Daniel Ortega for the Central American Summit, since it is he who has been supplying arms to the left-wing FMLN. But despite the riots and shootings related to the FMLN's demands for a postponement of the March elections, San Salvador is ticking over much like any other teeming tropical city. Or so it seems to those who wish it to be so.

I have heard that there is an interesting Englishman working as Curator of Reptiles at the San Salvador zoo, so having an afternoon to spare I go to see him. John Boursot is a blue-eyed man in his early seventies, frail-looking but still vital and talkative. He left England in 1939 and has been at the run-down zoo for twenty years. 'They don't give me enough money to look after the snakes,' he tells me one minute after meeting me. 'They're scamps and thieves in this country. They had a hole in the wall and the boys would push the lion's meat through to a friend. I tried to get the hole blocked up, but they said, don't you dare ... and they bring their chickens to feed at the zoo. That's my own tortoise there. This is a Californian rattlesnake, very dangerous.' We are walking along behind the cages and John now opens the back and starts digging in the earth with a scoop. 'You have to remove their excrement or they get sick.' The rattler is tasting my irritating new smell with its flickering tongue. 'Don't worry,' says John. 'I've been bitten several times. My body swelled up for a month, but they don't have any antibiotics in this wretched country.'

As he goes along opening the flimsy doors on the backs of the cages – his boy was supposed to fix them – he tells me in detail how the elephant killed his keeper the other day – threw him down and stood on him, blood coming out of his eyes. On the other side of the cages the spectators are looking straight past the seedy reptiles under their crumpled newspapers to the far more interesting sight of two gringos, talking animatedly, lit up by neon, one with a horrified expression on his face.

John went back to England a few years ago and was very impressed by how clean London was. 'All the buildings were newly whitewashed, with baskets of flowers hanging in the stations. The trains are incredibly smooth-running with big picture windows and they always arrive bang on time.' As he speaks I wonder if he is talking about London, England. It makes me realize that my impressions of San Salvador are even more selective. As we leave the reptile house he shows me a putrefying jacket hanging near the door, just near a rack of old snakeskins. This is one of John's cast-offs. 'It used to belong to my father in India,' he says. 'Sometimes it has mice nesting in it.' At this moment something live falls on the back of my neck. 'Look,' says John agreeably. 'A cockroach.'

Nicaragua is the poorest country in Central America. The government keeps lopping noughts off the cordoba, but as fast as they do the country's 300 per cent inflation

*The scaling down of internal conflicts has led to a shared hope of more
peaceful times ahead for both the Indians in Guatemala and the Sandinista
soldiers returning from the front in Nicaragua.*

puts them back on again. There is a depressed, bedraggled air to the place. I didn't meet anyone who didn't want to leave, and the government lets them go because they send back dollars.

At first sight, downtown Managua isn't there. It was destroyed by an earthquake in 1972 and they haven't got round to rebuilding it yet. Once-busy streets wander through scrubby fields. Addresses tend to be by landmarks, but the landmarks – a dairy, an old tree – often don't exist any more. The odd ruined cinema or laboratory remains, too tough to clear away, squatted by Indians in hammocks. But many people simply camp out still, at least in the dry season.

Nobody seems to know why rebuilding hasn't started yet, but everyone seems to agree that it is the fault of the Americans for financing the Contras. The next year or so will show whether they are right.

I heard it said that Daniel Ortega is adept at maintaining the spontaneous, improvisatory appearance of his socialist revolution while quietly exercising a steely efficiency. There is a welcome absence of advertisement hoardings and Mr Donut forecourts in the capital – faded lettering announcing an old Grundig concession strikes a ghostly note – but a commercial desert seems too high a price to pay for ideological purity. 'Only the workers and *campesinos* will go to the end,' says the ambiguous inscription on a vast and hideous statue of a well-muscled worker, one of the only new constructions. We take a ride through the outlying area where the administration lives and find it comfortable and leafy, much like any other well-to-do suburb. As in the Soviet Union, the privileged few shop in the chain of 'Dollar Shops' which have a $12 million-a-year turnover. There is soon to be a nightclub with two sides, one selling beer and cane liquor for cordobas, the other a holy of holies selling anything you like for dollars.

I must admit that it proves easy enough for us foreigners to attend Ortega's pre-Summit press conference, but then according to our interpreter he isn't saying anything worth passing on, so it is a waste of time. While I am waiting I sit outside with the Swiss-Guatemalan manager of our hotel, who is kindly driving us around. He rises to greet a man coming down the bleak stairway of the administration building. It is the Foreign Minister.

Two of the buildings in Managua that survived the earthquake were the Intercontinental Hotel and the cathedral. The Intercontinental, a sort of informal world embassy, is right-wing and sinister with spies. The cathedral is the haunt of lovers, an area of peace. The roof has fallen in and small trees grow in its nave. Birds and stray dogs live there. But the feeling of the church lives on.

I climb out of a window and sit on a pediment watching the Sandinistas coming home from three months on the coffee front. A great cheer goes up from their families as the convoy of lorries enters the plaza and the sunburnt young men and women jump down into their arms. I am joined by the very different Teofilo, sickly but friendly, an *hombre de negocios* who wants to sell me his mother's gold pendant. He takes me to his squat in an old hotel and shows me his one British stamp. I understand that there is no place for Teofilo in the brand new Nicaragua.

As you drive south into Costa Rica, signs of prosperity gradually seep back into the landscape. Ads make a nostalgic return. The women put on weight and are fanciable again (notoriously so). The Sharatoga Hotel in Santa Cruz is like a mini-James Bond movie set with palm trees round the courtyard pool, macaws, two deer imprisoned in the stair-well and a spider monkey attached to a block.

I have just paid my bill and am walking back to where I left my luggage when I notice that all my things are scattered round the place. Peter is holding my notebook. My plaster quezals lie shattered. What is going on? It seems the monkey attacked my belongings, then bit our fixer when she tried to intercede. Our next task is to get her a rabies jab, which she isn't looking forward to.

The British Embassy doctor says, 'Why did you let him bite you?'

'For fun,' says Ana.

This is cattle country. We watch the Indian cowboys working – big stetson hats and Western saddles. Next stop is the Quaker settlement of Monteverde. After 30 miles of bumpy, twisting dirt road we meet Bob Law at the Quaker School and he explains to us how these three hundred Americans come to be living on a mountain in Costa Rica.

It all started in 1948 when America introduced its first peacetime military draft. By what seemed like a gift from God, this was also the year that Costa Rica changed its constitution, abolishing the army. In 1950, fifty Quakers from Fairhope, Alabama, drove down to San José – there was no highway then – and started looking for land. On 15 April 1951 three of them rode up this mountain. It was the end of the dry season, yet the land was still green. It was a perfect place for dairy farming, but how to get the milk down the mountain? The idea of making cheese, thus increasing the value of the milk (and taking advantage of the bumpy track?) soon followed, and today the cheese factory is the economic staple for miles around.

As prosperity increased, the Quakers began to realize the importance of the cloud forest over their heads. To the original 3000 acres purchased in lower Monteverde they added 1200 acres of forest. Since then, with donations from all over the world, the Monteverde Conservation League has purchased a further 150,000 scattered acres, connected by wooded corridors for the animals.

Their policy of ecological conservation also conserves their own privacy. The Quaker community is naturally wary of progress. They are fond of their wind-up telephone system connecting their houses and the mail that arrives twice a week with the returning cheese lorry. (Each family has a box at the factory.) Their problem is that their school of twenty-eight children is not recognized by the Costa Rican government: pupils cannot get into local universities, and those who go back to America often end up staying. Bob Law gave us to understand that this was not an insuperable hurdle for people who had come so far up the mountain. As we left, we saw several fair-headed kids delightedly tending saplings in plastic bags.

There is another very different English-speaking community on the Atlantic coast of Costa Rica, at Limón, where Columbus landed on his fourth voyage. These are the easy-going Caribs, descendants of runaway slaves, whose main claim to fame is their strange greeting, 'What happen!' pronounced 'Whoppen!'. We try this out

In Managua the angel of death still stalks the streets in the form of bold
revolutionary graffiti.

Right: Not far away, an ecstatic soldier salutes the cheers of a crowd
gathered in the main square to welcome the returning heroes.

on the first Limonade chick we see and she bursts into laughter. 'OK!' she says, (another Limón catchphrase). There is more hilarity in the café when I order beans, rice and bananas, three ingredients of the national dish, *casada*. Peter says it is like ordering Yorkshire pudding with a Bendicks mint. While we are eating, a deaf-mute appears at the grille of the window and does a long, musical mime show of the sloths which live in the nearby Parque Vargas. He moans and warbles as he imitates them climbing, biting and trying to grab his leg.

It is a great performance, which is hardly equalled by the sloths themselves when we finally manage to spot one, very high up in a banyan tree, slothfully cleaning its fingernails, hanging by its tail. After watching this thoroughly unsensational animal doing practically nothing for a very long half-hour, I retire exhausted to the Hotel Caribe where I watch the even slower-moving business of an albino prostitute working the street with her four-year-old daughter. After an hour, a very old man comes by and the three meander off to the Hotel des Déportés for some kind of lethargic dissipation.

Limón is the sort of place the disgraced Lord Jim might have holed up in before going definitively up country. There's a banana railroad from the interior and a big container port, but the town has a sleepy, passed-over air. Nobody, you feel, really gives a damn 'What happen'. And that is the place's charm.

Flame trees among the pure jungle on either side of the *auto-pista* to San José. Pools of flame tree petals under our wheels – then a still-living monkey that seemed to raise its poor head. We stay in a Chinese hotel where a ferocious Chinese Claude Rains barks my orders back at me, making me want to cry. In the middle of the night two drunk Scotsmen come home to their room next to mine with one or more *muchachas*, who speak only in giggles. One of the Jimmys seems to think Andy is sleeping in my room and keeps banging the wall, telling him to wake up. I yell back that he's already awake and has been for hours.

On to Panama. The Bridge of the Americas rises like a silver rainbow out of mist and jungle. Known as the Thatcher Ferry Bridge, after the only previous means of transport, this American-built bridge over the Panama Canal was opened in 1962 and is the longest steel arch bridge in the world.

This is the point where the Pan American Highway crosses from North America into South America: 'a country divided, a world united', as the saying goes. Panama was part of Colombia before a separate country was created for the canal and it still feels more like South than Central America.

This is the First, not the Third, World we're entering. To the right, downtown Panama looks like Manhattan rising out of the bay. To the left, the canal stretches away, the famous Manchester-built steam engines that used to haul the ships through the locks now replaced by ugly Mitsubishi tank engines.

Old Panama is supposed to be the most dangerous city in the world, but I was only told that after I'd been wandering round with my eyes on stalks for two days. The old timber tenements are incredibly vicious and decrepit and one whole quarter has long been condemned. But life on the streets is like one big musical about sex and drugs, if there are musicals about such things any more.

> You see me down in Panama
> some hot and dusty night.
> I was eating eggs in Sammy's place
> when a black man drew his knife. . . .

There are vultures everywhere in this town, real and metaphorical, on the streets and at corporation level. You go from steaming squalor half a mile down the promenade to screaming high-tech land, the colonial residences of the canal builders marooned between. The whole place is jumping with opportunism and intrigue. We have a car with Texas number plates and receive many unambiguous signals from Reagan-hating inhabitants. Gringos are unpopular at present due to US efforts to depose President Noriega. We don't outstay our welcome.

There's only a dirt road south after Panama City, so we decide to fly to the jungle town of Yaviza.

Dawn coming up at the Panama City aerodrome: *vuelos ala Darién*. Flight bags for villages in the little manifest office. Racks for things ordered: a basketball, some handlebars. A nun waits on the tarmac while others crowd round the breakfast canteen. '*Una sausage para me*,' says Tom, our newly arrived photographer. Our pilot honks and spits authoritatively, then climbs astride our flying canoe which I'm ecstatic to see has two engines. We fill in the emergency addresses in our passports and try not to wobble.

The first sight of Yaviza is not to be forgotten: a carless, wooden town built on stilts beside a lazy river fringed by mangroves. Families of negroes stand among their ducks and puppies, staring at the river as we cross in a canoe from the landing strip. They pull up the fronts of their shirts for coolness. This is the hottest place I have ever been to, but the young boys are playing basketball in the square as if to keep warm.

From Yaviza, we take a motorized canoe downstream to El Real, where we check into the Hotel El Nazareno. This seems at first sight to be a real hotel with all the usual appointments, if a little dusty. Four cane chairs are grouped around a large open picture Bible on a stand in the open-work lounge. There is the bar. And here is another room with a washing machine, which is good news all round. The walls are decorated with *Playboy* centrefolds and upstairs more pin-ups, with cardboard corner stiffeners, appear on the doors of the rooms, all of which have showers and lavatories.

It isn't until we have been here a while that we gradually realize the hotel is not what it seems. For a start, there are no other guests, no staff, no food available and no water of any kind. On closer inspection, there is no drink behind the bar, no ice in the fridge – which is not plugged in – and no barman, of course. There is no light in the non-functioning loo. And no chocolates in the large box displayed on the cocktail cabinet. 'What did you expect, soft centres?' says Peter. He finds a half-full bottle of Chinese hock on a smart rack in the lounge, but we think better of it. The

The cloud forest at Monteverde in Costa Rica.

Right: A Choco Indian girl in the jungle of the Darien in Panama.

boy who let us in says no need to lock your rooms as there is no crime in El Real. I've shut mine already, so keys have to be sent for. I dub the hotel's overall style (which is considerable) 'provisional-fantastical' and give it three stars. It is agreed by all that El Real is *más tranquilo* than Yaviza, where there is *mucha actividad*. In the house opposite, a crowd of people are busily watching a TV that doesn't work.

After pig's foot soup from a stall we pass along the dark main street, smoking cigars and enjoying the carless, domestic night as other lit cigars call '*Bueno*' to us from their porches. There is an Evangelist meeting going on in a darkened church. We sit in the dark square as the pico-pico starts up – the Saturday night dance to hot salsa sounds on guitars and accordion.

Inside the dance-hall we are joined by Manu, a small, drunk, very randy bush ranger friend of our guide, who asks for more and more beer and cigarettes. Later, after Peter has gone home, he says for $1 I can have a *bailar* – a dance. Am I interested? I don't get the point until he drags up one of his girlfriends to be introduced. I get down off my stool and find myself looking up into a fierce gorilla-face with a smile like a burning fiery furnace. She takes my hand into her paw and leaves it there. Manu says I can have her for $1. I say no-no-no, but the poor fellow has left himself no room for bargaining, so he dashes off and fetches someone else, a tiny, simpering Indian woman called Mary, who doesn't like the look of me. I plead *cansado*, tired, and the bush ranger looks at me with contempt. '*Una cerveza más*,' he calls. At least I can buy him another beer!

Most people in El Real stay up all night shouting, and on Sunday morning everyone is still drunk. Unfortunately this is the day we have to order the raft to take the 'action car' down river to the Indian village of Penabejawal when we return to film our journey. The raft-maker's wife assures us that her husband is away for several weeks, so our guide writes a detailed note for him about the raft's dimensions and we repair to the Cantina Rosa to regroup. Lots of jolly oil paintings of naked white women surrounded by cocktail glasses, bubbles and musical notes. No photography!

Suddenly the raft-maker materializes with his assistant and many more big Atlas beers are called to the raft-negotiation table. A four-wheel drift of an afternoon commences, climaxing in a cock-fight.

First it's into a back room for inspections: strapping on of spurs, which are sharpened with bits of broken glass. The birds are shivering with excitement or fear. One struts about and shits. The cockpit, like a big sandpit with sides, has imitation advertisements hand-painted round the side: 'John Player Specials. No a las Drogas. Yaviza, Pueblo de Futuro. Visita su Cantina. Prop. Ciro Ayala.' Fistfuls of money. Roars of sadistic glee. The referee hurls himself about for a minute and a half, then it's all over. The owner of the losing cock sucks its wounded wing and spits. The raft deal is solidified.

Dismayed to see that the tipsy bush ranger is to be our canoe helmsman on our river recce to Penabejawal. Every now and then one of us remarks, 'Amazing how stable these things are', meaning it's a miracle we haven't been sluiced to the caymans already. The bush ranger is still girl-crazy and drunk and swerves into the bank, whistling and blowing kisses at the slightest trace of womanhood. Worse, he has brought along a supply of beer. We spend our time righting his wobbles and giggling nervously.

Next time around I will be arriving by raft with a very tired action car and a pig in the passenger seat, a gift for the headman of the village. Lindo, the headman, is a man of perfect social poise, at ease in his hammock in his raised house, smiling among his extended family of children, women, old men and a strange 'rabbit-dog', which might be a capybara. He prepares coconuts for us to drink and shows us an old Gulf Oil calendar featuring himself in ceremonial costume.

He has a question for us. A 'thing' of some kind has been discovered on the outskirts of the village which looks to him as if it might have come from France or England. Can we tell him what it is? We struggle with the possibilities for a while – along the lines of Animal, Vegetable or Mineral? – while Lindo looks increasingly disappointed at Western intelligence levels.

Suddenly it occurs to one of us to take a look at the Thing, so we process out of the village to a rise overlooking a bend in the river. There, in long grass, lies a length of iron tubing embedded in a concrete collar. Someone has scratched the initials SPOC in the concrete together with the date, 1947, which is ten years before the village was founded and therefore historical. Mining equipment? I suggest to a derisive look from Lindo. Peter thinks it must have been a marker for some kind of survey, perhaps by the South Panama Oil Company. He is striding abstractedly about, testing the ground for possible camera positions. The rest of us troop back to the village for the next event – the cutting down, presentation to me and filming of a giant custard apple. Peter continues to ruminate on his hill, shading his eyes and gazing up and downstream from his vantage point. It seems the mysterious Thing from England or France has given him the perfect closing shot for our film.

Was this the end of our journey? Did we look at each other with a wild surmise – silent, upon a peak in Darien – and wonder how to bridge the 500-mile 'gap' to where the Highway begins again in Colombia? No, we couldn't be bothered to die in the snake and spider-infested jungles that the United States likes to keep between it and those hoards of marauding dagos bearing drugs, disease and revolution. We thought that would look a bit *too* keen. We had thought of loading the car on a raft and floating it a little further downstream into the wilderness as a gift for some rowdy tribe of barbarians, because Peter fancied the image of revelling villagers lighting a fire in the back seat and barbecuing the pig I had brought with me. In the end he realized that it would cost several hundred 'little old lady's licence fees' to sacrifice the convertible in such a casual manner. So we settled for a shot of me at the hypothetical 'end' of the Highway, staring moodily out across the river that seems to bar my way. It's an anti-climax of an ending, but appropriate to a road which begins undecidedly at a number of points (Nogales, Eagle Pass, El Paso and Laredo), achieves considerable beauty and grandeur in the countries it travels through (Mexico, Guatemala, El Salvador, Honduras, Nicaragua, Costa Rica) only to peter out in dirt-track, jungle and official paranoia. I had a feeling that one day in the not-too-distant future, when the Highway finally shoots through to South America, our ending would achieve a certain period charm, a retrospective fascination.

*The Pan American Highway peters out in the impenetrable forests of
the Darien Gap near El Real, a village populated mainly by descendants
of slaves brought over by the Spanish.*

*Left: Only the indigenous Indians can survive in the jungle itself, their
exclusive preserve until the road breaks through.*

THE BURMA ROAD

Miles Kington

Every capital in the Third World seems to have one hotel which is pointed out proudly as a relic of former grandeur, which is to say colonial days. I have never been to Singapore or Cairo, but the names of Raffles and Shepheards Hotels are well known to me. In Rangoon, capital of Burma, the equivalent is the Strand Hotel and a lovable old place it is too, but I hope for their sake that Raffles and Shepheards are in better nick than the Strand.

My bath was palatial, but there was only two hours of hot water a day. The bedroom was so long that the three lights in the ceiling cast pools of yellow light which did not even join up; walking down the room at night was a bit like going along a badly lit main road. When I asked a girl at reception if I could phone up to one of the second-floor rooms, she confessed: 'It is much quicker if you walk up and knock on your friend's door.'

The effect was that of a stately home whose family have fallen on bad times. There just wasn't enough money. The bar was spacious but the drinks you wanted were not always available. And yet the whole threadbare service was maintained with great charm and a complete lack of guilt. The Burmese hate saying 'No.' They hate it so much that they do not have a word for 'No', which means that when you ask a barman for a beer he does not say: 'I have no beer'; he says: 'The beer is not here yet' or, 'What I would suggest instead of beer is . . .' and you take it without feeling deprived or disappointed.

And there are unexpected bonuses. Every evening at 6 o'clock a man came to play the piano in the large hall, and what he played was Burmese music. Now, the

*The Schwedagon Pagoda, Rangoon, rising from the Sacred Lake
at dusk.*

Right: A monk on the steps of the Schwedagon, Burma's holiest shrine.

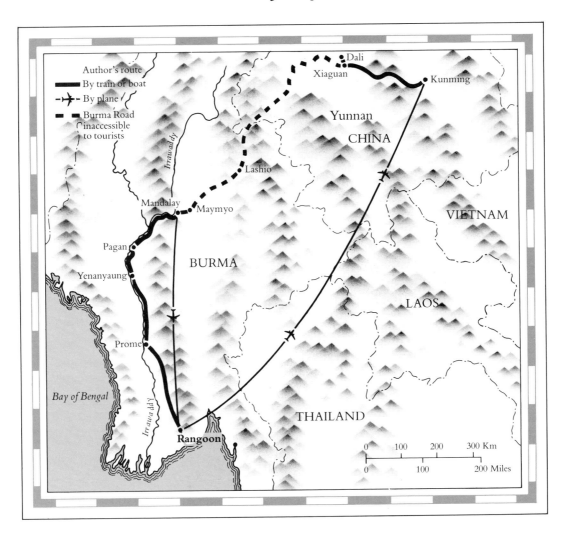

piano is not a Burmese instrument and it is totally unsuited to Burmese music, which has no harmony to speak of – only melody and rhythm. If you play two notes at the same time on a piano, you have harmony. This pianist did *not* play two notes at the same time; he played long streams of notes very fast to give a shimmering, impression-istic effect, like Debussy at speed or perhaps on speed.

I saw him as a kind of symbol of Burma. In any other country I know, that man would have been playing more or less debased cocktail music, but the Burmese don't make many concessions to the West. They are among the last people to resist trousers – it is still very rare to find a Burmese male wearing anything but the loose sarong called the longyi – and a man wearing a longyi and playing Burmese music in the foyer of the Strand Hotel seemed to me to represent a country which was not too bothered about jeans and rock 'n' roll.

What I was really looking for was a symbol of an *invisible* country. There are one or two countries in the world which fail to catch people's attention, like someone who can never hail a taxi or catch a barman's eye: Paraguay, Albania, Cameroon – nations like that. A hundred years ago Burma was in the British Empire, but it was an invisible part of it, being attached to India for administrative purposes. Fifty years ago our fighting men in Burma were known as the Forgotten Army. Forty years ago Burma went independent and promptly drew up its bamboo drawbridge against the world. Now you're dealing with a country which is *naturally* invisible and likes being that way.

One result is that nobody can remember what the Burma Road is, or was. Take Burma from the map of people's consciousness, and you take the Burma Road with it. Small wonder that people looked puzzled when I said I was off along the Burma Road, as they would not have done if I had announced I was off up the Khyber Pass or away along the Silk Road. A few thought it was a famous golf hole somewhere in England (it is, but not worth a whole film). Others thought it was the railway built for the Japanese of River Kwai fame (no, that's the Burma Railway and it's in Thailand) or the road to Mandalay (no, that's the River Irrawaddy). And there were those who remembered the Burma Road as being the supply route into China which kept alive Chiang Kai-shek's resistance against the Japanese.

This last lot were right in a way. When they invaded China in 1936, the Japanese rapidly conquered the whole country until they ran out of steam in the extreme south-western corner. China is huge, and there simply weren't enough Japanese, however superior in equipment and organization, to occupy every corner. Chiang Kai-shek's tactics were simple: avoid confrontation and hang on grimly until the Japanese went away or the Americans came and rescued them. The Japanese plan was equally simple: as they now occupied the whole Chinese seaboard, they could cut off supplies to Chiang Kai-shek and starve him out.

This particular corner of China, however, was just across the hills from northern Burma, which was just round the corner from India. With a decent road, lorries could bring in enough supplies from either place to keep the Chinese going. There was, however, no decent road – only a winding track designed for pack animals. So Chiang Kai-shek used forced labour and unashamedly dictatorial methods to get a road built, conscripting tens of thousands of Chinese coolies and working many of them to death in the process. The same methods were used later by the Japanese to build the Burma Railway, but in China no British prisoners of war were involved and so it was never made into a film starring Alec Guinness. The long white ribbon came up out of Burma twisting and turning, like a string of pearls flung carelessly over her coat by a lady back from the opera. It ended in Kunming, the chief city of the Chinese province of Yunnan, after passing across mountains, over great rivers and through towns that had never seen a motor vehicle before. It saved Chiang Kai-shek and his war effort, and it was called the Burma Road.

But it wasn't a new name. The old track had also been called the Burma Road. This I know because in 1930, six years before the lorry road had been built, a medical missionary called the Revd Neville Bradley had come all the way down from Kunming into Burma. In 1940 someone persuaded him to write an account of his journey and publish it, probably because the Burma Road was then in the news. So there he was, writing in Chiang Kai-shek's day about a journey along the very track which Chiang had replaced, and he called his book *Down The Old Burma Road*. And what you gradually realize as you go back through history is that it has always been

A Burmese girl with traditional sandalwood face decoration.

Left: A wreath seller in the back streets of Rangoon.

Pages 128 and 129: The temple-studded plain at Pagan.

the Burma Road, sometimes new, sometimes old, sometimes grown over and forgotten, but always there somewhere.

It was there when Marco Polo passed from Burma to China. It was there when Kubla Khan came rampaging down from China to conquer Burma and empty the great city of Pagan. It must have been the route along which Buddhism infiltrated into China. Never the same road, quite, never exactly the same twists and turns, never exactly the same path along which the last invasion or trade mission had come, but always following the same course, as a river may change its bed and still stick to the same river course. The Burma Road is not a road but a route, a passage between Burma and China which is used when wanted and allowed to green over when not needed.

It has not been needed since the end of the Second World War. Officially, not a single lorry has passed over the China–Burma border since 1946. That is not very surprising when you understand that no lorry has officially crossed *any* of Burma's borders in that time, because all the Burmese frontiers are in the hands of insurgent tribesmen fighting for independence. Unofficially, of course, it's quite a different matter, because those very same independence-seeking tribesmen are busy trading drugs, smuggling teak, levying duty off other passing smugglers and generally promoting the black market economy which keeps Burma supplied with basic goods. But theoretically all Burma's land borders are blocked, and unless you want to come in through the jungles as paying guests of the Karen or Shan tribes, you can enter Burma one way only: via Rangoon.

Don't stay longer than you have to in Rangoon, they told me. Get your black market money and off you go. There are some staggering pagodas in Rangoon, but it's a depressing place when you think what it used to be like. Used to be the Harrods of the East, they say, a shopping centre like Bangkok or Singapore today. Now, there's nothing worth getting at all.

So you seek out the black market to get your 36 kyats to the US dollar instead of the official 6 (actually, the black market seeks *you* out as you leave the Strand Hotel and says: 'Hey, mister – got any dollars?') and then you go to the station to start the journey northwards. The train for Prome leaves two hours late. Nobody seems surprised. We travel through hour after hour of countryside which manages to be lush and arid at the same time – the train raises dust going through villages bright with flowers and loud with dogs, at that respectable speed which allows you to put your head out of the window without being deafened, blown away or hit by a bridge. Water buffalo lumber about, young rice grows piercingly green, and on almost every rise there is the curve of a stupa, that licked vanilla shape peculiar to Buddhism. For an hour it is enchanting, but after three hours it becomes boring, so I retreat to my seat with my book because this train has something I've never seen in my life before: a travelling librarian. He hands out books for a small fee and collects them before the end of the journey. But they are all in Burmese except for a stray copy of *Wuthering Heights*.

'Do you have any other English books?' I ask.

'Yes.'

'What are they?'

'*Wuthering Heights.*'

'They are all *Wuthering Heights?*'

'Yes. It is very popular.'

That is not quite the whole story, I learn later. In fact, *Wuthering Heights* is the prescribed book for English students that year, and the Burmese book industry has risen to the occasion by producing several different editions, all annotated and all with the text considerably pruned. The cover artists do not seem to be familiar with the look of Victorian Yorkshire, as they all feature thatched cottages, smiling landscapes and girls in jeans and blonde hair with ponies. New readers may be in for a shock. The copy I buy has also a few poems by Alexander Pope, including the one starting: 'Happy the man, who free from care ...'. the editor explains that Pope is lauding the simple English farmer content with his small herd of water buffaloes.

Apart from their Brontë production, the Burmese book trade seems to have no interest in foreign books. I looked vainly for George Orwell's *Burmese Days*, his first novel based on his three years in the Burma Police. I gave up when a Burmese writer quietly took me aside and explained that, as Orwell had made it quite plain in the book that he liked neither the British nor the Burmese, they had preferred to return the compliment. The book was not actually banned, more forgotten.

This, surely, was another example of Burma's invisibility. India and China have had any amount of books written about them. Occasionally it seems almost an entrance exam for British novelists to have done at least one novel on India – Paul Scott, John Masters, Kipling, E. M. Forster, and so on. But apart from Orwell's unread first novel, Burma has nothing except Kipling's poem 'Mandalay', and that, as befits a poem written after a couple of days in Rangoon, is riddled with mistakes.

> On the road to Mandalay,
> Where the flyin'-fishes play,
> An' the dawn comes up like thunder outer China 'crost the Bay!

China is hundreds of miles away, the dawn doesn't come up over the bay, there are no flying fishes. ... But one thing he got right. The road to Mandalay is the River Irrawaddy. I was going to Prome to get on to the Irrawaddy.

Long ago, Prome was the capital of Burma. There is nothing odd about this. Almost every Burmese town has once been the capital, because when a new king took over he was usually so fearful of threats to his person that he had his nearest relatives murdered and moved the capital. But all the ex-capitals have one thing in common; they are all a stone's throw from the Irrawaddy, because although you could afford to lose all your family, and move all your possessions, you couldn't afford to be far from the river. It was the backbone of the country for hundreds of years, a broad, flat highway which reached up hundreds of miles into the north, the road to Mandalay and way beyond.

The British carried on this tradition when they arrived. Not only did they move

the capital from Mandalay to Rangoon (I don't know how many relations the British commander slaughtered) but they built up the river flotilla to over six hundred vessels – a bigger navy than Britain has today. It all vanished on the day the Japanese invaded Burma and the order was given for the flotilla to be scuttled. The boat I was hoping to catch, the ferry which goes from town to town up-river, had been built in Japan since the war.

'The boat leaves tomorrow,' said the man in the ticket office. 'At least, it comes tomorrow. Perhaps it leaves tomorrow.'

'At what time?'

He shrugged and burst into Burmese.

'He is saying that he does not know when it comes, so he does not know when it leaves,' translated the person behind me. 'It depends on the weather, the currents, the supply of fuel. . . .'

My fellow passenger, as he turned out to be, was called U Thein San and was on his way to Mandalay. Something to do with business, but you don't ask too many questions about people's business in Burma as it quite often turns out to be black market. The only people you can really be sure about are the soldiers with their rifles and the monks without anything.

'Perhaps you would like to have a stroll around Prome looking at things?' said U Thein San. It did not sound as if he was very keen on Prome, but nor did it sound as if he was warning me off the place. He just sounded politely neutral. Throughout I found this absence of raving enthusiasm for anything, the tendency to say 'It's OK' after an exciting experience; but this is compensated for (if it needs compensation) by a complete lack of overt fury. Never did I see a Burmese person lose his temper. Even when, later, our filming ran into problems, it was always the British who lost their cool, not the Burmese.

This is attested by a UN official who served three Secretary-Generals, including Burma's U Thant. Of them all, he reported, only U Thant reacted to disasters and wars with calm and Buddhist serenity. The most extreme emotional reaction he had ever spotted in him, at the height of the Vietnam War, was a soft drumming of his fingers on his desk. However, he also reported that when U Thant died the post-mortem revealed him to be suffering from more stress-related conditions than it was thought possible for one man to endure. . . .

'I think you should buy some sandals,' U Thein San told me. 'Burmese sandals are very good. They are better than those English shoes.'

He was quite right. I have a horror of dressing up in the English style, wearing sandals, socks and shorts, so I was trying to get away with long cotton trousers and Clark's desert boots. Quite apart from being a death trap in wet weather, Clark's desert boots are a bit hot in desert weather. But Burmese sandals, which are simply a sole and two leather thongs covered in velvet, are fine once you get used to them after the initial two days of agony. Now, even after a six-month gap, I can put Burmese sandals on again and not feel a twinge.

'You must give your sandals a bite before you put them on for the first time,' he told me. 'We consider it good luck.'

I bit them. They didn't taste too bad. 'Why are they called Tractor?' I said, looking at the thickish rubber base.

'Oh, probably they are made from old tractor tyres. Everything in Burma in a market like this is made from something else. Look at that hardware stall over there. . . .'

It was true. The watering cans, the money boxes, the candle-holders, the vegetable graters, the oil cans – they were all made from something else, usually beer cans, petrol cans or Coke tins. I still have the vegetable grater I bought there, which was converted from a tin of German insect-killer; that is probably why I bought it.

'Burma cannot afford to import things,' said U Thein San, 'and we have not got the raw materials to hand, so we have to recycle things. Nobody throws bottles away; they resell them on the black market. Someone will cut the top off and make them into very good glasses.'

As we walked down the friendly grid pattern streets of Prome, I realized that things like turning bottles into glasses do not happen in factories tucked away in industrial estates; they happen in front of your eyes, in people's homes. In one house people were outside, finishing off sandals (you could dimly see the chief cutter indoors, dealing out the sandal shapes with his mighty scissors). In another house people were boiling sweets, cutting them up and wrapping them, all in the same room. People were making umbrellas, rolling cigars, inventing toys, all in their own homes. If you think back to Victorian cottage industries, it was all very much behind the times. If you think of current efforts to get people to work at home, then it was way ahead of its time.

'Oh, it is Friday,' said U Thein San suddenly. 'I must go to the pagoda.'

Not, as you might think, because it is a special service day. Buddhists do not have services; everyone makes his own worship. But on the weekday on which they were born many Buddhists make a special point of going to a temple for a prayer and an offering. U Thein San bought some flowers outside (there they sell flowers outside temples, with us outside hospitals) and left them on one of eight such shrines.

'Hold on,' I said. 'There are eight weekday shrines, but there are only seven weekdays.'

He smiled a little sheepishly.

'Well, for the symmetry of the temple there have to be eight shrines, but as there are only seven days, we name the eighth shrine after a day that does not really exist – from Wednesday midnight until Thursday dawn. You will quite often find Buddhism stretching things a little. For instance, Buddha forbids us to kill any living creature. Yet we eat meat quite often. How is this reconciled?'

I still don't know.

The river at Prome is fat, sluggish and wide, a bit muscle-bound like many famous rivers. But as this is the dry season, it is not quite so wide or deep as usual, and there is a sandy foreshore which is not usually there. Up and down the foreshore charge buffalo carts, going up laden with sacks of concrete and coming back empty. I don't know where the concrete is going to, but it seems odd to find something so modern

Sunrise over Thatbyinnyu, 'the temple of omniscience', Pagan.

Left: The golden figure of Buddha in the Ananda Temple, Pagan.

as concrete being transported by wooden carts pulled by buffaloes, lashed on by men roughly dressed like the peasants in my old Bible illustrations, in that all-purpose oriental wrap-around costume. They charge up that bank without rolling back again. And as the dust and sand get kicked up in a swirling cloud, and the sun makes patterns through the trees and the murky air, it is suddenly the concrete which looks out of place. Everything else looks normal now.

So, too, does a raft which turns from being a blob on the river horizon into a 50-foot-square construction of bamboo carrying dozens of huge pottery jars, big enough to hide Ali-Baba in. Ten minutes later comes a raft twice as big, bearing nothing except two or three huts, half a dozen people and a camp fire smoking dangerously. It is like a village sailing past. But for the life of me I can spot no cargo.

'U Thein San, what are they carrying?'

'They are carrying bamboo. The raft *is* the cargo. When they get to their destination, they will dismantle the raft, sell it, and go back home.'

'How will they get home?'

'Oh, hitch-hike, I expect. Perhaps go on our boat, if they make a good profit.'

Our boat gets in at 6 o'clock the next morning. It's a grey, slaty dawn, barely light enough to see our feet as we walk the plank up to the ship. You can tell we are in a hot country, because the top thing on the boat is an all-embracing roof to keep the sun off, and under the roof is the passenger deck. On a cruise liner the passenger deck is where the passengers go out and play deck quoits, or stroll, or go to sleep in a deckchair while their Ludlum paperback falls off their knees into the sea, but here the passenger deck is where the passengers *live*. Purchase of a ticket entitles you to a space on the deck about 6 feet by 2; they are actually painted on the deck, these spaces, but we can't see because they are covered in bodies. If they get up there is nowhere to go but below, to the cargo, or aft, to a kind of tea bar with four stools, so they might as well stay where they are, and sleep.

U Thein San and I have gone up-market. We've paid to enter the only cabin, a single room at the prow with five dead hard bunks, a table and chair, and some privacy. In our case it also contains two *pongyis* or monks, one quite old and one a mere boy, but both instantly recognizable because of their orange robes and their shaven heads. The word 'monk' gives a wrong impression, because we think of monkhood as a kind of very special, terribly badly paid profession which requires a now-or-never decision. It's only one short of becoming a hermit or a lifer in a top-security gaol. But in Buddhist countries everyone becomes a *pongyi* for a while. Religion is so much a part of life that it's quite natural to go off to a monastery and meditate or learn full-time, and then come back to life again.

Certainly the community feels it is their responsibility to feed the monks, who are not allowed to have money and therefore cannot buy food. Every day in every town in Burma monks with begging bowls do a tour of the street. The strange thing to Western eyes is that monks never show any signs of gratitude, a trait shared by the Burmese at large, who accept presents as if they were letters from the Inland Revenue, and put them aside to open later.

'I do not like this monk,' U Thein San mutters to me after conversing with the older man.

'Why not?'

'I think he is a spy.'

'You *what* . . .?'

'Look at his chest. It is a military chest. Why would a poor monk be travelling with army property? He must be a spy.'

Quite why a spy would be disguised as a monk travelling up the Irrawaddy in the late 1980s is not quite clear, but that's not the point. The Burmese government has for twenty years imposed heavy censorship on the news and recruited informers everywhere. As always happens in a society starved of real information, rumours flourish, everyone is seen as a spy and the BBC World Service becomes very popular as the only source of unpolluted news. Personally, I feel that if the Burmese government runs its intelligence service as inefficiently as it runs everything else, there is nothing to fear from spies in Burma.

The sheer joy of moving up a big river outweighs everything else. Through those windows – wooden casement windows, rather nineteenth-century – you can always see something new on the banks – pagodas perched on unlikely outcrops, river birds making a living, farmers cultivating the new foreshore in the six months they have before the river rises again, villages, women washing. . . . And right below you, the top of a pole rising and falling as a sailor takes the depth measurement every ten seconds . . . five . . . five and a half . . . five . . . four and a bit . . . five. . . .

'If it goes down to three and a half, we're aground,' says U Thein San.

But mysteriously, even watching one of the world's mighty rivers palls after a while, and I look for other amusement. I decide to shave. Perched in front of the tiny mirror, I wield the tiny shaving brush I bought in Bangkok (it took me three hours to find a chemist's shop selling them) and as I tackle the stubble I gradually become aware that I am being watched. The older monk has his grave eyes fixed on me, for the very good reason, I suddenly realize, that he has never seen a man shave his face before. Shave the top of his head, yes. Monks do it two or three times a week. But the Burmese have very little in the way of facial hair – certainly not enough to make it worth shaving. They are a smooth-faced lot with enviably girlish complexions, and if one hair should suddenly decide to grow the Burman does not shave it off. He lets it grow as a symbol of manliness. U Thein San has one hair on his left cheek about 4 inches long, and if I should ever give way to the awful urge to lean forward and snip it off the offence would be dreadful.

Another thought occurs to me: all monks in Buddhist countries look, at first, vaguely threatening to Western eyes. Those sleek boxer's forearms, those robes which look ready for unarmed combat, that shaven head . . . yes, of course, it's the shaven head. In the West, a shaven head betokens aggression. The villain has a shaven head. Wrestlers have shaven heads. Skinheads have shaven heads. The only two nice guys who ever had shaven heads were Telly Savalas and Yul Brynner, and they weren't *that* nice. When a man with a dome-like skull edges up to you in Europe or America,

Bullock carts, still the most common form of transport in rural Burma.

Pages 140 and 141: A hill-top pagoda overlooking the Irrawaddy
at Sagaing.

you feel disposed to treat him respectfully in case he should start hitting you. But here in the East a shaven pate is a sign of holiness. There is something saintly to Eastern eyes about a bare skull, and when they see our skinheads on television, they must wonder why monks have suddenly dressed up in boots, jeans and braces. . . .

You get odd thoughts like this going up the Irrawaddy.

Almost everywhere the boat stops and puts out a plank and people run up and down it and then we go off again. It's a long-distance boat and a local bus service as well. It may also be a useful way to cross the river if you can't catch a ferry; in the hundreds of miles between Prome and Mandalay there is not a single road bridge. Most people are traders, or families, or people going up-country looking for work, but one or two travel as groups, such as the bunch of sad-looking prisoners who get on under armed guard and get off at Pakoko, where they are replaced by a girls' basketball team going up to Mandalay for a tournament.

I fell in love with all of them immediately. If Burmese men have nice skin, you should see the girls' complexions. But it was their smiles that got me – the clear, confident, laughing, unabashed smiles of fifteen-year-olds who seemed like women already. Luckily, I was proof against their charms. I had bought a small book in Rangoon which had been printed in 1945 as a guide for British soldiers.

'Tips on how to treat the Burmese', it said at the end. 'No. 14. Burmese women: Unlike many women in the East, Burmese women do not go around with downcast eyes. They are very independent, and will approach you in a frank and friendly way. Do not mistake this for an invitation to go to bed with you.'

'It's all right, girls,' I said as they chattered to me in a frank and friendly way. 'I know you don't want to go to bed with me. So what shall we do instead?'

What they proposed doing instead was showing me how to put on the distinctive face decoration they use, which comes from ground up sandalwood and gives each girl a big white circle on each brown cheek. To me, it always looked slightly Stone Age beside the neatness of their dress and their elegant poise, but they all adhere to it. You wet your little block of sandalwood, put it on your face, and fifteen minutes later you have a dry patch on each cheek which gives you a certain look halfway between an avant-garde clown and a Central American tribesman. Or, in my case, makes you look very stupid and gets you laughed at by entire basketball teams.

At Yenanyaung you can find what little is left of the once mighty Burma oil industry. Before the war, the landscape was festooned with oil derricks like the candles on a centenarian's birthday cake. Now only two or three drills are still working, producing enough oil to make a salad dressing. I paid a pilgrimage to the edge of the old oilfield, once worked by enough Europeans to form an entire dance band – I was shown a photo of an oilfield orchestra containing at least nine ukeleles. While I was sitting there, two men came up and spoke to me in courteous Burmese which I could not understand. Later I discovered that what they were telling me was that I was sitting right where dangerous snakes like to come and bask.

I found it slightly odd that the oil industry pre-dated European expansion by at least two hundred years. It was so thick, so plentiful, so near to the surface that it could be scooped or dug by hand. I was introduced to a family who had once owned a prime site but was now sunk in genteel poverty. They had put what little funds they had left into a printing press.

'We print mostly wedding invitations,' the father told me softly.

'How many guests come to the average Burmese wedding?'

He thought about it. 'About twelve hundred on average.'

U Thein San solved the mystery of the monk's military chest shortly before he and his boy companion left us. Apparently the man had been in the army until the age of fifty-four and now, a year later, had decided to become a monk. But he had kept his luggage. Now U Thein San did not think he was a spy. He merely thought he was a rather amateur monk.

'The boy is a better monk than he is,' he told me contemptuously.

The days, seven of them, came and went. There was not much sailing at night, unless we were hurrying for a destination – then the captain would switch on a huge searchlight, the beam of which he swivelled from one bank to the other while it attracted huge crowds of insects. In the morning, most of them lay in a sad, grey pyramid below the light, burnt to death. If it is possible to get an idea of timelessness in seven days, then a boat on the Irrawaddy is the ideal place to get it. Not only does the clock seem suspended, not only is there nothing to do, not only are you surrounded by people staring into space, but you are cut off from the riverbank world, the real world, the world of clocks, calendars and timetables.

You also pass the most timeless place I have ever seen, Pagan. I have been lucky enough to see a few of the world's great temple sites – Petra, Machu Picchu, Stonehenge, St Peter's – but this is the one. What makes it unique is that this plain was once the site of a great city studded with temples, 5 miles across. The capital, for once, did not move for over two hundred years and in that time they built huge temples out of glittering white stone and deep glowing brown brick, rising out of what must have been the Rome of the East. But when in our Middle Ages there was an invasion by Kubla Khan, the Burmese king simply turned tail and fled. The city was abandoned, and slowly all the houses, shops and palaces – made of wood – disappeared. (A Burmese friend who came to my house in Wiltshire, which has its share of exposed beams, exclaimed: 'My God! In Burma this wood would not survive a year before the ants and termites ate it!')

But all the stone and brick temples survived, and most of them still stand, like precious stones on a necklace from which the string has rotted. It is, of course, one of the collecting points for tourists in Burma, but there are not yet nearly enough to spoil the place, which is about as developed as it would be if Thomas Cook had been given sole rights and the year were 1895. There is still something very genteel and amateurish about it all, which is charming, especially the fact that the best and easiest way to get around, and get away, is to hire a bicycle for the day.

When people talk about Buddhist buildings in Burma they call them pagodas,

but the buildings at Pagan are called temples, and they are indeed quite different. The pagoda is always topped by a stupa, that gently curving, friendly mushroom shape which I think represents a major achievement: it is the only religious architectural silhouette which is not aggressive, phallic or forbidding. But none of the temples at Pagan comes into that dome-on-top bracket; they are all square, and you can climb to the top either via stairs inside or simply up the stepped exteriors, as if you were going to the top of some ancient Buddhist football terrace.

As the boat goes up-river again from Pagan the pagoda count seems to increase, and it rises to a great frenzy a mile or two before Mandalay; the establishment of one of the great holy places there has covered the hills on the left-hand bank with domes like a prize-winning display of meringues. The first sight of Mandalay itself is quite different: a waterfront full of dilapidated jetties and decrepit-looking boats, dusty and down-at-heel. For steam fans there was one sight to gladden the eye: the last remaining steam-driven paddle boat on the river, now converted to a dredger.

But once past the shabby waterfront Mandalay emerges as a city of green and leafy charm, a huge garden suburb awash with bicycles. As a farewell present, U Thein San introduced me to his cousin and arranged for me to borrow his bike to get around Mandalay. Cousin Jimmy was a sad-faced man who, like many Burmese, had a factory in his house. It was a cigar factory – in other words a small summerhouse in which three very old ladies rolled large cigars very slowly and patiently out of tobacco leaf that looked like thin and and not very clean dishcloths. Jimmy presented me with one of these cigars, and from the wrapping I learnt that they had carried off a silver medal at a tobacco contest in Hyderabad in the 1930s. I fear they have not won many prizes since. Mrs Jimmy, a jolly, laughing woman, also had a factory, or rather a schoolroom for teaching English to tiny tots, and in my honour she got them to sing 'London's Burning'.

Several years ago Mandalay itself nearly burnt down. It's quite easy to see how such a town of low, cheek-by-jowl, mostly made of wood, could be a high fire risk, though it was quite hard to see where the fire had been. It was the Chinese who got the rebuilding under way quickest, or so I was told by a professor at the university.

'I don't know where they get all their money from,' he said darkly. 'The Chinese always get things done quicker than the Burmese. Perhaps they know all the right people, or put their bribes in the right place. The Indians, too.'

In some countries the business seems to slip into the hands of the Indians, and in some the hands of the Chinese. In Burma, it's both. The casual, friendly approach of the Burmese businessman seems no match for the other two, with the result that whole areas of business life seem foreign-dominated, and the result of that is that at times of crisis the populace tends to turn on the poor rich foreigner. Twenty years ago there were rice shortage riots, and the Chinese community was victimized for it. When the Japanese invaded Burma in 1942 the first to flee from Rangoon were the Indian traders, calculating quite rightly that if they stayed behind they would be looted and lynched by the natives long before the Japanese got there. Many were.

'You know that cricket is banned in Burma?' said the professor, apparently totally irrelevantly.

'I didn't know it was played here, let alone banned,' I said.

'Only the Indians play it here. That's why the Old Man banned it,' he said, twinkling.

The Old Man is General Ne Win. In 1987 there was no sign yet of the popular unrest which would sweep Burma in 1988 and then recede, leaving things apparently much as before. Still in power behind the scenes is the remote figure whose twenty years of patient stewardship had brought the country from comparative prosperity and optimism to near-bankruptcy. People talked about him with the hopelessness and familiarity with which Russians discuss shortages or the British discuss the weather. They never referred to him as Ne Win, only by circumlocutions like the Old Man, but many stories circulated of the things he had banned in a fit of pique. Gambling, horse-racing, social dancing, cricket, any restaurant staying open after 9 p.m. the teaching of English in schools. . . .

'About dancing,' said the professor, 'the story is that one New Year's Eve the Old Man was kept awake by the noise of a party at a nearby hotel. About 1 a.m. he suddenly interrupted into the party, told the band to stop, ordered everyone to go home and decreed, almost as an afterthought, that there should be no more dancing in Burma. The teaching of English he banned, I think, because he wanted to keep Burma purer. It did the country great harm.'

'Why did he restore it?'

'Oh, that was a personal whim as well. His daughter wanted to go abroad to study, but she was not accepted at the colleges of her choice because she could not speak English, due to her father's own policy. So he rescinded it. Bit late in the day for her, though.'

Perhaps the reason that people haven't risen and strung him from the nearest tree long ago, as I would have wanted to, is that a nation so used to kings and emperors goes on treating its ruler as a potentate, even if he is only a general, and that he therefore behaves like one. Throw a Shah out and you quite likely end up with an Ayatollah.

Mandalay – you will be surprised to hear – was until relatively recently the capital of Burma, and the palace of the last king lies inside a vast square moat, about a mile long on every side, near the centre of town. Or rather, it did until 1945, when the retreating Japanese camped in it and the RAF totally destroyed it; but the walls and moat remain, and by themselves are wonderfully impressive.

The professor, however, like most natives of anywhere, was unimpressed by his own home town. What he wanted to show me was a precious photograph album from thirty years ago.

'Here is Buckingham Palace,' he said. 'This is Piccadilly. I think this is Paddington Station. . . .'

They were black and white snapshots of his student youth in London. His memory crackled with excitement as he talked about it, the last time he had been anywhere outside Burma. To me, Burma was exotic, strange and brand-new round every corner; to him, the most exotic thing in the world was the London I knew as an everyday routine.

A monk standing in the ornate archways of one of the 600 monasteries
and temples in the monastic city of Sagaing.

'Of course, those were the days of the colour bar in London,' he said impassively. 'There were signs in so many windows saying "No coloureds". 'Sometimes it was better. It said, "Sorry, no coloureds". And sometimes it said, "Sorry, no coloureds or Irish".'

He didn't seem too depressed at the memory. In fact, he suddenly chuckled. 'I remember one place was advertising a room to let and didn't say anything about a colour bar, so I went round to enquire. The man took one look at me and said he was sorry, he only let rooms to whites. So I said he ought to have the decency to mention that in his ad so that people like me didn't have a wasted bus fare and an afternoon down the drain.'

'Well, this took him aback slightly and he suddenly said, "Come in for a moment." When I got inside, he said he was sorry, I was quite right, he should have mentioned that in the ad. And he gave me a cup of tea to make up for me coming all that way. So I told him all about being a Burmese law student, and I mentioned that I didn't drink, didn't smoke, had no lady friends and just wanted to study, and all of a sudden he said, "You can have the room, you seem the ideal lodger to me."'

'We got on very well after that. I stayed for two years or more. In fact, as he had quite a lot of students and came to trust me, he put me in charge of all the rent arrangements, for which I got a rent reduction. So you see, having started wanting to ban me, he ended up putting me in charge!'

He roared with laughter. 'I reminded him of this once, and he said he really had nothing against coloureds at all, it was the *blacks* he didn't trust.'

Prejudice is many-layered, indeed. It flourishes in Burma as well. Roughly half the population is ethnic Burmese; the rest are well-defined minority tribes. The British tended to favour some of these tribes, certainly for soldiering purposes, and promised them quasi-independence when they left. They didn't get it, and many of them are still fighting for it. That is why the border between Burma and China is controlled by neither country and why the Thai-Burma border has been privatized by small independence armies. In the case of the latter there is another factor. The Burmese and the Thais don't like each other very much, a result of one of those strange historical fishbones which still stick in the throat – the sack and burning of Bangkok by an invading Burmese army two hundred years ago.

I thought there was nothing much to this Thai-Burma rivalry till a few weeks later, when my mind was changed in Phuket Airport. This is way down south in Thailand, where no Burmese has been seen for aeons, yet in the brand-new building there is a large brand-new plaque commemorating the bravery of two local heroes in the war against the Burmese invaders two centuries ago. I call *that* serious.

I mentioned the Thais to the professor, to see what his reaction would be.

'They are all right, the Thais,' he said, 'except that they do boast a bit too much. For instance, that they were the only country in Asia not to be colonized by the West, as if they had beaten off the imperialist invader by their own efforts. It was not like that at all. Quite simply, the French and the British decided to have a buffer state between the French Empire and the British Empire, and agreed that neither would occupy Thailand. It was good luck, nothing else.'

*Evening on the Irrawaddy at Mandalay: a girl pauses on her way to
collect water and a young boy swims beside his parents' bamboo raft
which they are floating downstream to sell in Rangoon.*

Right: Women wash away the heat and dust of the day.

There were white people in Mandalay. I hadn't seen a white man for a week. In fact, I had come to think of myself as small and brown, being surrounded by small, brown people, and it always came as a shock to look in the mirror and see a tall, gawky, big-nosed white man. One white man was an Australian in charge of Mandalay's new water supply, not yet built. The present water supply, he told me to my great surprise, was the old palace moat.

Is it not stagnant?

No, quite fresh on the whole. The *bad* water is in the Irrawaddy. When the river rises in the rainy season, watch out for cholera.

Unnerved by the presence of white folk I decided to move on to Maymyo. It's less than 100 miles away, or a morning by train, but it's a different world, because we had started to climb the hills. Barely 5 miles beyond Mandalay the last bit of flat land is left behind, and it's up and down for the next 10,000 miles. In Mandalay, the hotels have air conditioning and mosquito nets; in Maymyo they have electric fires and extra blankets. That's why Maymyo is there, actually; it was a hill station to which the British army retired in the hot season, and any British chap who was lucky enough to work for a company rich enough to send him there.

I had Paul Theroux's *The Great Railway Bazaar* with me, and as we chugged up the hill from Mandalay to Maymyo I turned to see what he had been doing when he chugged up the hill from Mandalay to Maymyo. Apparently he had bumped into the manager of the Candacraig Hotel. The Candacraig (I found later) is like something out of Balmoral, all curly beams and antlers and blazing log fires, not to mention Yorkshire pudding with the beef, and Paul Theroux had chatted to this hotel's manager all the way up – just enough to fill the journey. My feeling, as I spent the journey reading about what Theroux had done on the journey, was: *I don't believe it.*

Do you ever get those feelings when you read long conversations in travel books between the writer and this extremely interesting character he just happened to meet on this potentially quite boring journey? A feeling that it didn't quite happen that way? That, in short, he made it all up?

I do. Not just with Paul Theroux, but with all of them. I get the feeling that a lot of travel writing is fiction. I don't actually disapprove of this, but I had never before been in a position to check up on my suspicions.

There was nobody on the train who looked remotely like a hotel manager, but I sat next to a monk who was carrying a camera and spoke excellent English. Monks are not allowed to own personal property, but this turned out to be monastery property; his English he had learned from the BBC World Service, which is the source in Burma of endless conversation and all the news that's fit to repeat. Nobody in his right mind would look at a Burmese paper for information and nobody who was interested in the world would be far from a radio set at World Service news time. In fact, I believe the Burmese Service of the BBC gets more mail proportionate to the population than any other country. In Maymyo an elderly lawyer said to me sharply: 'And what is this new paper *The Independent* like?' This was a month before the first issue appeared.

The monk got off halfway up the line, and the only other noteworthy thing that happened was that, as I was staring out of the window, a pair of feet appeared a foot from my face. They wriggled down, bringing with them two legs, two knees and so on, until a boy carrying a tray of bottles finally came in through the window. He had been up on the roof serving the many passengers up there and was now coming in to serve us more staid customers. I bought a bottle of the local hooch, about which I had heard many reports, all bad. They were right.

Maymyo is a weird place, at least to British eyes. Our presence left behind a clutch of churches which wouldn't look out of place in Surrey, suburbs reminiscent of Sunningdale and rickety horse-drawn cabs straight out of Sherlock Holmes, as well as a thriving strawberry-growing industry and a healthy-looking botanical garden. Just when you have convinced yourself that it's all comfortably Trollopian or at worst Dickensian, the illusion subtly shifts; you spot bars with swing door entrances, moustached men upstairs on balconies, horses hitched to posts – and all of a sudden it's a frontier town. The Wild East! And those cabs aren't Sherlock Holmes – they're Wells Fargo!

And indeed it is in a sense a frontier town, because for us gringos this is about as far as we can come. The Burmese government will never admit to you straight that they have lost control of anything, such as their northern territories, so what they tell you as a traveller is that it is not in your interests to go any further and they cannot let you continue for the sake of your personal safety. In vain do you tell them that you are happy to risk your head; they refuse to hear of it.

But it is a frontier town also in the sense that many races mingle here and many religions co-exist. Just outside the town is a village occupied entirely by Gurkhas, descendants of the soldiers brought here from far-off Nepal by the British. The British went back home, but the Gurkhas couldn't; none of them has ever seen Nepal, but every family has a photograph of its ancestors and the homeland.

'Have you ever thought of going back?' I asked one of them.

He smiled the sort of sweet, sad smile that you smile when a foreigner asks an idiot question.

'What for? This is home now. And even if I could, I would have to take twenty relations with me. Twenty tickets to Nepal is expensive. . . .'

I should have been here, the elderly lawyer told me, when the rebels took over the town thirty years ago or more. Ah, these tribesmen were good fighters, they were. They held Maymyo for six months before the Burmese army drove them back. Very good at fighting, these chaps, but not so good at knowing what to do when they had won.

'After it was all over, I was the chief official prosecutor in the treason trials of the main rebels,' he revealed. 'I asked for the death penalty in all one hundred and fifty cases. And I got it! Unfortunately, the government commuted them all to prison sentences. Do you know what that means? It means that eventually they all got out and then there were a hundred and fifty chaps roaming the world whom I had got condemned to death!'

He laughed uproariously at the idea.

'Some of them still live here. I see them from time to time. We get on all right.'

An open-air class in the park for Chinese schoolchildren in Kunming,
capital of free China in the Second World War and terminus of the
Burma Road.

'Does everyone get on all right?'

'Oh yes, I think so. We worry sometimes about the Muslims. They are very keen on converting, you know, very proselytizing, and we Buddhists won't go in for that. But apart from that we have all creeds here. We even have a Christian Scientist here. He is a missionary, and a friend of mine. I do not think he is a very good missionary, as he is still the only Christian Scientist in Maymyo, but he converted me to being his friend, at least!'

More laughter. Later that day, an elderly Muslim leaped out on me in the street and I feared for a moment he was going to try to convert me. But he had other ideas on his mind.

'Are you English? You are? So you have come back! But where were you in 1942 when we really needed you? You left – and we got the Japanese in return, a terrible exchange. Ah, how I miss the British! Especially your Cadbury's Milk Tray!'

He was truly a man who spoke in exclamation marks. It turned out, on closer examination, that in 1942 he had not been here at all. He had chosen that year of all years to make the Haj, the holy pilgrimage to Mecca.

'It was terrible, sir! When our boat was off Egypt, we were torpedoed by the Germans! I lost everything – and I had to swim! I finally got to Mecca, but then when I got back here I found the Japanese had arrived in my absence! Ah, what a bad time!'

I finally made it to Candacraig Hotel, where there were two people staying, two tourists who had decided to use all their seven days at Maymyo and not see Lake Inle or Pagan or Mandalay or any of the other possible sights. They were not sorry to have come. I was too late to check up with the hotelier on the truth or otherwise of Paul Theroux's conversation, but I met one of the manager's sons, who was still basking in reflected glory.

'Tell me, did Paul Theroux meet your late father on the train coming up?'

'No, sir, he did not.'

Aha!

'No, sir, he had that conversation with him right here in the hotel. I suppose in the book he repositioned it because nothing else had happened to him on the train.'

And that, children, is how books get written.

'But I must tell you, sir, that my father was always amazed how Mr Theroux remembered everything he had told him so exactly – he could not see any notebook, any tape recorder, nothing! And yet he had got every detail right. And I will tell you another thing: we learnt things about our father from reading Mr Theroux's book which we did not know before, many things about his early life. You know, we had not even asked him. And he said all these things to a stranger, because the stranger asked him all the questions. And now we only know these things because we have read them in a book. It is very strange.'

Beyond Maymyo is black market country. Most people would only go up there, to Lashio and beyond, to get their slice of the action coming across the border from China. What I had to do, being European and not wanting to get on the wrong side of the authorities, was go back. Paul Theroux tried to go further, illegally, and didn't get very far. But before returning, I encountered several people who had been to Kunming and back along the Burma Road during the war. They were a Eurasian gentleman who had done it as a teenager in his sports car for fun and said it was a dreadful road – all those lorries, you know; an old lorry driver who said it was just a job and very boring; and an ex-policeman who had for two years run the border post where Burma joined China and had had to let through, or not, every single lorry that passed that way. He had quite fond memories of the time, not least because he had been speedily promoted when the Japanese came, and as speedily demoted when the British came back. His biggest memory was of the day he had had lunch with Chiang Kai-shek.

'The Chinese leader and his wife, and many important people, stopped one day at my control post, and they had brought a big lunch with them, so they invited me to join them. He was a very nice man; he pretended not to speak English very well, but he did. Afterwards, he gave me a signed photograph of himself. Alas, I no longer have it.'

He was the only man I came across who had a good thing to say about Chiang.

And there was a foretaste of China in Maymyo – a Chinese Buddhist temple. Chinese temples seem rather different – more smells, more bells, and Buddhas with beards, albeit straggly. While the Burmese do not have facial hair (therefore neither do the Buddhas), the Chinese can run to a mandarin moustache or a Confucian beard, so their Buddhas are encouraged to have just a little growth. I am afraid Jesus must look very hairy to them, rather like an early hippy.

There was also something I had not expected: a fortune-telling service. You rattle some sticks and take one. You follow the number and look it up in a big book. It is written in Burmese, so you haven't the faintest idea what it says. But a kindly bystander translates it for you....

'You will have troubles on your journeys.'

Hmm. Still, I don't believe these things. Never have.

'And you have a pregnant woman in your household, who will also be trouble.'

Ridiculous, isn't it?

The trouble was, my wife Caroline was actually three months pregnant.

I flew back to Rangoon from Mandalay, and stayed at the Strand Hotel. The piano player was still playing when I left for the airport and the Kunming plane. I didn't tell them about the black market currency when they checked my money, and they didn't ask me about it, even though they knew that I knew that they knew. We boarded a Chinese plane – once a fortnight it goes north to China – and we went north to China.

I think the reason I didn't like China much was that I had just come from Burma. Most people drop into China from home, or from Hong Kong or some modern metropolis, and so it looks exotic and different. Hardly anyone (judging from the

*Terraced paddyfields outside Kunming along the road westwards to the
forbidden frontier with Burma.*

*Right: A small boy in a remote walled village by-passed when the
Burma Road changed its course.*

dearth of passengers on the plane) ever goes into China from somewhere as warm and natural and happy-go-lucky as Burma; but if you do, China appears like just another modern, industrial nation. The people seem off-hand, the buildings charmless, and everywhere looks polluted and without grace, as well as humourless. By comparison with Burma, of course.

Actually, if you have to start anywhere, Kunming is a good place. It is mentioned in all the guide books as probably the one Chinese city which has most resisted mindless modernization, and great areas of the city still consist of green-painted, wood-fronted, low-roofed streets or alleyways. There are specialist markets everywhere – for flowers, for clothes, for fruit, for fish, for pet birds. At one I came across a performing parrot which had devised a great act. After doing one or two mildly interesting contortions on its perch, it would suddenly drop dead. It would fall off and dangle upside down at the end of the stout piece of string that bound it to the perch, like John Cleese's proverbial bird. After twenty seconds or so, it would suddenly recover and clamber back on to its perch, looking round slily for a standing ovation – though I think I was the only person who ever looked like clapping.

Hiring a bicycle to see Kunming is not really a fun thing to do as it was in Mandalay – it is a necessity. So few people in big Chinese cities have private cars and so many have bicycles that the streets are geared to the bike the way ours are geared to the car. This is, on the whole, bad news for a cyclist, because it means that you are strictly controlled at lights, shouted at by policemen, restricted to certain speeds and – incredible as it may seem – made to pay wherever you park. If you leave your bike in an unauthorized zone, you get it towed away.

It was in this handsome, broad city (though it wasn't handsome and broad then) that the supply lorries due to help Chiang Kai-shek finally arrived after their arduous, weeks' long journey up the Burma Road. The only person I met in Kunming who admitted to remembering that was an American, a missionary staying at my hotel.

'I haven't been here since 1943,' he told me. 'It was a dump then, and it looks great now.'

The reason that he was the only person to remember those days is that the Chinese don't want to remember that war, because it was fought by the reactionary Chiang Kai-shek, the arch-enemy of Mao Tse-tung and Chou En-lai. He may have been defending China – but only for his own ends, his capitalist power struggle. And the American missionary was here because in 1943 America was the ally of China against Japan, but from the point of view of present history the ally of the *wrong* China. So it all tends to get forgotten, except by the odd, lone, elderly missionary on his first return trip since 1943.

Things haven't changed so much out on the road. Once you get outside Kunming and start the long trek back towards Burma, you get transported back in your mind to those wartime days, because the road is still dedicated to the lorry. In Kunming, the absence of private cars is disguised by the locust swarms of bicycles. Out on the main road, all you are aware of is that every vehicle seems to be a lorry.

The road has a strangely military air about it, as if all this equipment is being moved somewhere for some urgent purpose, especially as the lorries are mainly old.

What gives the road an even more atmospheric feel is that all the trees within reach of the road are painted white for the first 4 feet of trunk. I think the idea is that at night it makes a substitute for our white line. In theory it's a good idea, but in practice if a lorry runs off the road it always runs into a tree. I saw four heavily impacted lorries during my time in China. Don't plant trees at the side of the road was my advice, but the Chinese don't listen to world opinion.

I travelled for two days down the road towards Burma, a road which twisted through hills and sped across plains. Occasionally it would go through towns, either small not very distinguished towns or big not very distinguished towns, black with smoke pollution and caked with industrial grime. But the countryside was quite beautiful, farmed still in the traditional terraced way with paddy fields and patient bullocks doing all the work. Compared to England, China is still medieval. People have all but vanished from the English countryside – somebody once worked out that an English field received a human visitor on only fifteen days in the year – but in China agriculture is still highly labour-intensive. Stop on any corner of the road, as I did once, and count the people within 100 yards of you – eight, was it? Ten? Not just passing by; these were people working in the fields or chasing an animal or carrying a load of produce on those agonizing-looking yokes.

Or look out across a plain from a hill and you will see twenty, thirty, forty villages, all smoking and steaming in the sunshine, where in Europe or North America you might see a tenth of that number. Listen hard, and you can hear the noise of the village, which very often is a tinny loudspeaker broadcasting correct Party thoughts to the people. Not Muzak, but Maozak. I never saw a single person listening to it, or even registering that it was there.

Quite often, along the road, I saw huge artificial mounds, steaming and belching smoke, looking like miniature Silbury Hills. The country is well endowed with brick earth, and here in these temporary kilns the local people were making and baking as many bricks as they needed for their house-building. No allowance is made for doors and windows – they simply build great expanses of wall, and then cut holes later. The conical kiln which produced the bricks is left to become part of the landscape when the cooking is over, and I found myself wondering if anyone has looked inside Silbury Hill with a knowledge of brick-baking to back them up.

It was down this road that the Revd Bradley travelled in 1930 by mule and leisurely packhorse and many of the villages he mentioned are still to be found. Many more are not. None of the inns is to be seen where he spent a night in the stables – he always made a point of sharing the stables with his animals, because, he claimed, it was more comfortable there than in a room, which he would have to share with lots of unpredictable strangers. Better a predictable and familiar animal, he thought. The Chinese have still not entirely grasped concepts of basic comfort, I'm afraid to say, especially in plumbing. I could give you the names of several hotels where the bath plumbing was inextricably mixed up with the lavatory, and others where the food was so dreadful that you wondered how Chinese cooking ever got a reputation for being edible.

But to trace the missionary's exact course would be impossible, especially as the

A Chinese tourist on the medieval gateway of the walled town of Dali.

Right: One of the Three Pagodas outside Dali.

road, like a river, has changed course again since Chiang built it. As you travel from Kunming back to Burma you see, almost out of the corner of your eye, shadows of where the road used to be, bridges now going nowhere, absent curves going round a hillside. Go closer and you sometimes find that what look like old farm tracks are lined with massive slabs of stone, as the old Imperial Chinese highway is supposed to have been. Sometimes the abandoned roadway is a flat embankment high up on a slope, suspiciously flat, too flat for a mere road, which means that it must be an old railway, and that is ridiculous, because there has never been a railway in these parts. . . .

Much later, I learnt that there almost was a railway. Kunming, a desirable railhead, could be reached by rail from either Vietnam (if the French cared to build a track) or Burma (ditto the British). The British started building their track, but the French finished theirs, and the trip from Hanoi to Kunming is said to be among the best of all railway journeys in the world – at least, it was once, because this is one of the unspoken victims of the Vietnam War and the current lack of love between the Chinese and their Vietnamese neighbours.

After two days' travel the houses are no longer built from red earth but become handsome stone edifices. We are coming to Dali, an ancient fortified town which, when Bradley came this way, still had its town gates closed every night – though not to much avail as the walls were crumbling and grassed over. It is being painted in glittering red and gold now for the beginning of the tourist trade. The handsome local mottled grey marble is being made into eggcups and inkstands and things that you and I would never find a use for. You turn right here to go to Tibet, and you go straight on towards the Burmese border. But only if you are Chinese; here too, the foreigner is not welcome yet, and a road which was open to all in the middle of a horrendous war is closed to almost everyone in peacetime.

Not everyone who lived round here would consider himself Chinese – there are many minority tribes, and small pockets of Buddhist monks. It was not so very long ago that this part of Yunnan was independent, and Dali was fortified against the Chinese in the first place, not by them. As you go towards Burma the feeling becomes less and less Chinese; up there in the borderlands they enjoy near-autonomy, and even the Chinese officials admitted to me that the border was only closed to people like me and them; the tribesmen themselves moved freely in and out of Burma.

And if you want to know what Dali looked like sixty years ago, when Bradley was walking to Burma and Chiang had not started rebuilding the road, there is a small walled town lost down a valley about two hours' drive from Kunming. It was bypassed in the 1930s, and left to survive as best it could. It is the nearest thing to a medieval town I have ever seen, with pigs and chickens wandering the stone main street – it's inaccessible to cars – and men threshing corn with flails in front of their houses. It has ancient gates, and ancient walls, and I saw nothing else remotely like it between Dali and Kunming.

Perhaps even the Chinese felt there was something special about this place, because the oldest man in the town had been commissioned to write its history. He spoke no Chinese, only the local dialect, but through an interpreter he told me of his memories of the Burma Road coming that way . . . the first lorries anyone had seen

. . . the first Americans . . . the forced labour . . . the deaths among the navvies . . . the fact that some people still hadn't been paid for their work.

'Of course,' he said, 'I remember even better the days before the road was built. The gates of the town were closed every night, then.'

'Against what?' I asked him.

'Why, against bandits,' he said, amazed that anyone should not know.

In the street outside his house, where he sat in a sunny window carefully dipping his pen in the rich black ink and tracing the elegant characters, the children gawped and raced after me. They had never seen a foreign devil, a long nose, before. And yet they were not entirely uninformed about our doings, because one of them was carrying an English-language textbook home from school. I borrowed it from him to see what they were being taught. The book started:

'Where is Mr Smith?'

'He has gone to Washington, I believe.'

'Will he be there long, do you know?'

A month or two later we came back to film what I had seen and met, and we saw entirely different things and met different people. But the pianist was still playing at the Strand Hotel, and the producer agreed to get him in a shot. However, at the only time he could film him, the pianist was not available – he was doing another job.

'Never mind,' said the producer. 'Here's what we'll do. We'll get someone who can play the piano, and shoot Miles walking past him and then walking out of the hotel front door.'

The only man in the hotel, it turned out, who could play the piano passably was a Japanese student who was staying there. From behind he did look vaguely as if he might be Burmese. But all he could play was Beethoven.

'Never mind,' said the producer. 'We'll record the pianist later and dub him over. Now, Miles, just walk it through and go out the hotel door.'

Outside the hotel door the crowd of black market dollar buyers was waiting for guests to leave. Every time we tried the shot, the same thing happened: the hotel door would open, releasing distant echoes of Beethoven's 'Für Elise' and, I would be set upon by anxious hands looking for my currency. A distant cry of 'Cut!' would come, and I would disengage myself from the hands and go back in.

After five or six takes, the black marketeers got the idea that I was a mad Britisher who had got into the habit of putting his head out of the hotel door every four minutes and then going back in again, and they had come to ignore me totally. The only person who took an interest in me at all was one currency dealer who had arrived on duty late. When I came out of the hotel the seventh time, he rushed towards me. The others dragged him away, warning him that I was a dangerous lunatic.

Needless to say, this sequence was not used in the film. The sequences you remember are the ones that were not used. Everything I have written about here really happened to me and not to Paul Theroux, though not always in the order mentioned. The things I have completely forgotten about are in the film.

A Bai woman visiting Dali to celebrate an annual festival. Close to the border with Burma, the town is dominated by minority hill tribes.

Right: A young Yi girl in the unyielding mountains surrounding Dali which run unbroken to the gates of Mandalay.

FROM THE BALTIC TO THE BLACK SEA

Norman Stone

Leningrad in the snow is one of the finest sights on earth. With its vast, dreamlike palaces it is still very obviously the capital of Imperial Russia. The greatest of them all is the Winter Palace, the centre of old St Petersburg, as Leningrad was originally called. With its hundreds of rooms, and the adjoining Hermitage which now contains one of the greatest picture collections in the world, it was the main residence of the tsars, where they spent the winter when weather conditions made other palaces difficult to reach.

The tiniest details of the palace symbolize the grandiose ambitions of tsarist Russia. Look down, and you see parquet flooring in a pattern of extreme complexity; look around, and you see one extraordinary artefact after another – rococo clocks, huge vases made of impossible-to-extract minerals from remote mountains, delicate porcelain, tables of Italian marquetry; look up, and you see ceilings decorated with exquisite murals and highly elaborate mouldings.

In the eighteenth century, when it was built, and in the nineteenth, when it was filled with ever more elaborate artefacts, the Winter Palace expressed the dream of a Russia that would be greater than those European powers which had provided its inspiration. The resources to create it came from a huge country which had been opened up over the centuries – Siberia in the sixteenth, the Baltic provinces in the seventeenth, the Ukraine in the eighteenth, and the Caucasus and Central Asia in the nineteenth. By 1917, when the Communists seized power, the Russians occupied one-sixth of the world's land surface and had a population approaching two hundred million.

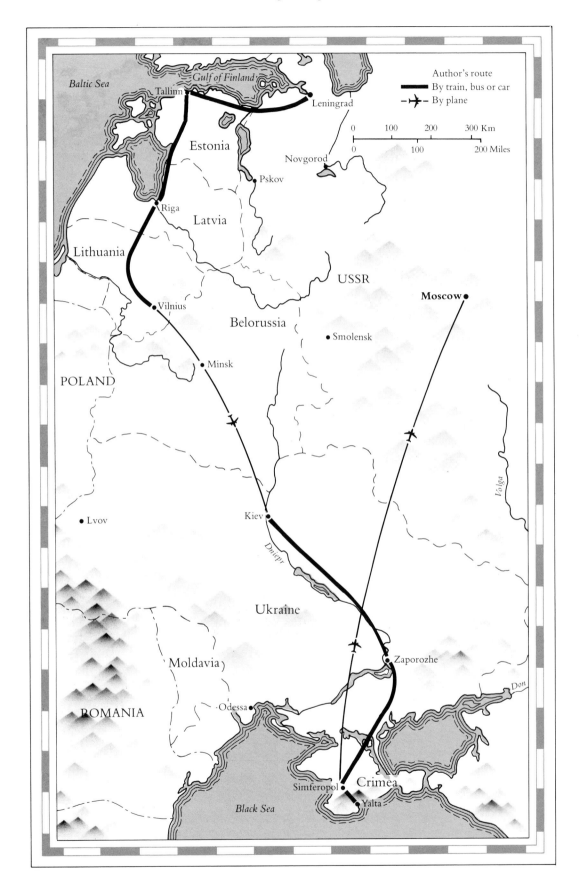

The Winter Palace is only one – though the largest – of the Imperial palaces. There are others, summer residences of the tsars, in the surrounding countryside. Peterhof, now Petrodvorets, overlooks the Baltic; Gachina stands on the banks of the River Izhora in the midst of large pine forests, and is now a grim place dominated by army barracks; and Tsarkoe Selo, in the town of Pushkin, 19 miles from Leningrad, is where the last Tsar was kept under house arrest until, with his wife, children and dog, he was carried off to be murdered in the Urals in 1918.

The land on which the city was built was reclaimed from marsh at the beginning of the eighteenth century, and the canals which drained the city's foundations – the Moyka, the Griboyedov and the Fontanka – are still there, as are the grand eighteenth- and nineteenth-century buildings, once the noble palaces of the aristocracy, which lined their banks. Through the city long straight boulevards were driven, the principal one being the Nevksy Prospekt, 114 feet wide, which starts near the Winter Palace and runs south-east for $2\frac{3}{4}$ miles, ending at the Alexander Nevsky monastery. In the adjoining Tikhim cemetery the great writers, artists, composers and poets of Russia are buried – among them Dostoevsky, Musorgsky, Rimsky-Korsakov and Tchaikovsky. This place is the Westminster Abbey of old Russia. You often hear, nowadays, that great art is not appreciated in its own lifetime, but it is surprising how many of the nineteenth-century Russians whose work is still enjoyed are buried in this national cemetery. Obviously, these men were revered in their own times.

Peter the Great built St Petersburg as his new capital because it was much closer to civilization, as then understood, than messy, 'Asiatic' Moscow, where he had had endless trouble controlling the mob in general and in particular religious dissenters, who opposed any reform on the principle that what was already in existence was God-given. The new city, looking out over the Gulf of Finland towards the Baltic, joined Russia with the West, which Peter wanted to imitate. He recruited Scots, Germans, and, above all, Dutchmen (the Japanese of the seventeenth century: St Petersburg was originally a Dutch, rather than a German, name), and these men taught the Russians how to build a navy and how to trade. In this they were the successors, in a sense, of much earlier north-west European invaders of Russian land: the Vikings.

My journey was intended to cover the route that these Scandinavian adventurers took in their colonization of Russia: from Leningrad and the shores of the chilly Baltic, down through the rich and fertile Ukraine to sub-tropical Yalta on the Black Sea. The Vikings would have sailed their tough longboats along the Dniepr; I had to make do with the trains and planes of the Soviet system. But essentially both our journeys, though separated in time by a thousand years, were journeys of discovery. And while the Vikings began their incursions into Russia from the Black Sea and then moved northwards, back towards their homeland, it was important that my journey was done in reverse and began in Leningrad, Peter the Great's 'window on the West', because that city symbolized so much of what was to come.

In the ninth and tenth centuries, the Vikings sacked and raped their way around the coasts of Europe, including the Mediterranean. The 'Danes' took over a swathe of

Pages 166 and 167: The Winter Palace in Leningrad, built by Rastrelli
between 1754 and 1764, centrepiece of the Imperial capital St Petersburg.

Above and left: Magnificent palaces and shops devoid of fresh food stand side by side on Nevsky Prospekt in Leningrad.

eastern England, as well as much of Scotland and, for a time, Dublin: their traces remain in endless place-names. They even ventured as far as Greenland and, it seems, Newfoundland and Maine, although these settlements were too remote to survive. The Vikings were endlessly adaptable; with time, they learnt from the peoples they had defeated, and established vigorous but civilized states – Normandy in France; the mixed Anglo-Saxon-Norman monarchy in England, taken over by William the Conqueror in 1066; and the spectacular Norman Kingdom of Sicily, which had a large share in the success of the early Crusades in the Holy Land. But the Vikings also had a powerful impact on Russia.

The very name 'Rus' seems to be of Scandinavian origin: it meant, very roughly, 'men in boats'. My journey through the western part of the Soviet Union was, essentially, the Viking Route – one of the great historical trails, but also one along which you can rightly ask questions both about Russian history and about what is now happening in Gorbachev's Soviet Union.

In various places I was asked on Soviet television what my purpose was. The journey itself looks, now, very 'political'. It took me to Tallinn and Vilna (or Vilnius), both centres of reviving and vociferous nationalism, since they are the capitals of what were respectively the independent republics of Estonia and Lithuania until engulfed by Stalin. I went on to Kiev, the greatest city of the Ukraine. This country, larger in size and population than France, is a republic within the Soviet Union, and its language is close to Russian (not the case with the Baltic republics). Here, too, nationalism is stirring: there are people who want sovereignty; and since the Ukraine is so important a part of the Soviet Union, officials are very, very worried. When I appeared with a BBC team, in Kiev and further south in Zaporozhe, I was often asked whether the journey's purpose was not really political, and to do with the present. It was not easy for me to explain that the journey was about both the past and the present, the old question of West and East. It was about the relationship between Russia's past and the Communism of today: and many of the themes are coming alive again. The Viking Route, like the city of Leningrad, is an apt symbol. Just how 'Western' is modern Russia?

Judging from the hotels and travel facilities, it is not very Western at all. Since 1917 the Communists have been very suspicious of foreigners, and until a few years ago you might well have been followed, had your telephone tapped, maybe even had your hotel room bugged. Even as late as the seventies, people were careful about contact with foreigners – if spotted, they might have to account for themselves to the KGB.

I was struck when one of our helpers, with whom I got on very well, made a point of telling me not to telephone from the hotel if I wanted to reach him, and not to send anything through the post – advice, incidentally, very widely tendered by other people, who said that parcels of books would be opened, and some of the contents removed. Letters from Finland to Estonia, only 50 miles away, take thirty days, and are often obviously opened by censors. Nowadays, the press and television themselves protest about this, and younger people especially do not mind what they do or say. But there is widespread fear that the bad old ways might return.

The suspicion of foreigners also meant that, though they might be needed to bring in hard currency, they must be isolated in special hotels. There are not many of these, and, with the present vast increase in Western visitors, they are often swamped. Ordinary Russians are kept out by a Cerberus of a porter; inside, typically, you find an extraordinary mixture of Macedonian students in a group, French or American senior citizens, journalists, TV crews, and businessmen prospecting for a 'joint venture' with Gorbachev's economy. Formalities of various sorts, difficulties in telephoning out to the West (you have to order a call in advance, sometimes two hours, though in my experience less), and trouble getting taxis must make life unnaturally difficult for joint ventures – not to speak of the currency, which is surreal. At the official rate of exchange, the Soviet Union is as expensive to visit as Japan; yet outside tourist hotels there are throngs of none-too-discreet black marketeers. Caviar has virtually disappeared, but on the black market a tin costs £6, not the £35 you would otherwise pay.

To say such things in the past classed a writer as anti-Soviet. Now – and it is the greatest merit of Gorbachev's era – you can criticize as much as you like. People do. The Russians resent the knowledge that they are far behind the West in terms of living standards. They know that, in Western eyes, the shabby clothes and empty shops and crowded transport and street-sweeping old women are a condemnation of the system. Time and again on my journey I would come across spoilt American youths in floppy plastic clothes, and with faces of that curious livid pink that marks the children of the rich, sneering at the poor Russians. They hardly think of Russia as a civilized country. Is it a part of the European world at all?

That question haunted Russian minds in the nineteenth century, and dominated my 1000-mile journey from Leningrad to Yalta. The question of the Vikings' involvement was a matter of intense political debate in Russia, a debate which often took on nationalistic and racial overtones about the nature and character of the Russian state. Were the northern Aryans – in other words, those of Gothic or German extraction – superior to the Slavs from Russia, Poland and the Balkans? Was Kievan Russia – the first Russian state – a creation of Germanic outsiders? This idea became popular in Central Europe later on, particularly with Hitler and the ideologists of the SS.

The original Russians were a Slav-speaking people who settled in the great plains of Russia, an area bounded now by Moscow, Leningrad and Kiev. In the eleventh and twelfth centuries the Mongols, otherwise known as Tatars, from Central Asia over-ran Russia, enslaved the Russians and ruled until the middle of the fifteenth century. The Mongols gave to Russia an element of the Asiatic to which later writers often called attention: the word for executioner – *palach* – for example, is of Tatar origin, as were several of the great Russian aristocratic families.

The Mongols swept over the principalities of 'Kievan Rus' and set up an empire that lasted in some regions, including Moscow, for two centuries, and elsewhere, as in the Crimea, for four or more. How strong was the 'Asiatic' influence on the development of Russia? Did it make the Russian monarchy, when it arose, equivalent to the other great 'Asiatic despotisms' of India, China and Persia: immobile, ruled by

The dome of St Isaac's Cathedral, rising behind the River Neva in Leningrad (above), contrasts with the Central European feel of Vilnius, capital of Lithuania (right above) and the Germanic architecture of Tallinn, capital of the Baltic republic of Estonia (right).

terror and religion, and unable, in the end, to achieve the technological change which ultimately caused Western empire-builders to destroy them? What was the role of Viking state-builders in old Kievan Rus as against the role of Mongols in Muscovy later on? Did they 'colonize' barbarians, and teach them how to build a great state – Kievan Rus – or was that state a 'native' creation? The debate, involving place-names, burial practices, archaeology and the interpretation of hideously difficult medieval texts, has still not been resolved.

This also raises the perennial question as to whether Russia belongs to Europe or not. The country's history has been punctuated with gross cruelties, often described as 'Asiatic' by writers who wished to put a distance between Russia-as-Europe and 'Asia'. There was Tsar Ivan the Terrible in the sixteenth century, who murdered his own son and sent a bell to Siberia because it had tolled the news of one of his defeats. There was Stalin, the greatest mass-murderer of the twentieth century. And between these two there was Peter the Great, surely the epitome of the Russian paradox: inspired by 'civilized' Western ideas he dreamed up the fabulous new city that bore his name, yet in the process of constructing it he drove endless serfs to death. Were these rulers 'Asiatic'? Is Russia a barbarous country? If so, how are we to account for the technical, literary and musical achievements that have distinguished the country for the last two hundred years?

This debate goes on in another form – one which has reached the centre of today's incarnation of the old Russian Empire, the USSR. In the nineteenth century there was a great rift between those Russians who looked to the West for inspiration, and those who looked to their own past and to the East; the two parties were called Westerners and Slavophiles.

The Westerners wrote off old Russia as primitive, Asiatic, peasant-dominated, obscurantist in religion and slave-minded in politics. They believed that the best models to follow came from the West – liberalism, parliaments, commerce and religious tolerance along Protestant lines. They looked partly to France, but especially to Germany, and many Russian intellectuals spent time at German universities.

The Slavophiles, of whom the best known is Dostoevsky, conceded that the West was technically superior – but they did not have a very high opinion of such achievement. Rather, they said, the West was corrupted by materialism, dominated by a bourgeoisie counting out its money, whereas Russians were closer to spiritual values. Sometimes the Slavophiles talked high-sounding nonsense – close, in spirit, to what has been heard in recent times from the Ayatollah Khomeni.

Dostoevsky himself hit upon a truth, that there is a certain shallowness of spirit in the West: 'progress' to him was just silly, liable to lead to social disintegration and a warping of individual virtues. In the Pushkin memorial speech which he delivered to a vast and ecstatic audience shortly before his death in 1881, he said that Russia's way forward was through cultivation of Russia, religion and autocracy. This – and taking tea with Grand Dukes in the Winter Palace – was a very strange end to a career that had begun, in the later 1840s, with revolutionary talk that had landed him in gaol, and with a death sentence that was dramatically commuted at the last moment to long years in a labour camp.

Maybe we should not take the politics of Dostoevsky any more seriously than we might take the politics of other writers – who in my opinion have been more wrong, politically, than any other profession. But in his case the politics formed a piece with the Orthodox religion and the anti-individualism. He thought, like Turgenev, that in the next generation liberalism would give rise to shallow revolutionaries who, finding that the ordinary people remained refractory, would then engage in totalitarianism and general mayhem. In Russia he was right, in the sense that the progressives of the 1860s produced sons who, as revolutionaries, produced Stalinism. For Dostoevsky, the evil came from the West.

These attitudes are nearly incomprehensible to modern Westerners, but they made a certain amount of sense in nineteenth-century Russia. For a very long time tsarist Russia did not suffer from the troubles of class and industry that Western Europe knew. The population was mainly peasant, and the system allowed anyone land when they had mouths to feed. The Slavophiles may have been prejudiced and antediluvian, but they did understand a thing or two. The tsarist government may have looked, to outsiders, quaintly oppressive. But the fact is that it abolished the death sentence in 1864, and ran a police force, even in 1900, that consisted of about seven thousand men, two thousand of them in the capital. The system fell apart in the later nineteenth century, when liberals and socialists and education and railways and journalism and banks and dynamite ruined the old position of the tsars. But for years that position was immensely powerful, even if based on values that the West did not understand, let alone share.

Of these, easily the greatest was Orthodoxy. In Leningrad, I went to the Sunday evening service in the main church of the Alexander Nevsky Monastery at the end of the Nevsky Prospekt. In Kiev, later, I spent two days discussing Orthodoxy with the monks of the Cave (Pechora) monastery; it lies within the 100-acre site of the earliest Christian foundations of Kievan Rus, a magnificent collection of churches and cathedrals, kept (so far as I could judge) in excellent repair. A few months earlier, the monks – three dozen – had been allowed to return to the monastery, to look after the miles of underground passages where the mummified remains of Kievan princes and medieval monks are kept.

Fortunately, the Communist state has largely abandoned its persecution of Orthodoxy. I remember on my first visit to Russia, in 1976, being prevented from entering St Isaac's Cathedral in the middle of Leningrad. Now, the attitude is quite different. Raisa Gorbachev has planted a tree in the grounds of the old Kiev monastery; there are now eight or nine working Orthodox churches in the city, and a small Catholic one for the Poles who were once a substantial part of Kiev's population. In Moscow, forty churches now hold services – though once there were over four hundred. The bad old days, when Communism (even under Khrushchev, whom we now regard as a good guy) persecuted religion, have largely gone, except as far as the separate Ukrainian Catholic church is concerned – it is seen as a buttress of Ukrainian nationalism. True, there is still much difficulty in relations with the Vatican, and the Pope has still not visited Lithuania, a largely Catholic country. On the other hand, the Catholic churches of Vilnius, once the headquarters of the Counter-

The new face of the Soviet Union in conservative Kiev.

Left: The entrance to the ancient Pecherskaya Lavra in Kiev, a hundred acres of churches, cathedrals and monasteries, where Christianity first took root in Russia in the tenth century.

Reformation in Northern Europe, have been lavishly restored and in most cases reopened. Like the Orthodox ones which I visited, the Catholic churches were full.

Church and State are coming together now in Russia. The reason, my archimandrite in Kiev said, is clear enough. Communism has not resulted in the 'classless society' of model proletarians which it was supposed to produce. On the contrary: article after article in today's press talks of laziness, shirking, stealing, drunkenness, divorce. Gorbachev calls for a new Soviet man, and wages war on drink and cigarettes (you are not supposed to smoke in airports, aircraft, hotel restaurants and so on). The church is a useful ally in this, whatever the difference in motivation.

In any event, this is a good thing. For years the official attitude was that religion was mumbo-jumbo. Now – as an article on a theological philosopher, K. N. Leontiev, in the best-known literary periodical showed on the day of my departure – you can talk openly about the importance of Orthodoxy in the making of Russia. As with all religious subjects, this one is difficult to discuss. Each religion has its 'spirit', but that is usually indefinable. Besides, it divides into a good side and a bad side. There is, for instance, the Scottish Protestantism of dismal Sundays and hell-fire sermons; but there is also the Scottish Protestantism of scrupulous honesty and high education. Dostoevsky wrote about the dual spirit of Russian Orthodoxy in *The Brothers Karamazov*: there is the crazed mystical hermit, Father Ferapont; and there is the wise old man, Father Zosima. Orthodoxy's spirit, like the spirit of any Christian religion, is best expressed in music rather than words, and the two-hour-long chanted liturgy, with hundreds of old women prostrating themselves, is the heart of it.

This is a religion which does not offer any hope for earthly existence. It was not usually much good at education, and it was hardly concerned with politics. It called for deep personal relations – Russians were and are good at that, not wasting time on small talk – and it encouraged peasants in particular to share and share alike. One of the peculiarities of the Russian land system was that the idea of private property never developed, as it did in England in the Middle Ages or even earlier. In England it was a recognized principle, enshrined in common law. In Russia they took a different view: a man should have land when he needed it – when he had children to feed (and, by the same act, hands to work the land). When the children grew up, the land dropped back into the village pool, to be reallocated according to need by the village elders. Up to 1914, not even one-fifth of the arable land had even been surveyed. Of course this made for great problems with agriculture. But in terms of Christian economics, it made some sense; and it is not an accident that the Russian word for 'peasant' is *krestyanin*: Christian. The counterpart of this attitude to the transience of earthly things was a very tolerant attitude towards sin of various sorts. Russians have an interesting belief that the major virtues are likely to coincide with the minor sins – drunkenness, fornication, improvidence and so on.

For centuries this religious attitude went together with tsarism, and tsarism flourished. In Western eyes it was tyrannical, even absurd. But to the tsars, in the splendours of the Winter Palace, the system as a whole made sense. They, and Orthodoxy in general, regarded politics as a lie and progress as a corrupting illusion. Dostoevsky, for instance, thought that modern medicine was a nonsense, liable simply to prolong the lives of old people to the point of parody; he despised Western liberalism, partly on the grounds that it would corrupt relations between the classes, and partly because it would corrupt people's relations with each other. He would not have been surprised at the autobiography of John Stuart Mill – the greatest exponent of nineteenth-century liberalism, a man who knew a great deal about a great deal, a scholar who believed in facts, and yet emotionally so warped that his autobiography is the bleakest document of the century. Tsarism had its own – we should now say 'ideology', and it took over one-sixth of the world's land surface.

How could this vast state just disintegrate? And what did Marxism have to do with it? The question is never far away if you are in Leningrad, where the principal acts of 1917 took place. It was the most advanced industrial centre of the country, with huge factories (by the standards of the time: nowadays, they look remarkably compact, and are often rather splendid buildings) and a working class that lived in squalid circumstances. The city had grown up quite quickly in the nineteenth century, and the most populous quarters – the *Petrogradsky rayon,* say, and most of Vasilevsky Island, in the River Neva – were notorious for bad housing. Every spring, when the thaw came, floodwater invaded the basements where many families lived; and besides, the water of the canals was so polluted that cholera was a great danger into the twentieth century, whereas in other Western cities it had been overcome.

There was another feature, too, peculiar to Petrograd, as it was renamed during the First World War, when German-sounding names went rapidly out of fashion. In the middle of the nineteenth century, before there were undergrounds and cross-town railways, the kind of suburbs which were growing up around the edges of other major cities did not develop. An entrepreneur who put up a building would try and fill it as profitably as possible. This meant a noble front, behind which would be grand apartments; but squeezed together behind these would be a huddle of courtyards with smaller flats into which artisans would be crowded (just as once happened in the Gorbals, Glasgow's – and maybe Europe's – most notorious slum).

In St Petersburg this situation carried on until revolutionary times, because the city council worked badly, failing to develop a tramway system, let alone an underground railway. The reason was characteristic: tsarist government did not wish councils to build up a debt, because it did not trust the councils with loans – and anyway, not until relatively late were there sufficient middle-class people who could band together and pay the interest. Besides, the government was not at all keen on letting such political independence develop. As a result, public transport remained quite backward, suburbs were not built, and outside the grand government quarter there was a mix of social classes which other cities had not seen for a generation.

Now the Bolsheviks were very consciously and aggressively a working-class party, and in 1917 class hatred was very strong. It was true that other parties claimed to speak for the working classes, but in practice they were much more inclined towards the intelligentsia; in 1917, as chaos mounted, they lost support. The strength of class feeling in Petrograd was such, even in March that year, that 'the masses' distrusted the parliament, led by intelligentsia and the educated, middle-class element.

*A packed mid-week service in the Orthodox Church of St Vladimir in
Kiev (left) demonstrates new-found freedoms, and challenges the
traditional Party line that religion attracts only the elderly (above).*

They set up a parliament of their own, the Soviet of Workers' and Soldiers' Deputies: a huge, inchoate assembly which met in the Tauride Palace, built for a favourite of Catherine the Great's. The Bolsheviks captured a majority in this soviet – and others throughout Russia – by September 1917, and although they never took a majority of votes in a parliamentary election, control of the towns was enough to guarantee power once they had taken it in November. Within weeks of the coup in Petrograd, they had taken control of most of the other chief towns and cities, even as far off as Vladivostok on the Pacific coast.

The Bolshevik Revolution expressed a huge variety of discontent – here a peasant wanting land; there a Jew in a ghetto, fearing the next onrush of the Cossacks; here a student in a university, listening to some tyrannical but comical figure with a beard droning on; there an NCO in the army, despising the mess made at the front by the remote and elderly generals; here a bewildered and despised Muslim from Central Asia, disliking his mullahs as much as he disliked the tsarist police; there a married woman, having to put up with the drunken tyranny of an adulterous husband and the habit of employers of paying married women about the same as a prostitute. Lenin knew, somehow, how use might be made of all this – how the ideology of Marxism could be adapted to take it far beyond the industrial proletariat to which it had originally been addressed. He somehow explained – although it did not quite work in the countryside – that everyone is a proletarian of a sort, put down by 'capitalism'. Capitalism, in the Marxist scenario, would eventually make so much profit that their own workers would be impoverished by the act of sustaining the profit. Therefore, everyone would get poorer and poorer. Marx died in 1883, and by 1900 Lenin could see that this theory was simply not being borne out – on the contrary. The situation was that, apart from an 'underclass' of maybe 10 per cent that one gets in any industrial society, even today, everyone was getting steadily better off. Why? To Lenin, the answer could only be that Western capitalism was taking unfair advantage of the non-industrialized, 'native' countries – India, Africa, China, Latin America, Australia. *They* were being exploited, to pay for the transference of goods and cash that could be passed on to the workers of 'capitalist' countries and so stave off the crisis of 'capitalism'. In other words the imperialists, who enslaved the countries of what came to be called the Third World, both saved 'capitalism' and gave it new enemies.

Lenin's discovery made his appeal far broader than Marx's, because he could include as 'proletarian' any downtrodden peasant from the Third World. The ideology had a consistency that was illustrated in 1917 but was still well and truly alive in the Vietnam War, when young boys of sixteen would take on the Americans, for all of their military hardware, with a ferocity and resilience that won the day. Nowadays, Leningrad itself is boringly full of reminiscences of Lenin – endless statues of the man with hand upraised in greeting. An effort was made, in the thirties and later, to move the centre of Leningrad from the tsarist palaces to a new quarter out to the west, with huge, regular, concrete buildings of the kind we now call Stalinist-classical. These enormous edifices line avenues of shattering regularity, and it is all quite hideous – as everyone now admits. Soon, the role of the old government quarter was restored, because the Party people themselves could not really stand it. But the move, and its subsequent rejection, are symbolic of something much bigger.

That something was, once upon a time, very powerful. The spirit of the Russian Revolution carried on: Lenin proclaimed, and certainly believed in, a new society which would do away with all the troubles of capitalism. There would be no more want; there would be no more war; there would be no more empires; women would be emancipated; religion would cease to fuddle people's brains with irrelevancies; everything would be 'scientific'. That was his appeal in a desperate corner in 1917 – and, against most of the odds, his Revolution survived famine and civil war.

The costs of that victory are still being counted. In the first instance, up to two million people emigrated from Russia between 1917 and 1926, when it became forbidden; but the casualties of the Civil War and the famines of the early 1920s and 1930s, together with the victims of political persecution between 1917 and Stalin's death in 1953, have never been properly assessed. For many years people were forbidden to discuss such matters – and Western sympathizers with the Soviet Union played the figures down. However, in 1988 the Soviet press itself started to discuss these matters, and historians now talk of forty, perhaps fifty million.

There is, to this Western observer, a certain melancholy satisfaction in this, for Soviet sources are themselves now saying what we were once denounced for saying in the West, on the grounds that it encouraged the cold war mentality and so forth. In any event, it is one of the strangest phenomena of our times that the very country where dictatorship over opinion, over the written and even the whispered word, was most absolute, now has few secrets about its own past. The Russian Revolution went wrong: despite Lenin's claims, it created a new society only in the sense that there was horror and terror on a scale that no one had hitherto experienced.

Even in Lenin's time – he died relatively soon after the Revolution, in 1924 – the system was well and truly in place. He himself made no bones about it: he was not in business to serve the ends of Christian morality, and told the Ministry of Justice in 1922 that 'for us, anything is moral that serves the cause of the dictatorship of the proletariat'. In Lenin's time there were already camps in which people were worked to death; already there was arbitrary hostage-taking and execution; the peasant's grain and lifestock were subjected to requisition; the trade unions were closed down. Inside the Bolshevik Party, a system known as 'democratic centralism' prevailed. This meant, in the first instance, that decisions of the Central Committee, and then of its chief committee, the Political Office or Politburo, became binding on all; there was to be no disagreement. Secondly, the power of the Party's central office (of which Stalin became Secretary, again in Lenin's time) was extended over the provinces. The central office *chose* the candidates, who won power by currying Stalin's favour, not by making themselves popular locally. In this way, a machine was built up that could easily lend itself to a regime of terror. In Stalin's time the Party, and its police, ran the country arbitrarily, opening up a system of concentration camps – the Gulag Archipelago, in Solzhenitsyn's phrase – that took in uncounted millions. During and after the Second World War entire ethnic groups were shifted to somewhere else in this vast state, and after 1946 the machine turned against the Jews as well. Nowadays,

Stalinesque heavy industry at a steel plant in Zaporozhe, with working conditions and environmental standards unthinkable now in the West.

as you go through Russia, you come across memorials to these victims, but it is only very recently that these wrecked lives have received any acknowledgement.

Why did the Russian Revolution take this direction? In the old days, there was quite an easy answer. I heard it myself, when I began teaching Russian history at Cambridge over twenty years ago, from E. H. Carr, then the best-known Western historian of the Russian Revolution. It is an answer which, apart from anything else, has the convenient advantage that a lecturer in his mid-twenties can construct an hour's reasonably coherent talk on it. It runs like this: tsarist Russia was a backward place, with lots of peasants, most of them illiterate. There was some industry, but most of it was created by get-rich-quick foreigners, collaborating with a state machine that really wanted an arms industry. The government was mainly comic opera. When it took on the Germans in the First World War, it collapsed, and various waffling liberals took over. By an act of will, the Bolsheviks were the only group with the understanding and energy to take power. But they had to create a new society. This meant dragooning people – creating modern industry, educating the masses, in particular calling a halt to what Marx called 'the imbecility of rural life'. Agriculture was collectivized. There were millions of casualties, true. However, these 'excesses' were really justified, because after all big industry was created, and the Soviet Union became a superpower with everyone crammed into tower blocks.

For all that I know, this line may still be peddled in British universities. But George Orwell had the best answer to it when he remarked that you cannot make an omelette without breaking eggs, but where's the omelette? My own understanding of these things came in 1970, when – in the course of writing a book about the First World War in Russia – I turned up some statistics on the Russian war economy. I had to find them in the Hoover Institution in California, because at that time there would have been no possibility of using Soviet archives for the period. They showed that Russia already had quite a good war-industrial machine, although for various reasons it was more slowly mobilized than that of Germany or France. In other words, the notion that Russia in 1914 was somehow backward was not really true. I told Carr about it, and after that we never really spoke again. The fact is that pre-war Russia was a very go-ahead place, overtaking France in fourth position in the world's economic league.

On my last day in Leningrad I went to look at the Museum of Russian Art, housed in the vast Mikhailovsky Palace 100 yards from the Nevsky Prospekt and the enormous Kazan Cathedral. Look at the portraits: here are faces, nineteenth- and early twentieth-century, that are as 'European' as anything you might see in Paris. Serov was the society portraitist of the age, the Russian Sargent or de Laszlo. Here is Prince Yusupov, seated grandly on a horse; his son, the husband-to-be of a Grand Duchess and murderer-to-be of the Tsarina's sinister favourite, Rasputin, effeminately fondling a pussy-cat; the poetess Anna Akhmatova, in semi-demi-Cubist version; and the 'moderns', Larionov and Gontcharova. It is a completely European world, and the idea that Russia lacked Western sophistication in 1914 is nonsense.

Towards the end of my journey I put these points to historians in Moscow.

Nowadays, they have no difficulty in admitting that pre-1914 Russia was a very promising place. In fact volumes of the *History of the USSR,* written in the 1960s, said as much – although the historians who compiled it were dropped in the 1970s and, I am told, ended their days as demoralized drunks teaching in far-off provincial schools. Under Brezhnev, a pale version of the Stalinist line came back into vogue in that decade. Nowadays, things have changed. It is old Russia that is very much in vogue. There are sales of antiques in Leningrad and Moscow. History examinations in schools were suddenly cancelled on the grounds that the textbooks were being pulped: a new version of the history of the Communist Party of the Soviet Union is being written. I wish its compilers well, and have no doubt that this time they will make honest statements.

It may seem that I have deviated a long way from the idea of a physical journey from the Baltic to the Black Sea. But I am a historian and in a sense I was also tracing the course of one aspect of Russian history – the influence of the West. And that in turn is inextricably tied up with the seeds of the Revolution. Without some understanding of Russia's complex past, it is impossible to appreciate what is going on in the USSR today – to see the small freedoms that are tentatively being introduced, and the attempts at reconciliation with the West, in their true context.

As you wander around Leningrad, a great paradox strikes you. Here is a European city, in many ways the grandest of them all except for Paris. Every epoch of European architecture up to 1914 is splendidly represented – the Art Nouveau here, as in what is left of old Moscow, or Kiev, or even the back streets of Yalta, is magnificent, though much of it is in bad repair. Yet the population looks desperately poor. In Moscow, it is even worse. Crowds of people with bad complexions trudge around, filling the streets at all times of the day – does anyone, you wonder, have a job to do?

The undergrounds, the buses, the trains, the planes are always full to bursting point in the rush-hour. On one occasion, when we flew from Vilnius to Kiev, the pilot had to ask the front six rows of passengers to move to the back, otherwise the nose of the plane would not have been able to lift off. No one to whom I spoke failed to talk of the tremendous difficulties of ordinary living. Housing, food, clothes, travel: all are similar to what was experienced in war-time Britain, without the sense of national effort that made it worthwhile for us, and without, I suspect, the sense that fair-does are being measured out by the people in power. A van driver to whom I spoke made no bones about this. 'They talk about "reconstruction",' he said, 'but we get nothing out of it. It's all lies, designed for the benefit of you in the West.'

Why did Communism end up in this way? It was, after all, supposed to offer a better life for the working classes – in fact, Lenin said, for everyone who was downtrodden by capitalism, whether workers, peasants, starveling intellectuals or oppressed peoples. In the Soviet Union, everyone now admits that it has not worked out. The press is full of the country's shortcomings. They are at present being blamed on the 'administrative-bureaucratic' system, in other words ultimately on Stalin who is 'panned' day after day in the press (it really cannot be long before he is removed from the Kremlin Wall of revolutionary dignitaries).

Even the Crimean resort town of Yalta suffers shortages – no suncream or sunhats, but there is a table (above left) where you can be photographed with Soviet luxuries such as oranges and instant coffee.

But Lenin, though still officially sanctified, was really responsible for the system of power which made Stalinism possible. How long will he remain sacrosanct? How can Communism really be reconciled with the talk of free markets, of private agriculture, of joint ventures with capitalism? Everyone admits that to reform the whole system, a degree of private reward and responsibility must be introduced. How? Where? Here, the question of the nationalities is inseparable from Communist reform. For Russia is a country of nationalities. Over one hundred languages are spoken. For the moment, the flash-points are in the west: Estonia, Latvia, Lithuania, the Ukraine, as well as in the Caucasus.

When I first planned my journey through western Russia, the idea was simply to follow the Viking trail in reverse, from the Baltic to the Black Sea. I wanted to look at the traces of the influence of the West upon Russia, beginning with the Vikings. In my view, Russia is a European country on much the same lines as Great Britain or Greece – on the fringes, but European just the same. Communism I see as an import – something that was thought up in Germany and France, which defeated the native revolutionary tradition as well as the native regime. I had taken the view, in a theoretical way, that Communism would be challenged by nationalism, but it was a theoretical argument. When I applied for visas to go to Tallinn in Estonia, Vilnius in Lithuania, and Kiev and Zaporozhe in the Ukraine, my intention was to look at them in a historical context. But then, history came alive. Since September 1988 the West has been well aware of the demonstrations in the Baltic republics. National flags, betokening independence, have been hoisted above historic buildings. On 16 November 1988 the Supreme Soviet of the Estonian Socialist Republic proclaimed sovereignty. All of a sudden, a film intended to be about history became a topical one.

Tallinn, once called Reval, is very obviously a north European city, Protestant, well ordered, with its sixteenth- and seventeenth-century merchants' houses. Like Riga and other towns along that part of the Baltic coast, it thrived on the Russian trade. Vikings, trading between the Baltic and the Black Sea along the river route, established settlements which in time developed into independent towns with their own commercial law, usually modelled on that of Magdeburg in Germany. Later, the towns of Novgorod and Pskov in Russian territory developed along similar lines, in effect until they were sacked by Ivan the Terrible in the later sixteenth century.

The Baltic coast and interior were themselves colonized by Germans – the Teutonic Order, the Order of the Sword and the Hanseatic League; by the middle of the sixteenth century, they had turned Protestant. In the eighteenth century they were taken over by Russia, but always with a big element of autonomy. Baltic Germans, and Germanized Balts, had a disproportionately strong influence in the development of Russia: names such as Manteuffel, von der Ropp, von der Osten-Sacken, Lieven, Benckendorff and Kauffmann-Turkestansky were common in the state machine, and in the eighteenth century the army used German as well as Russian in its manuals. These Baltic, Protestant skills were essential for the Russians' exploitation of the Ukraine.

As you travel in Estonia – it is a seven-hour train journey from Leningrad (and, since they play their equivalent of Radio 1 over the tannoys, it is rather uphill work) – you see the difference of landscape and orderliness; the same is true as you travel south through Latvia. Nearly fifty years ago the Baltic republics, which had been independent between the wars, were taken over again by Stalin. His response to any potential opposition was to crush it mercilessly in advance: he deported 20 per cent or more of the population, and moved in Russians or Ukrainians to take their place. Tallinn itself is half-Russian; Vilnius in Lithuania is very largely Russian. The countryside round about is still quite heavily 'native', just the same, and in the past twenty-five years there has been an attempt to defend the national heritage. Vilnius and Tallinn have been quite successfully restored.

Now, under Gorbachev, the Baltic nationalists have taken wing, and we were amazed at the openness with which local Baltic people talked of 'sovereignty' – meaning, really, independence in association with the European Community. Estonians know from Finnish television how much easier life is for their cousins across the Gulf of Finland, who not so long ago were the poor relations of the Baltic. To them, the Soviet Union has meant huge, polluting factories, ghastly tower blocks, police tyranny, empty shops, and mass immigration by the worst sort of Russo-Ukrainian riff-raff. In Lithuania, the popular reaction is similar.

Both are cautiously led, for, as an old Lithuanian historian told me, 'The giant can do anything he wants.' The Balts have allies in Moscow, if only because there are people who believe that they have a key role to play in the economic regeneration of the USSR. Allow them to return to their original position, as middlemen for the Russian trade, as educators of the backward interior, and the entire USSR might well prosper. That the present, sovereignty-sympathizing head of the Estonian Party is high in Soviet counsels – he was recently ambassador to Nicaragua – is a good sign that Baltic nationalism will not just be crushed, as the nationalism of the Caucasus peoples in the south is (at the time of writing, in April 1989) being crushed.

The problem, of course, is that this example might prove infectious. Travelling south from Vilnius to Kiev, I was aware of a different atmosphere. The Ukraine is still under something resembling the old management. Its head, Boris Shcherbitsky, is one of the few surviving Brezhnevite appointments in high places, and Kiev is still quite tightly controlled.

On the surface, it is a characteristic Soviet city. Great concrete blocks march, mile after higgledy-piggledy mile, as you come in from the airport; then you arrive in a spectacular nineteenth-century city, with golden domes glinting in the sun as you cross the wide River Dniepr. There are the usual masses of Soviet crowds, trudging the length and breadth of Kiev's most famous street, the Khreshchatik; the shops are pitifully empty, and there are few cafés, those few rather repellent (although, in a side street, there was a sort of Soviet MacDonald's, with not inedible pizzas: there was a long, long queue). In Kiev I talked chiefly to the monks, although also to Western businessmen and a Ukrainian civil servant. They were hopeful about the progress of joint ventures with the West: taking up contacts with the million-strong Canadian Ukrainians, and able, now, to promote joint ventures without reference to Moscow.

The onion domes of St Basil's Cathedral in Moscow (left), built by Ivan the Terrible in the sixteenth century, look down on parties of newly-weds who collect in Red Square every Saturday (above).

It was in Zaporozhe that I was best able to talk about the present-day Ukraine. The problems of sorting out its economic problems emerge there in strength. In the first place, the journey from Kiev by rail takes an inordinately long time: it is as if the trip from London to Glasgow took twelve hours instead of less than five. The trains are comfortable enough and people are friendly – for years, trains were the only place to talk openly. But the infrastructure of the Soviet Union is obviously a great obstacle to any modernization: the roads and railways are simply insufficient. Zaporozhe is, I am afraid, rather a showcase of the problems of the Soviet Union – a typical instance of yesterday's solutions becoming tomorrow's problems.

Historically, it is important. The island in the River Dniepr here, Khortitsa, was defensible, and in the sixteenth and seventeenth centuries it harboured people who were escaping from the clutches of rapacious Polish landlords. They were known as Cossacks, since some of them came from what is now Kazakhstan in Central Asia; the name spread. Cossacks were at the heart of the Ukrainian (and Orthodox) national movement that expelled the Poles from the Ukraine in the middle of the seventeenth century and attached it to Muscovy. These Cossacks were, in the end, tamed by Catherine the Great, and formed a substantial part of the Russian army.

The name 'Zaporozhe' means 'beyond the rapids'. These rapids were a formidable obstacle on the Vikings' trade route; traders had to trans-ship, a difficult business surmounting which was an important element in the establishment of the earliest Russian state. In later years the town – renamed Alexandrovsk, with a fortress attached – was the place at which the first Russian Black Sea fleet was built, to challenge the Tartars and the Turks who, until the late eighteenth century, ruled the Crimea and along the northern coast of the Black Sea. When Russia conquered them, Alexandrovsk declined in significance.

Renamed Zaporozhe, it came to occupy an essential role in the Communists' industrialization plans. For these, hydro-electricity was essential; and the river at Zaporozhe was the ideal place to construct a great dam, the Dneprostroy (now Dnieprogez). It was an astonishing feat of engineering – the more so as there was no heavy machinery, and much had to be done by hand (the museum has a good reconstruction of the process). Factories mark the Zaporozhe skyline. They also mark the Zaporozhe air: it has one of the worst pollution problems in the world, by all accounts. We were able to film one of the steel factories, a great monster of a place, where people work in the hellish conditions that used to prevail in our own Consetts and Pittsburghs two generations ago. The dam itself, rebuilt after the war, causes great problems with the water-table, which in turn harms the fertility of the soil. Here, in microcosm, was the problem of the modernization of Soviet industry and agriculture. Where do you begin?

The people whom I met were all splendid: we had a very good welcome, and I was interviewed several times by television and the press. Out of a deep sense of respect for the people and their past I forced myself to talk in Russian – rather an ordeal, for, although I had learned the language quite well in the late 1960s, I forgot much of it in the later 1970s and early 1980s when the Soviet Union became restrictive and inaccessible, and its historians pedalled only the Party line.

After Zaporozhe, I travelled by train to Simferopol in the Crimea, and from there by car to Yalta, a three-hour journey (although less by trolleybus). Yalta was the Bournemouth of tsarist Russia. The tsars' palace at Livadia, a short drive away, was put up in splendid style just before the First World War – and built, as the curator told me, far faster than a modern building of that size and elegance could be built today. It was the scene of the famous meeting between Churchill, Roosevelt and Stalin in February 1945 to decide important elements in the post-war world. The room in which the three men talked is preserved as a museum, and there are interesting photographs of the event.

On Crimean television they asked me if I regarded Yalta as a sell-out – after all, we agreed in effect that Eastern Europe would become Communist – and I had to say, no. In the West, there was a great tide of pro-Soviet feeling because of Russia's enormous part in the war; people hoped that Stalin would mend his ways; anyway, he was already in full charge of the area; and we thought that we needed him against Japan, which showed no signs of surrendering in those days before the atomic bomb was tested. I could really only answer that the problem became severe, turning into a cold war, because Stalin maintained full military strength after 1945 and imposed his rule savagely on the places which he took over. This is our orthodoxy in the West – unshaken, so far as I am concerned, by the shelf-loads of American revisionist literature that endeavour to prove that the United States caused the cold war by being imperialist and militarist.

What *is* happening in the Soviet Union? In my five weeks' journey, the question came up again and again. *Glasnost* is splendid. What a relief it is to open a Russian newspaper – even *Pravda* – and to read human beings talking in plain language about real things. But will the economic reconstruction of Communism prove to be possible? Can you inculcate habits of responsibility, hard work, honesty and so forth in a workforce which, especially on the land, has been so badly demoralized under the old systems? Will the more westerly nationalities be given, in effect, a separate economic status, so that they can bring back a free market and joint-venture technology to a country that, by its leaders' admission, has fallen so badly behind the West and Japan?

It is, of course, much too early to say. Most people to whom I talked were deeply worried by the nationality question, the possibility that the state would break up. Most people were pessimistic about economic reforms. Talking on my way back to historians and theatrical people, I asked them what they would like the West to do now that the cold war was receding. They said, just go on criticizing. Criticize the awful way our people live, the bossiness of the system, the empty shops, the overcrowded transport, the working women lugging their babies halfway across the cities in the tube, having collected them from the child-minder, and returning to some tiny flat with a drunken, demoralized husband and nothing much to cook. I pass this message on, and accordingly criticize. But I do so in a spirit of deep respect for the Russian people's past. I felt, for the first time in my adult lifetime, that I had passed through an historical moment of real significance.

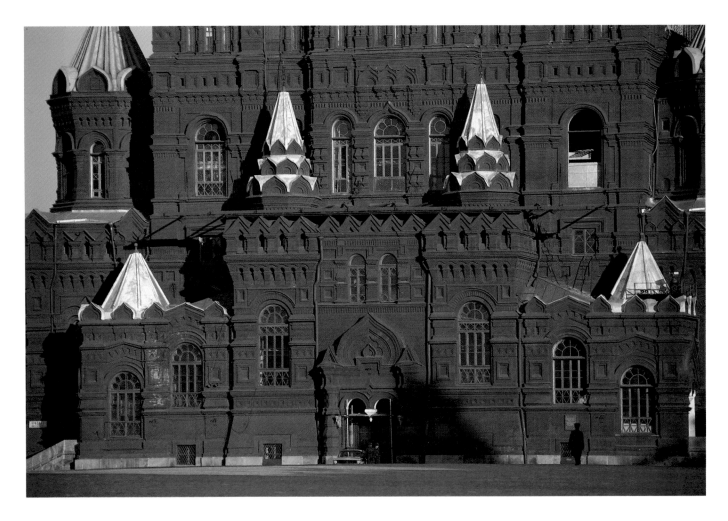

Soviet soldiers patrol past the History Museum at the north end of Red Square in Moscow.

Right: Sunday fishermen gather in the chill dawn on the banks of the Moskva River.

THE SALT ROAD

William Shawcross

Apart from a short and anguished visit to Ethiopia during the famine of 1984–5, I had been almost nowhere in Africa before, so my search for the old salt road across the Sahara was based on total ignorance. The Sahara was an uncharted ocean as far as I was concerned: my perceptions were a blurred mix of Beau Geste and St Exupéry. I knew nothing, but nothing at all, when I began my journey in Fez. There I had my first surprise.

I tumbled like Alice into a brilliant and unchanged medieval world, a labyrinth of tiny streets and shops and stalls and alleys where no car has ever been. The ways were all overhung and crumbling, no wider than a heavily laden donkey; there were cubicles for shops, mud (at that time of year) on the cobbles, stalls, workplaces, caravanserais, tanneries, palaces, teahouses, olive presses, coppersmiths, shoemakers, carpet sellers and a million other pursuits besides.

My white rabbit on this almost free fall was Abdul Latif, a Fezian whose acquaintance I had made through Bruno Barbey, a French photographer whom I had met some decades ago – or so it now seems – in Vietnam. Bruno was effortlessly elegant as well as talented; he appeared to parachute into battle in an Yves St Laurent suit, take fine photography and parachute out again. Abdul Latif had been his guide around the maze of the old *medina* (town) of Fez, and he became mine as well. He was not an official guide – those fine gentlemen stood close to the porch of my splendid hotel, wearing gowns and fingering their bronze badges of office. Abdul Latif did not have their status; he had to lurk, *en civil*, some 50 yards from the hotel, pretending to be doing nothing while in fact waiting in hope for tourists. We found

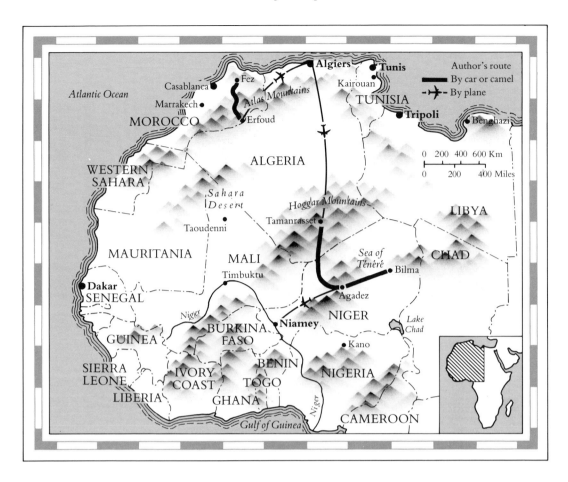

each other and set off. He loped beside me, his head askew, his shoulders up and his eyes revolving like windmills, talking all the while about his town.

Fez has been an active, indeed vital meeting place between East and West since the ninth century, when the Arabs began to spread west across North Africa from the Nile. Morocco's huge plains and open pastures made it one of the most fertile places the invaders had discovered, and they founded permanent settlements from which they went on to conquer Spain. After that had been accomplished, Morocco became a vital meeting point between Eastern and Western Islam – a confluence of travellers from Europe and the Orient. Nowhere was this more obvious than in Fez. Early in the ninth century, several thousand people from Kairouan in Tunisia settled on one bank of the river; a few years later thousands of people expelled from Cordoba settled on the other bank. Out of these two communities, the Kairouanis and the Andalusians, sprang Fez, which created one of the finest universities in the world and became the intellectual centre of North Africa.

Morocco was not just a lynchpin on the Islamic arc between Spain and Arabia. For centuries, the country also benefited from north–south trade over the Atlas Mountains and across the Sahara Desert. There, below the sand, was the unknown kingdom of Ghana. The trade was principally of gold, of slaves – and of salt. Ghana has always lacked salt, and thus the gold miners often would not trade their metal for anything but salt; indeed, one Moorish proverb had it that 'The price of a negro is salt.' By the beginning of the nineteenth century the Moors bartered at the rate of one pound of salt for one ounce of gold.

Taghaza, the main saltmine, was lost in the sands midway between Morocco and Timbuktu. In the middle of the fourteenth century the extraordinary Muslim traveller and chronicler, Ibn Batutu, described it as an unattractive village where the houses and mosques were built of blocks of salt and the roofs were camel skins. No one lived there except the slaves who dug for salt, who survived on dates brought south in the caravans, camel meat and millet. 'The negroes use salt as a medium of exchange,' he wrote, 'just as gold and silver is used [elsewhere].' In the late fifteenth century the Moorish traveller Leo Africanus also passed through Taghaza on his way south. He described the slaves as living in little cottages by the mines; they sold salt to caravan merchants, who brought them food in exchange and took the salt on down to Timbuktu. 'Neither have the said diggers of salt any victuals but such as the merchants bring unto them; for they are distant from all inhabited places almost twenty days' journey, insomuch that oftentimes they perish for lack of food, whereas the merchants come not in due time unto them.'

The trade across the desert lasted well into the nineteenth century, drawing merchants and Christian shipping to the Barbary coast from Tripoli to Agadir. But the age of imperialism changed everything. The white man's roads, river boats and railways opened new outlets to the Guinea coast and drained trade from the caravan routes across the Sahara.

All of this history depended to an extraordinary degree upon the camel, which is something I wish to discuss further. But I am being diverted from my journey around Fez. . . .

Fez used to be packed with caravanserai, a word which, I discovered, I had never used properly. They were the vast boarding houses or inns in which the caravaneers stayed with their pack animals before and after their journeys across the desert to the kingdoms in the south. Leo Africanus, many of whose descriptions stand up well today, is worth quoting again. He noted:

In this citie are almost two hundred innes, the greatest whereof are in the principall part of the citie neere unto the chiefe temple. Every of these innes are three stories high, and contain an hundred and twenty rooms apeece. Never to my remembrance did I see greater buildings, except it were the Spanish College at Bologna, or the pallace of the Cardinall di San Georgio at Rome . . . yet they afford most beggarly entertainment to strangers: for there are neither beds nor couches for a man to lie upon, unlesse it be a coarse blanket and a mat. And if you will have any victuals, you must go to the shambles your selfe, and buie such meat for your host to dresse, as your stomach stands to.

Today the caravanserai, decaying like the rest of the medina, are still in trade: they give shelter to young artisans coming from the countryside to learn a skill like leathercraft. Abdul Latif led me into several, pointing out door hinges shaped like the hand of Fatima, the daughter of the Prophet. The open courtyards were now used as stables for donkeys. Upstairs, many of the old doors were padlocked; others

A Berber village in the Atlas Mountains south of Fez.

Left: The Medrassa ben Yussef, Marrakech's ancient Koranic university.

Pages 202 and 203: The medieval city of Fez.

were open and inside sat men making shoes and cheap wallets. Scattered over the yards were piles of rubbish and bales of leather and wool.

It was a cold, grey day which seemed more Balkan than African. From next door to one caravanserai came the rumble of heavy machinery. Through the darkness of walls covered with grime we saw an ancient machine with huge cogs, flywheels and fanbelts whirring and turning two large wheels in a huge black vat. This was an olive press. The wheels were mushing up the olives, which came out of the bottom looking like nothing but thick mud. A man scooped this sludge out into a little bucket, sloshed it on to a straw mat, smeared the 'mud' over that as well and then placed a whole pile of muddy mats under an ancient press. Hey presto – and the mud was transformed into clear green olive oil which was poured into wooden boxes by the door. The owner of this turbulent press, Sidal Hassan, took great pride in drawing us a glass of the translucent liquid to drink. He said he had inherited his work from his father and had done it since he was a child. His own son was now in the countryside buying olives.

Later Abdul Latif took me to an upstairs tea house where men sat all day playing cards and drinking tea, green, sweet and deliciously scented with orange blossom. He explained that he was a happy man: he had his crust and that was enough; he had a wife and he loved her; he loved his king, Hassan II, as well; all he now needed was the badge of an official guide, so that he could ply his trade more openly than presently he was able. This seemed to me an excellent idea, though I had my doubts after he subjected me to the pleasures of a steam house – no, I am not being fair, for my director wished the experience upon us. Suffice it to say that the steam through which loinclothed men grappled with their meaty masseurs and slipped upon the floor, and flung buckets of cold water over themselves or the steaming coals, was not something that I found enormously attractive.

When it was time to go, Abdul Latif handed me a small bunch of pink flowers and wished me well across the Atlas, on the first stage of my retracing of the old salt routes south and east from Fez.

The drive across the fertile plains of northern Morocco was lovely, taking us past masses of vegetable gardens and orchards that were growing all sorts of fruits in abundance. The fertility of the country was beautiful and astonishing and would, I imagined, contrast strongly with the condition of its neighbours south of the Atlas. The bus took us up the mountains and through the ski resort of Irfane in which King Hassan maintains a vast castle which lowers in Ruritanian majesty over the town. Then it was over the top, past the snows and down towards the desert.

The south-eastern side of the Atlas is, literally, the high tide mark of the Sahara, a different zone entirely. Amongst the palm trees, the sand, and the old, thick-walled kasbahs, or forts, I met in the town of Erfoud a brash man named Basha who works for the film units which come here – to do *Scoop*, for example, or a James Bond movie set in Afghanistan. He was a hustler with none of the gentleness of Abdul Latif.

Basha was not best pleased when I met by chance in the crumbling kasbah a thin young man in a green tweed jacket who peered at me from behind his spectacles and told me he was a poet. His name was Abdou, and he said he had studied French literature as well as English. To my relief he took me off through the black lanes of the kasbah, where the mud ceilings of the houses roof all the passages and where women sweep the dust from their portals in the dark.

Upstairs in his bare room, he made a cup of tea on a little stove and told me that his parents lived in the kasbah. He had gone away to school and then joined the army to study further. All he wanted was to be a writer. He had written four books, he said, and he produced one for me to read. It was a solid exercise book, an inch thick at least, crammed with scrawly writing in English. It seemed to be filled with philosophical reflections on the meaning of life, its glories and difficulties.

Abdou had decided to return from the other side of the Atlas, from modern Morocco, to this simple life in the kasbah because here he could work and write more cheaply, he felt, than in a city like Casablanca. His calling was unusual here; most of the people in the kasbah earned their living from dates grown in the brightly coloured fields, which reminded me of Vietnam. In the old days these dates were exported south on the caravans; now they go north to Europe.

The loneliness was such that he had to have a wife, he said. She was fifteen when they married; now this young child had a young child of her own. On the roof of their home Abdou had a tiny study, also constructed from mud, in which he kept his treasure – a vast old Remington typewriter on which he was gradually transcribing some of his poetry. This was necessary, because his handwriting was even worse than mine: 'I have to write fast to imprison the idea on the page,' he said.

Horses were once used in the desert; so were oxen and so were elephants; but desert travel was revolutionized by the introduction of the camel in late Roman times. Unlike any other animal, the camel can walk through the desert for days on end without water; but it does need either to carry its own fodder or to be able to forage. For a camel, hunger is death.

Powered by camels, different tribes of Berbers, the principal indigenous people of North Africa, reached into the desert conquering oases inhabited by the negroid people from the south. The Tuareg Berbers went furthest south, reaching the Hoggar Mountains in what is now southern Algeria and eventually the River Niger near Timbuktu. The nomads on their camels, and in particular the Tuareg, became the masters of the desert; the blacks in the oases, their slaves.

Throughout the Middle Ages, camel caravan trails across the desert developed. Slaves, gold and leather came north from tropical Africa, while weapons, cloth, tea, spices and sugar went south. And so did salt, which the caravans picked up at the mines of Taghaza and Taoudenni (both in modern Mali) and Bilma (in modern Niger). Until the nineteenth century about ten thousand slaves were traded every year across the Sahara: European travellers were horrified by the numbers of human skeletons they came across along the way, for only the fittest of the slaves survived the march north across the desert. By the time they reached Fezzan (southern Libya today) those who were still alive had been reduced to skeletons, and had to be fattened up for the Tripoli and Benghazi markets where they might fetch a 500 per cent profit.

*A wandering minstrel in a cafe in the southern Atlas, where the
mountains start their descent to the Sahara.*

*Right: A veiled woman at a small market near Erfoud, from where the
caravans set off on their long desert marches.*

An important and appalling part of the slave trade was in eunuchs. In the Sudan it was the custom to geld the most robust youths captured in slave raids: the operation was done very crudely and brutally, and only about one in ten survived the assault. The Mossi were the most skilled at castration, and kept their technique a close secret.

The British abolished their own slave trade in 1807, and encouraged other governments to do the same. In 1842 the Bey of Tunis agreed to prohibit the export and import and slaves, and in 1857 the Ottoman Turkish government agreed to do the same in its domains, which included Tripoli. The Moroccan government was less susceptible to pressure, but as the French empire-builders advanced into the deserts they stopped the export of slaves from the Sudan. But the slave traffic still continued on the easterly route through the Sahara up to Benghazi, the chief city of Cyrenaica in north-east Libya until the Italians occupied the area in 1911.

Throughout the centuries the caravans had to travel *en masse* – size was the only protection from the Tuareg raiders. The best trodden north–south routes were from Marrakech to Timbuktu, from Tripoli to Bilma and Lake Chad, and from Fez to Kano via Agadez. Of all of them, the most celebrated was that between Morocco and Timbuktu, via the salt mines of Taghaza and Taoudenni. Taghaza is exhausted today, but Taoudenni, in Mali, is still operated. Worked by political prisoners, it is a sort of Saharan Siberia and must be one of the most wretched places on earth.

Next day I went south into the fringes of the desert. Out in the sand we came across a cheap flop house which caters for coach parties of German tourists come to see the Sahara. It was a good spot, for nearby some wonderful dunes soared out of the desert floor. A family of Tuareg with camels to rent hoisted me aloft on one of them and we teetered up the slopes, rather absurdly I thought. About sixty days' walk to the south was Timbuktu.

Its importance throughout the centuries lay in the fact that it was a mid-point on the north–south trade route. Moreover, it is on the northernmost bend of the Niger, which turns there to flow south towards the Gulf of Guinea. Timbuktu grew nothing and made nothing. It was an entrepôt, where the highway of the Niger is most accessible to the fertile plains of North Africa. From about AD 1000 it was the distribution point for salt, foreign goods and ideas coming south on the caravans.

Even so, the reputation which the town gathered in the minds of Europeans was a little excessive. Timbuktu became a sort of mythical metropolis in the desert, a Xanadu or an Atlantis. It was said to have fabulous buildings and limitless wealth. Throughout the eighteenth century, European explorers tried and failed to reach it. The Scotsman Mungo Park travelled down the Niger to the town, but was forbidden by hostile Tuaregs from disembarking at its river landing. Imagine his disappointment! Finally the town was reached in 1826 by the French explorer René Caillié, who was appalled to find a mud village rather than a great city. 'I had formed a totally different idea of the grandeur and wealth of Timbuktu,' he wrote. 'The city presented, at first view, nothing but a mass of ill-looking houses, built of earth.' But such testimony did little to diminish the myth of the fabled palaces of Timbuktu: Victorian travellers continued to expect gleaming turrets and resounding cymbals.

As I sat precariously on my camel and looked out over the great rolling dunes south towards Timbuktu, I thought it would have been very fine to have made the trip, however meagre the town is today. I was reading Geoffrey Moorhouse's staggering account of his lone voyage from west to east across the Sahara, *The Fearful Void*. His was an appalling ordeal which produced a magnificent book. But it would have been far more gruelling than a trip for a television film would have justified. And there were other problems. The land border between Algeria and Morocco was at that time closed on account of the war between Morocco and Algerian-supported Polisario guerillas over the Southern Sahara, which Morocco had annexed. So we flew instead via Algiers to Tamanrasset in southern Algeria.

During the Second World War, Charles de Gaulle used to speak of '*la France Libre – de Dunkerque à Tamanrasset.*' Only twenty years later he gave Algeria back to the Algerians. Even at independence, Tamanrasset was still cut off entirely from the world – a tiny French fort hundreds of miles south of Algiers, an immense journey across the desert. The *département* of Tamanrasset is actually bigger than the whole of metropolitan France. The town has always been a vital oasis on one of the main trans-Saharan caravan routes. Until recently it has also been a home to the Tuareg.

To the Victorians, the Tuareg were perhaps the most romantic or at least best-known of the desert tribes. For centuries they had preyed upon the caravan routes, and they decimated the French army columns sent into the burning sands in the late nineteenth and early twentieth centuries in an absurd attempt to conquer the desert and to lay a railway in the sand. They were the legendary 'men of the blue veil', who dashed on their camels out of the mirages, butchered their prey and disappeared again across the dunes. They were the wicked infidels who terrorized Beau Geste and other Victorian heroes; and they really did kill large numbers of Frenchmen.

They are a gloriously good-looking race, but now they have been domesticated. Today some of the Tuareg men in Algeria still wear their magnificent blue robes, and they still strut on their camels in the sand – but mostly for the benefit of tourists: they now service the grandchildren of the foreigners they killed. Both Algerian socialism and drought have compelled them to abandon their nomadic lives and become more and more sedentary.

Today Tamanrasset is the subject of a sudden explosion of tourism. The airport has already made it accessible to Europe, now it is being expanded, and very soon the holiday charters will fly direct from Paris. The little oasis will be transformed by backpackers and the Range Rovers and Toyota four-wheel drives that they need to make the spirit of their adventure holidays realizable.

One of the main attractions of Tamanrasset are the extraordinary Hoggar Mountains a score of miles away. This spectacular formation rises blindly, sheer and bare out of the desert. Quite unexpectedly, after thousands of miles of flat or undulating sands, a huge granite fortress appears, with domes and pinnacles and cliffs and cataracts reaching to the sky. The peaks are in fact plugs of cooled volcanic magma which fill the exit pipes of now-extinct volcanoes.

The Hoggar Mountains, in the heart of the Sahara, at dawn.

Like other tourists, we took four-wheel drive vehicles up into these dry brown mountains, where we stopped at a little encampment of Tuareg tents made of lamb- and goatskins sewn together; blankets were hanging over posts as windbreaks. There were only old men, women and children around. A pretty girl scraped a hole in the earth and lit a little fire. An old woman in black and white robes poured filthy-looking water out of a plastic can into an ancient kettle which she hung from an iron tripod. They brought out an old wooden box in which they kept the tea. Slowly she boiled the grey water and brewed the tea, and ceremoniously an old man poured it from a great height into little glasses. We drank, as is the custom, three glasses. Then off we set again, higher into the bare mountains.

Towards the end of the afternoon, we stopped for the night at a little inn a few hundred feet below the summit of a mountain called Assekrem. We walked from there to the summit, where we found a tiny stone chapel built some eighty years earlier by an extraordinary Frenchman named Charles Foucauld. He was soldier, roué, poet and priest. At the turn of the century, when the French were attempting to conquer the Sahara and especially the Tuareg, Foucauld decided that it was amongst the Tuareg that he wished to live. He built a mission in Tamanrasset, and this tiny hermitage on top of a mountain in the Hoggar.

Foucauld kept intricate and comprehensive records of his life and of the Tuareg. He loved them and immersed himself in their lives and culture, compiling a dictionary of their language. But he was also a patriot, and inevitably he was suspected of spying for the French in their struggle against the tribesmen. He was killed by a Tuareg in a skirmish in 1916.

Since then the little chapel has been staffed by priests of the order which Foucauld founded, Les Petites Soeurs de Jésus. Today, only three remain. Brother Antoine had been at Assekrem for six years, Brother Edouard for fifteen; Brother Jean-Marie, who had returned to France for the winter, had been on the mountain top for over thirty years. In the old days they had been surrounded by Tuareg and there had been very few tourists; now it was the other way round. This was an obvious matter for regret.

A wind blew around the little chapel. The view was superb — a peaked and jagged landscape stretching away as far as the eye could see. Flutes and towers, teeth and pinnacles of rock, rising and falling. Humps, crags, escarpments, domes, towers. All brown and grey, the colours softening into the distance until they met the sky in a soft uncertain haze of dust and refracted light. As the sun lowered, the haze crept closer, the wind strengthened, and the faces of the mountains grew darker until they were only silhouettes. The light turned yellow; the pale blue sky above the sun shading into grey and almost fog over the hills to the west. At 6.20 the sun finally set behind the mountains and I thought of it rising over California, where my son was then living, at just the same time.

We climbed down the mountain to the little inn. By the time we reached it, the sky was all shades of yellow and purple and a crescent moon was starting to shine brightly. We ate at a long table with other guests and wrapped ourselves in sleeping bags against the cold of the mountain night.

Before dawn we climbed the mountain again. The light began to rise in the east,

A Tuareg feeds his camels at the camel market in Agadez.

and when I reached the top the sun suddenly came sailing up like a great red and gold ship, out of the hills, between two peaks named Hadeor and Tidiame. Within two minutes the black bowl of the night was alive with flame and I could no longer look to the east, except by shading the eyes. Up and out of the mist soared the sun, its rays bursting through the crags and gullies and sending great shafts of light towards us, so that some valleys were all alight and some still sunk in mist. Black and white, hard shadows and soft. Ten minutes later there was a great separation in the heaven – above the sun the sky was brilliant blue, and below it was a mass of silver: there was a rigid line between the two.

Foucauld wrote of the spectacle from his mountain top, 'Nothing can give an idea of the forest of peaks and rocky needles which one has at one's feet. One cannot see it without thinking of God. At the same time, its solitude and its savage aspect shows how one is alone with Him and how one is only a drop of water in the sea.'

Brothers Antoine and Edouard are self-conscious about being a tiny Christian drop of water in the vast Muslim ocean. They keep alive the memory of Foucauld, but they do no missionary work. To make themselves useful to the Algerian authorities, they, like Foucauld, take meteorological readings – which tend to confirm the increasing dryness. In the Sahara the drought caused, it seems likely, by the Greenhouse Effect is becoming a catastrophic problem for everyone, and is one of the factors which has led to the death of the Tuareg's camel caravans. The last caravan south from here was in 1973. Since then the only desert work that the Tuareg have managed to obtain has been with tourists.

We set off south again towards Niger. I now had a driver called Mohammed, a Tuareg who had been brought up to be a caravaneer like his father. He had made five or six trips to the south, each of them lasting about six months, but now worked for one of the tourist agencies in Tamanrasset. Mohammed liked the new generation of invaders: he did not really miss the long trips, and preferred to be away from home for only a week rather than months at a time. 'Why would we go on caravans now?' he asked. 'There is nothing in Niger.'

This part of the Sahara is an international highway, with scores of tracks cut into the hard sand by the hundreds of trucks and cars that pass north and south every week. The various *pistes* were marked by vertical posts which stood out of the sand like buoys in the sea. Indeed, driving through the desert seemed very like sailing, a sport I have always adored.

By this stage we had fallen in with a group of English palaeontologists from the British Museum and Kingston Polytechnic; they had been on an expedition searching for dinosaur bones, and for a good part of our route they went in convoy with us. Their search had been successful: one of their trucks, filled with English foods and decorated with the banners of their supermarket sponsors, was also carrying the dorsal vertebrae of a dinosaur which died in the age when the Sahara was lush and verdant, some twenty million years ago.

At one point we grew careless and the cars became separated. We waited in the midday sun by a small hill. Two large trucks roared past us to the north and a couple of ancient Peugeots, driven by students from Cameroon, puttered south – after stopping to ask us, of all people, for directions. Finally our companions caught up with us – their cars made two dark shapes as they sailed out of the mist and mirage on the horizon. South through the sand we drove, past the wrecks of many cars which had not survived the long journey. We came across one group of tanned and wolfish-looking Germans, stripped to the waist, pushing and pulling a Volkswagen camper out of the sand.

The most common modern caravan is a fleet of old cars (Peugeots and Mercedes are favoured) being driven towards Nigeria for sale. The profits to be made from such a voyage, even allowing for the breakdowns and the shakedowns which are awaited almost every mile and every border crossing, are immense.

The border between Niger and Algeria was marked by one of the most doleful and widespread symbols of the twentieth century – a refugee camp. These people had fled from drought and desperation in Mali, Niger and elsewhere; for the lands to the south, Algeria today represents a kind of cornucopia. That is not, however, how it seems to Algerians. A few weeks after my visit the streets of Algiers and other towns were filled with demonstrators protesting against shortages in the shops and demanding an end to the socialist direction of the economy.

The Algerian border, a lone hut on the sand, we passed easily enough and then drove a few more miles to the customs post of Niger. This, a few huts grouped around a couple of trees, was altogether more bustling – a couple of coaches, old cars, a few camels ambling over the hillocks, a pleasant little café with one table on the sand. A gigantic soldier in a yellow T-shirt took our passports into a hut which was equipped with two narrow beds and a large ledger into which all our names were entered. With a flourish of bonhomie we were free to enter Niger, and so, with great pleasure, we adjourned to the café for cold beer, omelette and chips.

Other travellers were less lucky: one old man carrying boxes of cutlery for sale had at least one of them 'liberated' by the military. And when our German friends arrived, they at once began to have a hell of a time because the sergeant in charge decided he wanted to 'buy' one of their cars. Alas, when we left they were still imprisoned under the trees.

We went further and further on a course of south-south-east. By now I had lost count of the days of our voyage. At one time I remember sailing blithely along with Tchaikovsky's First Piano Concerto on the tape and seeing the lone and level sands stretching infinitely, shimmering with mirages; the car in front of us looked as if it were driving on the edge of the sea, with the water lapping at a vast golden beach. In the heat of the day, the mirages stretched up and up so that the silver water lying on the horizon simply rose into the sky in an unbroken sheen. Occasional trucks passed, like tankers on the ocean, occasional posts marked the channel. One day in particular had for me all the splendid isolation of crossing an ocean which was charted but, to me, completely unknown. As the sun fell, the cars cast great box-like shadows until the day suddenly dropped from sight in the west, leaving in the east, to which we were headed, a powder blue-grey sky with a band of purple above it – and then the dark.

Desert Tuareg (left) meet black Africa (above) in the streets of Agadez.

Civilization took the form of a vast uranium works, built by the French. Its silvered towers and tanks were covered with lights and looked, in the dark, like a great aircraft carrier looming off the starboard bow. And then, because of the uranium, we were on a metalled road and the emptiness of the ocean was, for the time being, lost. Now we seemed to be travelling on a narrow strip of twentieth-century logic, inspired by military desire. And so we came by night to Agadez and the ice cream parlour in the middle of the desert, which seemed to be a fine title for a novel.

Agadez is an exquisite town built of red mud, the capital of the Tuareg in Niger, hard by the Mountains of the Aïr which, even though pronounced Eye-ear, has a magical ring to me. In the days of the Songhai empire, which flourished from the eleventh to the sixteenth centuries, Agadez was the chief entrepôt for the gold trade between Gao (in Mali) and Tripoli and Egypt. A Moorish invasion in 1591 killed this trade and impoverished Agadez, but it still remained important politically as the capital of the Tuareg. In the nineteenth century its income derived principally from the trade in salt which was mined in Bilma 300 miles to the west across another, self-contained part of the desert called the Sea of Ténéré. This was now our destination.

Today Agadez is no longer independent; the Tuareg are ruled by Fulani and Hausa people, the men from the south of the country who now control Niger and whom the Tuareg used to drag north across the desert to be sold as slaves. Tuareg society is now breaking down, but until recently it has had a rigid class structure. This differs between Tuareg from different areas, but basically it embraces Ihaggaren: nobles, men of the sword and camel owners; Isekemaren: vassals of mixed Tuareg-Arab origin; Inaden: blacksmiths and artisans (the descendants of former slaves, usually dark-skinned); and Imrad: religious men (the Tuareg have resisted the march of Islam more strenuously than other peoples of North Africa).

The French defeated the Tuareg, but they attempted to preserve the social structures of the tribes; since independence, however, those structures have been under assault. In both Niger and Algeria, economic development has led to urbanization. In Niger, Tuareg men have found that, with the death of the caravans, they can only find work in or near towns – or building roads or working in the uranium mine at Arlit. On top of that, the appalling droughts of 1968-74 destroyed thousands of the nobles' camels – their principal source of wealth and authority. Many Tuareg have found work as nightwatchmen in factories or homes in towns. In Mali they have been brutally persecuted; in Niger they have occasionally protested their fate and attacked local police stations.

Here, in Agadez, the Tuaregs' Sultan still lives in his palace in the centre of town, but his duties are largely honorific. None the less he remains a fount of information on the caravans, and I wanted to see him. I made an appointment with his door man and then went for an ice cream. The ice cream parlour is named after Vittorio, the Italian who founded it. He is married to a Tuareg and lives happily in Agadez, serving pistachio and strawberry and banana ice creams as well as excellent milk shakes. He has a young, hip staff, who were listening to Michael Jackson tapes most of the time I was there.

Ice creams over, we walked into the Sultan's fort and were shown through a massive, battered, planked and repaired wooden door into a dark and musty passageway which had a large fireplace in the corner, with a small but delightfully warm log fire burning. We sat along the wall and waited. The door was held open by a rock. A servant tended the fire. The walls were pale green and very dusty, not painted for years; there was sand on the floor. A few electric wires poked aimlessly out of a wall. Cobwebs. A bell on the wall. A telephone on a little shelf. Along the far wall were stacked a deckchair, an old tyre, blanket, bottles. There was silence except for the man tending the fire.

Eventually, through the door from the palace itself, came first the shadow and then the tall figure of Sultan Ibrahim, dressed all in blue. His *chèche* or headscarf was of a lustrous deep indigo. His hand was cold, his fingers very long. Gracefully he sat himself down on a little blanket by the hearth.

I asked the Sultan some general questions, which he answered with the help of a refined-looking man in white – a historian, perhaps, or chamberlain – who came to crouch beside the hearth. The Sultan, one of the most elegant men I have seen in years, twirled a silver snuff case in his pianist's fingers.

He explained that the grazing grounds around Agadez and in the mountains of the Aïr used to support huge herds of camels and were vital to the caravans. Nowhere in the world, it is said, has there been seen any such commercial spectacle as the annual camel caravan from Agadez, the Azalai. Even in 1908, when it was in its decline, twenty thousand camels took part. In the early autumn the camels and their owners began to gather in the foothills of the Aïr, near the village of Tabelot, where the grazing was good. In October the vast fleet set out under the command of the Sultan of Agadez; it carried corn and cloth from Nigeria to barter for salt, as well as large quantities of fodder for the three-week round trip.

'In the old days the Sultan would go with the caravans as far as Tabelot,' said the chamberlain. 'In the old days it was very dangerous. That's why the Sultan went too, to give his protection. That is not necessary now. Now the caravaneers still come to salute the Sultan before they leave. They buy ropes, mats, *jerbas* (waterskins) in the market here, and they cut the fodder for the camels.'

I explained our purpose: I wanted to cross the Sea of Ténéré to Bilma to meet up with one of the few caravans which still traded salt between Bilma and Nigeria. The Sultan said that there might be a problem. I had arrived late in the season – caravanning begins in October; it was now the turn of the year, and the desert was becoming hotter every day. Nevertheless, he thought we would find a caravan in Bilma if we proceeded swiftly. But to cross the Sea of Ténéré and to film there we needed the permission of the central government in Niamey. So we said goodbye to this extraordinarily distinguished man who had given me a glimpse into the old glory of his people, and made our way south to the capital.

It is a long journey by road, but an ancient Hawker Siddeley 748 made occasional and unpredictable flights between the capital, Agadez and Arlit. We were in luck: it was in service. The plane, which had belonged to the army and was now repainted

Fulani warriors in ceremonial dress in Agadez.

Left: A Tuareg shepherdess in the desert. Traditionally nomadic, both Fulani and Tuareg are increasingly being forced to settle in towns as a result of political and environmental pressure.

in the colours of Air Niger, was surprisingly full, mostly of square-faced Frenchmen who worked in the uranium mines at Arlit. The two stewards stood, hanging with grim smiles to the straps, as the plane lurched its way low across the sand.

Niamey seemed, compared with Agadez, a somewhat desolate town on the banks of the Niger, slack at this season. I saw a few vainglorious ministries built in the seventies, a vast barn of an 'international' hotel, and dusty paved streets in between sandy humps and hollows which housed trees and garbage; food vendors were grilling meat over charcoal braziers and there were wood sellers about – which led me to thoughts of desertification. The loss of trees everywhere is helping the onward march of the desert.

We had to visit several different government offices, and the easiest way was to walk. I thought about how different the procedures were in each of the three French-speaking countries we had travelled through. In Morocco we relied upon sharp fixers; we had hardly set our bags down in our rooms in Fez when we were called by a smooth talker from Casablanca who promised us that for a certain percentage of the costs (a very modest percentage, he promised) he could assure all our permits from all the relevant ministries, and our journey across the Atlas besides. At first we had doubted the need to pay the percentage; our doubts were misplaced.

South of the Atlas, Basha, a less polished clone of the thoroughly modern man from Casa, had picked us up and hustled as hard as he could. In Morocco, where King Hassan controls his Muslim subjects far more skilfully than the Shah of Iran ever managed, and has so far succeeded in running an Islamic state allied to the West, there are no problems that cannot be soothed with a handsome gift.

In Algeria arrangements were different. Telephones did not work. We had to beg many different permissions from many different ministries and they all had to be co-ordinated. The bureaucracy was far more constricting, but it has to be said that in the end the permissions were granted, and with a good deal of charm.

Niger was different again, a country which was much more easy to warm to. Even the customs men at the airport were the least officious we had met, and Niamey was the poorest capital we had yet seen.

In the winding streets, stalls sold at some profit the sort of cheap digital watches which in England are given away with a few gallons of petrol. The influence of the French, evident everywhere we had been, was most obvious here. The larger shops carried cheap French goods, all obviously dumped in this, one of the poorer parts of the former French empire. The only modern shop was a photo-printing emporium which, like everywhere else in Niamey, had a sense of being unfinished. The floor was covered in large cardboard boxes from Korea, and the huge automatic developing machine in the middle of the room bore the legend: 'Challenge to new photography – humanized computer processing'. Upstairs there was a little brocade seat on which people could pose for Polaroid snaps.

At the Treasury, where we had to go to buy stamps for our film permit, there were long lines of people, mostly old, in different head-dresses, waiting with great patience. The Prefecture, the Ministry of Information, the Ministry of the Interior, the Television Station – we visited them all. I was struck by the ease with which it was possible to get to see senior functionaries – and then by the grace with which they received us. (Just imagine a film crew from Niger coming to Britain and managing to see all the officials they needed in just a day or two.) In Niamey everything seemed possible. Everywhere we went we were wished upon our way with the French expression '*Courage!*' And so our run around the dreary, unpainted offices in this apparently listless and impoverished town turned out to be both simple and pleasant.

From our hotel, I called the various United Nations offices in town: I wanted to find out about salt. A charming Italian from UNICEF came to see us; when I worked in Southeast Asia, UNICEF always seemed the best of the international humanitarian organizations. We started the conversation lightly and agreed that Italian women were the best in the world. About Niger, he said the terrible recent years of drought had forced the nomads south out of the Sahara and into the towns where many of them begged. Things were bad in Niger – but nothing like Mali, next door, where nomads were put into a concentration camp at Timbuktu.

Altogether his views, and those of his colleagues who kindly came to talk to me, coincided with my own brief impressions of Niger – that it was a relatively relaxed and liberal country. Relatively. 'Political co-ordination' was the name for the secret police, who were said to be less officious now than they had been. But life was harder and harder. Niger's best years had been in the seventies when uranium prices were high; since then it had all been downhill into debt and drought. Now everything seemed lost. Recently the new President, a reasonable man, had asked the senior United Nations official in Niamey, 'But what hope is there for Niger, *monsieur?*' The UN man smiled back in embarrassment and said nothing.

Another United Nations man, Paolo Bildan – another Italian as it happened – came to our hotel, and we perched upon the lavish leather chairs in the international bar while he talked about our principal interest: salt. He told us that salt was as vital today as it had ever been, and that the United Nations had a salt project. Its aim was to try to persuade the people in the south, around the capital, to use the same techniques to extract salt as the people in the desert used. This meant using brine evaporation rather than boiling – because it is much cheaper in fuel.

Niger needed about 30,000 tons of salt of year. Bilma, where I was headed, produced about 2000 tons. More and more salt was being imported – sea salt from Ghana and France were both becoming cheaper. Moreover, the Belgians had found another site which could produce a large quantity of salt – enough for the uranium mines – by brine evaporation. This was another threat to Bilma and the camel caravans. But most of the salt produced in Bilma was sodium carbonate and was suitable for animals only. Perhaps the market for this would survive the modern techniques of the Belgians, said Paolo Bildan.

There was another dimension to the mines of Bilma. The government of Niger was anxious to keep as many people as possible in the area, partly because it was close to Libya, and so was encouraging the UN to run whatever projects it could devise there. There was an airstrip nearby, which was being upgraded – for geopolitical reasons, I was told. The Americans were doing it. St Exupéry replaced by the CIA.

The oasis dwellers of Bilma, isolated in the central Sahara at the source of the salt trade, carrying water, a more precious commodity even than salt.

Nigerois waiters hovered quietly. One UN man said that he thought in fifty years' time we would look back on these years as the time of ecological disaster. The UN was trying to protect dunes by growing shrubs, but this was like putting a finger in a Dutch dyke. 'Look at the rainfall curve for Zinder in south Niger,' he said. 'Its been falling since the beginning of the century. It still hasn't bottomed out. It's a terrifying thought to project that over the next twenty years. If we did so, we would be making quite different plans.'

We finally managed to get tickets back to Agadez. The night before we left, we walked along the banks of the Niger and found a Russian restaurant. There was a roaring fire set in the garden and Christmas lights on the tree. The owner, Madame Mahinc, looked like an uneven-tempered *concierge* whom one might meet on a December morning in a *boulangerie* in a suburb of Metz, but she smelt of an expensive perfume. She said that she had been born 'by accident' in France but was 'pure Russian'. She had been in Niger for forty years and had had her restaurant for twenty-five of them. Did the staff of the Soviet embassy eat here?' I asked.

'*Eh bien*,' she said. 'In the old days [by which she meant before the Americans became interested in Niger] there used to be a Soviet embassy of about fifty people and the ambassador was "*un grand monsieur*".' His chauffeur was KGB, she said, rolling her eyes and pursing her little red lips. 'We used to drive Russian diplomats back to their lodgings, wait outside with the motor running, just in case of trouble, and then leave after they got in.' Things were less good now. Niger inclined to the West these days: the CIA, not the KGB. The Soviet embassy was nothing and the ambassador was a nobody. '*C'est dommage*.'

We drank several vodkas with her, and she asked fondly about a BBC broadcaster whom she had heard during Second World War. Next day we rumbled through the sky back to Agadez, our permits in our pockets. I was glad. I wanted to dive into the Sea of Ténéré.

Not so easy. When we landed, we discovered an extraordinary change. '*Le Dakar*' had arrived in town.

The Sahara was conquered by the motor car, not by the French army: it was an expedition by Citroën in 1921 which really spelt the end of Tuareg dominance of the sand. This feat is marked every January by a great invasion of the Sahara as thousands of French drivers take their cars and trucks and motorcycles in a race across the sand from Paris to Dakar in Senegal. The route differs each year, but it almost always passes through Agadez – to the obvious delight and enrichment of the townspeople.

Satellite dishes were being fixed on to the mud roof of the Hôtel de l'Aïr, opposite Vittorio's, where the new espresso machine had been installed just in time. Hundreds of Tuaregs had come into town bearing sacks full of Tuareg swords and knives, both flashily new and carefully distressed for those foreigners who preferred antiques, with worked blades and handles and leather scabbards. They also flashed handfuls of earrings and crosses to sell to the invaders. '*Regardez le qualité! Mais non, regardez!*' The travel agencies were renting out their four-wheel-drive cars at vastly inflated rates. Hundreds of mattresses had been made, every house in town had been rented out to the foreigners, and a thousand extra sheep had been slaughtered just outside the walls.

The invaders were clothed in gleaming anoraks; many of them had bought the traditional Tuareg veil or turban, the *chèche*, and had it wrapped around their heads; A French TV crew were all in white fatigues; the reporter wore a képi and his colleagues called him Rommel.

The race was started by an advertising man, Thierry Sabine, in 1978. It was a relatively low-key affair, the sort of outing you were supposed to be able to do in your Deux Chevaux. But it had grown inexorably since then and had become a French obsession second only to the Tour de France. Sabine himself had been killed in a helicopter crash one year and the race was now in the hands of the Organization, which itself was clearly in the hands of marketing men. By the time we saw it, Le Dakar was a vast business monster, sponsored by Coca-Cola and Panasonic, Camel cigarettes and other combines, roaring out of control across the desert. Every year the machines had become more powerful, the day's runs longer and more tiring, and the race more dangerous. By the time it reached Agadez this year a turbo-charged lorry had cartwheeled across the desert, killing at least one of its drivers; several other deaths had been incurred.

The little airport usually takes at most one flight a week. With Le Dakar, it looked more like a fantasy version of Orly. Parked along the sand were thirty-seven planes bearing very different markings: Baltic Airlines, South East Air, Brit Air Ferries, European Air Services, Air Charter, Air Vendée, Dakair Air Méditérranée. The press plane was filled with men and women of letters placing satellite calls to France, charged at great expense on their Organization credit cards, which bore the symbol of a veiled Tuareg head. Computers had taken the place of battered Olivetti typewriters, but some of the journalists wore Tuareg swords. At the finishing line there was a Japanese film crew wearing khaki and what looked like military caps from the Second World War. They were shooting with 35-millimetre cameras, while everyone else was using video. 'They're the only ones who can afford 35-mill for documentaries today,' sighed my director.

The Paris–Dakar had one day of rest in Agadez, during which the merchants made more money than they would for the rest of the year, and then it passed on towards Senegal, via Mali. The town and the airport emptied, and all was as before. I set off towards Bilma in cars from a travel agency owned by the only Tuareg rally driver, a large and delightful man named Mano Dayak. His 4 × 4 car, gloriously decorated with the images of a fat Italian chef bearing pizzas in the parlour which had sponsored Mano, had not got past Agadez; he had overtired the gearbox.

Mano was one of the few Tuaregs who successfully spanned Western and Tuareg society; he had a French wife and spent part of his year in Paris, the rest in Agadez. He was very gloomy about his brethren; he felt that Tuareg society was finished and that they would more and more become bound to a sedentary if not begging existence in the towns.

On the first morning in the desert a young attendant grapples to pull a
camel to its knees in preparation for loading.

Left: At the salines in Bilma, Afanou, leader of the camel caravan,
helps load the pillars of salt, wrapped in straw and sewn into sacking,
on to the camels.

Our approach to the Sea of Ténéré was on tracks through scrub and rock; we were rather disconcerted at one stage to see across the sand the brightly coloured sails of two sandsurfers coming towards us. These contraptions, piloted by two young French people from Le Touquet, were attempting to sail back to Agadez.

A little further on the tracks became fainter and we arrived at length at '*L'Arbre du Ténéré.*' This was a single tree which had marked the edge of the great desert which stretches to Bilma and beyond towards Chad and Libya. I say 'was' because, although it stood in proud isolation, years ago it was run over by a car. The remains of the original tree are now in the National Museum in Niamey, and it has been replaced by an iron tree with battery-powered lamps attached to its top to alert travellers to the fact that they are entering, or leaving, the Sea. The base of the tree was alive with flies and filth deposited by travellers.

I was happy that we had with us in our convoy to Bilma a formidable young American woman called Susan Braatz, who worked for the United Nations there. She was responsible for an afforestation programme, planting trees in the sand around the oasis to try to stem the inexorable advance of the dunes into the town. She had rented a little flat over Vittorio's ice cream parlour in Agadez and frequently made this crossing of the Sea; her Nigerois driver was very skilled at finding the route.

This was not obvious, for now we were in the purest, cleanest desert I had ever seen: for hundreds of miles around the sand stretched in unmarked billows and waves, and there were no tracks to follow. Our drivers picked ways up and down, around and along the dunes, always hoping to keep to well-packed sand but often sinking. The wheels would spin and we would have to dig the sand out, place the sand ladders under them and attempt to rush the car off along the ladders and away.

On and on we went. The dunes ran in ridges, and in the glare of the day it was impossible to tell which might make a good route. They formed corridors which gradually ran towards an apex, which forced us to take a run up on one side. All had different shapes and textures – some were rounded, some sharp, some pyramids; some were smooth, others flecked or pitted or rutted by the wind. The finest time of day to drive was the late afternoon. On one day we were driving along a ridge and saw the dunes below us stretching as far as the eye could see in an infinity of shapes and shades of yellow and shadow in the setting sun.

We camped every evening and cooked rather disgusting English food over a fire made of wood which we carried with us. The nights were cold and bright and we slept under the stars. Waking before dawn was like awaking to the midday sun, for the moon filled the sky with a marvellous silver light which had a strange and unearthly sheen to it.

Eventually, after several days, we arrived at the 'shores' of Bilma. In the distance its cliffs rose out of the sand as out of the sea. There were buoys out in the ocean to mark the channel, there was a lighthouse to guide travellers in, and gulls wheeled overhead. In the old days it was said that one of the cliffs started singing as the caravan, the Azalai, approached. I felt as if I had come to an island after a long sea voyage. It seemed astonishing that we had navigated successfully such a large and unmarked ocean.

In the dusk, we wound through the narrow streets and called upon the *sous-préfêt* to register our arrival. A tall man, he came out on to the steps of his house; he seemed surprised to see us, but courteously asked us in for 'hospitality'. He was a man from the south, from Niamey, and it was clear that he did not enormously enjoy the isolation of Bilma, where he had already spent two years. (The entire family of his predecessor had got lost and perished of thirst in the Sea of Ténéré.)

There were just eighteen hundred people in the oasis, growing dates, working in the *salines*, helping Susan Braatz plant trees, and tending gardens. The people of Bilma are either Kanari, who had always worked the saltmines, or Toubou, who came from Chad. They were both former slaves and nobles; now they worked side by side.

Salt was still the main industry of the town; but there was a danger that the *salines* were being over-exploited. Much more salt was being produced than sold. Indeed, the grey *salines* on the outskirts of town were packed with piles and piles of pillars of salt, each about 3 feet high and shaped like traffic cones. There were simply no longer enough camel caravans to take them away. And that was partly because of drought. Drought meant a scarcity of pasture for the camels; and it also meant the death of a large part of the livestock in the south of Niger and in Nigeria, which diminished the market for the salt. Ten years ago, about eight thousand camels would have left Bilma carrying salt; by 1988 there were only about two thousand.

Remote though it is, Bilma used to be at the centre of a long-standing trading circle – with Libya to the north. But the border with Libya was now closed, and so Bilma was no longer even a distant island on a trade route. The closure of the border in the late seventies, on the grounds that Colonel Gaddafi was aiding rebels against the government of Niger, was a terrible blow to Bilma. Young men from Bilma used to travel across the sands to work in Libya, taking with them henna, pomade, kola, plastic shoes and camels to sell. They would return with their earnings and such goods as blankets, clothes, sugar, petrol and radios. Now there was no through traffic and life in the *salines* was hard and poorly paid, so young people drifted off to Tamanrasset or Niamey.

There was said to be a lot of drinking in Bilma – not much else to do. There was one football game a year, between the school and the military base or the civil servants. The few dances were grim events because hardly anyone danced. Visiting dignitaries were treated to 'cultural evenings' which seemed to cause everyone pain. I could imagine one sort of pain after Susan Braatz took me for a drink in the Oasis Bar, one of Bilma's very few places of entertainment. This was a dark room with a concrete floor, two plastic chairs, one glass, a few ancient mugs and, in a dark corner, six large flagons of wine. 'From France,' said the owner of the Oasis. It was apparently a rosé and was thin, rancid and quite horrifying in taste.

In the *salines* we found, as the Sultan had predicted, a caravan of about thirty camels led by a man named Afanou from the village of Tabelot in the Aïr Mountains. He had half a dozen men and boys with him. They had bought their pillars of salt and wrapped each carefully in straw, and now the bundles were waiting to be piled upon the backs of the camels. Afanou was preparing to set out to sea, across the

The camels complain vociferously while being loaded. Once moving they quietly recede into the vast wastes of the Ténéré Sand Sea.

Pages 240 and 241: First light on the last day with the caravan; we return, leaving them to march to an uncertain future.

Ténéré, towards Agadez and Nigeria. The next day we would leave with them: at last we were with the salt caravans which we had sought since Fez.

On the morning of our departure the camels, well rested and watered in Bilma, were loaded with fodder which had been brought all the way from the Aïr Mountains. Afanou and his companion, Sethi, were dressed all in black and wore plastic flip-flops. Their sons accompanied them. They walked all day and long into the night, never stopping to eat, pausing only to pray, while the camels marched ahead. They covered up to 20 miles through the furnace of the day. As the hours passed, I became mesmerized by the steady swish of the camels' feet, rhythmically sweeping the sand.

Every morning the camels roared loudly in protest at their loads. But when they walked, they affected a certain serenity or at least resignation. In the early morning the sun cast thousand-mile shadows as we walked; the camels were silhouetted against the dunes far away. Then, when the sun went behind a rare cloud, the desert suddenly turned flat.

The dunes, with their curling peaks, looked like the waves in an old Japanese print. As we crossed up and down them, one of the boys kept a constant watch on the ropes of each camel, testing them like the rigging of a ship. If a load slipped, they brought the camel down to its knees so they could refasten it.

Afanou clearly knew the way, for he had made this trip dozens of times before. But I was never able to discover just what combination of instinct, experience and stars enabled him to do it. The day did not end for them when the sun fell swiftly into its gold and crimson bowl. The caravan continued through the cloak of darkness.

As we walked along, I was reminded of a verse from a poem by Paul Valéry. I had been introduced to it as a teenager by my greatest and most long lasting friend, and I have remembered it ever since:

> Ces jours qui te semblent vide,
> Et perdus pour l'Univers,
> Ont des racines avides,
> Qui travaillant les déserts. ★

Every night the camels were brought down to their knees to be unloaded. They roared in gratitude as the packed pillars of salt were removed and stacked on the sand. Then they were given the forage they had carried and sat around munching happily. David Wallace, our director, thought that they looked like gentleman in a London club.

After seeing to the camels, the boys in the caravan began to pound millet for the gruel to be eaten during tomorrow's march. We mixed up in filthy pans our rather nauseating packaged food from London,. The caravan had also brought a goat from Bilma, which travelled in style atop a camel. On the third night it met its end. The body was undressed very carefully from its skin, the front legs sliced open and the skin slid down the torso, so that, unpunctured, it could be fashioned into a waterbag. The meat was boiled and the head was braised on its own on the campfire.

★ The days which seem empty to you/And lost for the Universe/Have ardent roots/Which work through the deserts.

Over dinner we talked of the poverty of the Tuareg, a people to whom the twentieth century has been harsh. They have an extraordinary nobility – and almost nothing else. Afanou made it clear to me that he felt our lives were utterly different – I was a rich man and he was not.

At dawn the next day, the men quietly arose and the camels began to roar again in anticipation. When the bundles were tied we set off once more. In the middle of the Sea of Ténéré they were turning south towards Nigeria, weeks away. We had to go back to Agadez and London, in order to meet deadlines – a ridiculous concept, it seemed at the time.

I was extremely sorry to leave these kind people into whose past I had first tumbled in Fez, so many thousands of miles away across the sand. The pace of my life seemed absurd when contrasted with theirs. I gave Afanou's son my watch when we left; he had no idea how to read it. I watched as they walked rhythmically across the sand; they were over a dune and away with surprising speed. We turned the Japanese car towards Agadez, and were soon stuck in the sand. Clumsily, we left the past walking majestically to its uncertain future.

THE HO CHI MINH TRAIL

Philip Jones Griffiths

The Ho Chi Minh Trail has been described as the greatest feat of military engineering the world has ever seen. It was not a single trail but a series of pathways, dirt roads and river crossings covering an area 500 miles long by over 30 miles wide, leading from North to South Vietnam. The network itself consisted of over 12,000 miles of roadway down which flowed the men and munitions to fight the Americans in the South during the Vietnam War. The mass of tangled routes threaded westward out of three passes in North Vietnam, and continued southwards along the Truong Son mountain range that runs almost the length of the country. And to provide petrol to keep the supply lorries running, a 3000-mile network of pipeline was built.

The Americans became obsessed with stopping supplies getting down the trail, and the amount of bombs poured on it was greater than the total tonnage dropped during the whole of the Second World War! But the more they bombed, the more supplies got through. In the end the trail became the stage where the ingenuity of a nation of rice farmers was pitted against the brightest of the 'Post-Newtonian Mandarins of Technowar'. And the rice farmers won because they were smarter.

During the war the trail was something only seen by pilots with their finger on the bomb-release button. To us correspondents in Saigon it might as well have been on the dark side of the moon – it was an almost mythical place subjected to a daily destruction which none of us witnessed. In a war in which the enemy was rarely seen, it was easy to fantasize about being magically transposed to the trail to photograph from a hideout, with the rumble of the lorries disguising the sound of the camera.

At the main market in Hanoi an old lady sells lilies.

Right: A man hawks feather dusters from his bicycle.

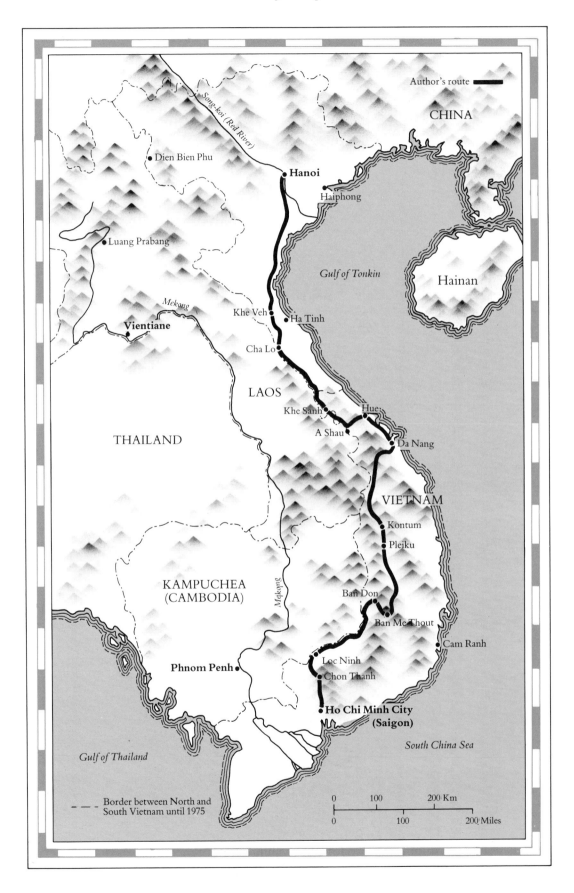

Author's route

CHINA

Song-koi (Red River)

Dien Bien Phu

Hanoi

Haiphong

Gulf of Tonkin

Hainan

Luang Prabang

Mekong

Khe Veh

Ha Tinh

Vientiane

Cha Lo

LAOS

THAILAND

Khe Sanh

Hue

A Shau

Da Nang

VIETNAM

Kontum

Pleiku

KAMPUCHEA
(CAMBODIA)

Mekong

Ban Don

Ban Me Thout

Cam Ranh

Phnom Penh

Loc Ninh

Chon Thanh

**Ho Chi Minh City
(Saigon)**

Gulf of Thailand

South China Sea

— — — Border between North and
South Vietnam until 1975

| 0 | 100 | 200 Km |
| 0 | 100 | 200 Miles |

Then, in the spring of 1968, I got my lucky break. To my consternation, the American general commanding the 1st Armored Cavalry Division became friendly towards me for no apparent reason. He invited me to visit his headquarters at Camp Evans, not far from the demilitarized zone that divided the country, and tipped me off that I should 'Hang around for the Big One!' A few days later I was relieved to hear that we were not invading North Vietnam (I didn't have my passport with me) and delighted to be told we were off to see the Ho Chi Minh Trail.

Operation Delaware, as it was called, had as its goal the destruction of the major terminus and staging area on the trail in the A Shau valley. The general described the valley as the North Vietnamese army's 'Cam Ranh Bay', after the huge American logistical base on the coast. The valley was the place on the trail where munitions and supplies were stockpiled for delivery to the various battle fronts. Its main defence was the weather: located between two monsoon systems, it was often covered with clouds which frustrated the American bombing.

The operation was scheduled to start on 19 April, but cloudy weather prevented our 'airborne assault' taking place until the 25th. The valley was well defended – one-third of our helicopters were hit by ground-fire: I photographed an ammunition-filled cargo plane exploding when it was hit by radar-controlled anti-aircraft guns.

On the ground, the camouflaged trail was easy to see because the surface was covered with bits of metal sheeting taken from an old American runway. I accompanied a platoon of soldiers as they set off down the trail, and after a mile or so we noticed tyre marks turning into the bed of a stream. We followed for 300 yards and discovered the first Chinese lorries ever found in South Vietnam, hidden in a tunnel of trees.

At last the myth became reality. Jubilation set in, and before long the GIs were looking incongruous wearing Russian helmets and waving Chinese AK47 assault rifles which they had found on the back of one of the lorries. We explored what was a rest camp for drivers, with food still warm in a cooking pot – a delicious beef stew. The hilarity subsided when ammunition for sophisticated machine guns not yet seen in the South was uncovered; we all knew we had to leave by helicopter, and here we were examining some of the most advanced anti-aircraft ammunition in the world.

The next few days were spent riding around the valley in the lorries that were easily 'jump-started'. We explored more of the trail, found another five lorries, dug up barrels of petrol and feasted on cans of Hungarian goulash from a cache found in the wall of a bomb crater. The occasional incoming mortar shell could be ignored, since our lorry was well protected with screens of bamboo filled with soil. Night was so cold in the valley I slept in the cab of the lorry. I remember thinking, 'If I must die in Vietnam, this is certainly the most intriguing place to choose.'

And so, twenty-one years later, I set out to return to the Ho Chi Minh Trail.

From the beginning things augured well for the journey. A small point for most travellers, but an important one for a travelling photographer, was being given seat number 1A near the door on the flight from Bangkok to Hanoi. Laden down with

Legacies of a turbulent past abound in Hanoi: a bicyclist in a French-built boulevard sports a beret (left), while children in Lenin Park play in miniature MIG fighters.

camera gear, I always try to sit near the front of the plane to avoid dragging camera bags down the aisle – in this case the very narrow one of an ageing Russian Tupolev jet. As often happens, when I boarded the plane seat 1A was already occupied – this time, not by a mother with a small child but by one of the military giants of the twentieth century, General Vo Nguyen Giap. Here was the man who had defeated the French at the decisive battle of Dien Bien Phu and had gone on to triumph over the most powerful nation on earth, the USA. The experience was not unlike a modern version of finding oneself sharing a stagecoach with Napoleon – except that this general avoided a Waterloo and has played a crucial role in guiding his country from colonialism to independence.

To understand the history of Vietnam and the war that brought about freedom for the country you need some knowledge of the geography of Southeast Asia. As one academic put it, 'Geography, geography, all is geography!' The Vietnamese belong to a rice-growing culture that was first identified in about 500 BC as a Chinese group living in what is now northern Vietnam. Over the next two millennia they worked their way down the fertile plains, with the sea to their left and the mountains to their right. They displaced all before them: the Chams, a Polynesian people who originally inhabited Vietnam, and later on the Cambodians, who lived in the huge expanse of the Mekong Delta in the south. The result of the French occupation of Vietnam in the latter half of the nineteenth century was to freeze the borders of what the French called 'Indo-China' (Vietnam, Laos and Cambodia) in their present positions.

When the Vietnamese revolted against the French colonialists they organized and attacked from the safety of the nearby mountains. Later, the Americans were to discover that what they aptly named the 'triple-canopy' forests that covered the mountains would conceal whole divisions of enemy troops, not merely a few guerrillas – and these troops could swoop down into the lowlands instantly to fight. The supply system that got the soldiers down from the north, armed them and fed them was the Ho Chi Minh Trail, and the man who masterminded the battles was Vo Nguyen Giap.

As the plane landed at Hanoi's Noi Bai Airport the sprightly, seventy-seven-year-old general was greeted by a large welcoming committee. I was met by Madame Tuc, who was to be my guide. She introduced me to the general and explained that I was in Vietnam to go on a journey down the Ho Chi Minh Trail. (She referred to it, as do all Vietnamese, as the Truong Son Trail – after the Truong Son chain of mountains along which it runs.) He welcomed my interest and wished me good luck; this endorsement was to prove invaluable as I sought help along the way.

We cleared customs quickly. Then, as we went off to find the Russian jeep that was to take us on our journey, I was approached by a taxi tout, another 'first' for rapidly changing Vietnam. When I declined his offer he countered with a sneer, 'Why, you have no money?' This was my eighth trip to Vietnam since the end of the war, and each successive visit had revealed the speed at which society is being transformed. Private taxis in the citadel of Marxism would have been unthinkable a few years ago. The Revolutionaries who began the drive for independence from the

French and directed the war against the Americans are now very elderly, and are delegating control to younger men who have more liberal ideas about running the economy. The result is a Vietnamese *glasnost*, with much more freedom in the private sector for business ventures. On my last trip I had met a boat-person now living in New Jersey. He had left Vietnam in a leaky boat in 1985, braving Thai pirates and stormy weather, only to return two years later on an Air France flight to finalize details for the importation of Vietnamese fish products into America.

After the war ended in 1975, the enormous task of reconstructing the devastated country began. After the Second World War America gave generously to the rebuilding of Germany and Japan, but war reparations promised by the American government to Vietnam were not forthcoming. In fact, under pressure from America a virtual trade embargo was imposed with the result that Vietnam has become one of the poorest countries in the world.

Hanoi is the capital of Basic Living. The city itself is built in the French colonial style, with no sign of fresh paint in recent memory. There is little noise – it must be the quietest and least polluted city in Asia. It is also the only capital in the world where women can be found on street corners refilling ballpoint pens with a hypodermic syringe full of ink. Unlike Western shops dedicated to selling things you don't need at prices you can't afford, the market in Hanoi only sells the indispensable at very affordable prices; the annual income in Vietnam is less than £100 a year. Luxury goods are almost non-existent – the most technologically advanced thing I saw was a hand-operated sewing machine. Most things for sale – such as scissors, mirrors, fish hooks and gardening tools – are produced locally. Food is available in abundance, with a section for each type of produce, making comparison shopping easy and therefore keeping prices down. In the poultry department, where only live birds are sold, it was wonderful to see an old man, who could well have been a university professor, choosing a chicken by fondling each one with the practised touch of a diagnostic physician.

With few of the trinkets of modern consumerism to distract them, the people fall back on their own devices. It's a society where if one isn't writing poetry, then one is certainly reading it; and the central bookshop was full of people buying such best-sellers as *The Life of Lenin*. Children play inventive games with home-made toys.

Before setting out on my journey there were places I wanted to visit and people I needed to see. First I paid a visit to Ho Chi Minh's mausoleum, the huge granite structure, modelled after Lenin's tomb in Moscow, built to hold the body of 'Bac Ho' (Uncle Ho) after he died in 1969. While I was there, streams of schoolchildren paid their respects to Uncle Ho, the leader who gave his name to the trail.

Then I went to see the man who had originally set up the trail and who had named it. Seventy-four-year-old General Vo Bam now lives in retirement with his wife in their modest house near the centre of Hanoi. Sweet, rose-flavoured drinks were served as the general showed me a painting depicting the occasion, exactly thirty years earlier, on which President Ho Chi Minh had visited the very room in which we sat. He had come to ask Vo Bam to explore a route through the Truong Son mountains from what was then North Vietnam to South Vietnam.

A guard at the notorious 'Hanoi Hilton', where captured American
pilots were imprisoned.

Left: An old man finishes an ice cream, a rare luxury in Hanoi.

In 1959, five years after the defeat of the French and the signing of the Geneva Accords that temporarily partitioned the country pending the outcome of elections, the country was still divided. The southern half was ruled by Ngo Dinh Diem, who had been installed by the Americans and had shown no interest in holding the promised elections because it was obvious that the great majority of the people would have voted for Ho Chi Minh and reunification of the country. Diem, a Catholic with Manichean leanings, had grown more aloof and dictatorial. He was fanatically anti-Communist and soon implemented a plan to liquidate those who had fought against the French, the Viet Minh; the mobile guillotine was making its grim rounds with increasing frequency. As the arrests, torture and killings increased, the authorities in Hanoi sought for their comrades a means of escape to the safety of the North. So the somewhat startling revelation made by Vo Bam was that the first travellers went north up the trail, not south.

The general travelled 1000 miles to set up the trail. 'We were hungry, thirsty and tired. Insects bit us day and night,' he explained. 'I was chosen because of my experience in mountainous areas. I can carry a great weight on my back. Even the Minorities cannot keep up with me.' (The 'Minorities' is the name given by the Vietnamese to the hill-tribe people who inhabit the Truong Son mountains. They are more commonly known as Montagnards.) 'We had to smoke under a blanket so as not to be seen from the air,' he joked. He had given up smoking ten years earlier, for medical reasons. I found this out when I asked him whether the silver bracelet he wore on his forearm had been given to him by a Montagnard chief. 'No,' he replied. 'It's a Polish magnetic device to ward off hypertension!'

At the Museum of the Revolution the recent history of Vietnam is laid out with graphic clarity – from Ho Chi Minh's Mauser pistol and the dusty trombone played during the independence celebrations in 1945, to the SAM missiles used against the high-flying American bombers. Outside in the misty sunshine a Russian MIG fighter plane sits on a pedestal above the remains of a downed American B52 bomber with its eight engines displayed as proof of its parentage. This computerized flying machine spewed out 1000-pound bombs like confetti all over the trail. A soldier from Hanoi, fighting in the South, was once asked if he feared the bombers. 'Not at all,' he replied, 'but they made my heart beat very quickly.'

Inside, a group of small children was standing before a scale model of the city lying in darkness. The air-raid warning sounded, red lights appeared, and in the beams of searchlights Phantom jets whizzed above on piano wires. In tune to martial music SAM missiles were fired, and a few seconds later the Phantoms, now with red feathers attached, plummeted to the ground to the clash of cymbals. The children danced with glee. Finally the pilots floated down on tiny parachutes.

To familiarize myself further with the original conditions of the trail I visited the army film unit located at 17 Ly Nam De Street, to view archival footage taken during the war. The unit had twenty camera teams that covered the conflict. They and their families were at one stage moved out of the unit's headquarters – not for their safety, but to vacate the premises so that they could be used to house captured American pilots: 17 Ly Nam De Street was better known as the 'Hanoi Hilton'.

Now, the film-makers and their families are back. However, it was only two years ago that a visiting American Congressman, eager to score points at home over the phoney MIA issue (MIA, 'missing in action', nowadays implies that American servicemen are held in captivity by the Vietnamese), leaped out through the window of the main building during a press conference and ran to the residential block. He banged on doors and, when the TV cameras caught up with him, shouted 'Open up! I know you have our boys in there!'

Today, to supplement their income, the staff show videos every night. The day I was there they were showing 'on a 26-inch screen' a Kung Fu movie advertised as 'Made in Hong Kong'. The admission charge was 500 Dong, about seven pence.

Having once practised pharmacy, I have a healthy disrespect for modern medicine. Still, a journey down the tangled trails and unlit tunnels of Vietnam could never be thought of as hazard-free. Malaria is endemic in this part of the world, so a weekly dose of anti-malarial drug was my compromise. I also took the precaution of visiting an old friend, Dr Cuu The, who has never let what he considers my persistent disregard for his principles of good health come between us. His surgery is an open-fronted shop that overlooks the lake in the centre of Hanoi.

The doctor's fame is based equally on the fact that he looks very much like the late Ho Chi Minh, that his wife is young enough to be his grand-daughter, and that his diagnoses are always correct. (One colleague was told, after a brief pulse-taking, 'Your liver is damaged.' He turned to me in complete consternation and said, 'How *can* he know!', then revealed he had just been treated for a month for amoebic dysentery in the London Hospital for Tropical Diseases.) Dr Cuu The's diagnosis of me was by now familiar – body overheating, pulse irregular and breathing too shallow. The prescription? Lemon juice on waking, and fresh fruit three times a day.

My last visit was to the Truong Son army division at their headquarters 10 miles south-west of Hanoi. On the way we passed a funeral procession, led by a band playing traditional brass instruments. The coffin, draped with a red cloth, followed on the back of a huge lorry. The deceased was an old man, and his tearful children followed behind. The clashing, discordant music was not helped by the raucous horn-blowing of drivers held up by the cortège. My guide, Madame Tuc, was pleased with our encounter: 'In Vietnam we say that seeing a funeral at the beginning of a trip brings good luck,' she explained.

At the army camp I was greeted by the commander, Lieutenant General Phan Quang Tiep, a remarkably young-looking sixty-four-year-old veteran of the trail. He quickly gave me a business-like rundown of the facts.

There were three modes of travel. In the early days everyone travelled on foot and wore 'Ho Chi Minh' sandals made from rubber, a raw material always available from worn lorry tyres. This footwear, however, left soldiers susceptible to snakebite and leeches, so everyone carried anti-snakebite serum. Men carried their ration of cooked rice in 'elephant's intestines' – a linen tube hung around the body. Then bicycles came into use. A bicycle can carry 440 pounds of rice, he reminded me, Finally, five thousand lorries supplied by China and Russia, each able to carry up to 6 tons, took up the task.

A man sells snakes for medicinal use on the wide, uncongested streets of Hanoi.

Right: A girl in make-up, still an unusual sight in Hanoi, and a young boy wearing a traditional north Vietnamese hat.

Lieutenant General Tiep enumerated the steps taken by the Americans to stop the flow of men and supplies down the trail. First they tried seeding clouds to try to make rain wash out the roads. This was a failure. Then they tried dropping 'chelating chemicals' designed to make the surface slippery. This also was not a success. Then they tried bouncing searchlights off clouds to light up the night so that they could see to shoot the lorries. But it seems that when there were enough clouds to bounce light the clouds also prevented planes from seeing the illuminated targets. Then the Americans used planes flying overhead with infra-red sensors to detect the heat given off by the lorries. More often than not they mistook for campfires shell-holes filled with rainwater that heated up during the day. The bombing and shelling that resulted in turn produced more 'camp-fires', that resulted in more bombing. During the dry season the Vietnamese heated up anything metallic to mislead the sensors. The Americans tried defoliating the trail to reduce the cover, waiting for the trees to die, then using napalm and white phosphorus bombs to burn what remained. The lorries simply moved at night.

The American lack of success led to the installation of the triumph of American technology, the 'Electronic Battlefield'. This was the way wars were going to be fought in the future, using sensors, lasers and computers. The project was code-named Igloo White and designed by a Pentagon agency, innocuously called the Defense Communications Planning Group, at a cost of $2 billion. 'We've wired the Ho Chi Minh Trail like a pinball machine and we plug it in every night,' said a technician at the time.

Hundreds of thousands of sensors that looked like plants were dropped from planes to detect lorry and troop movements. The sensors, which were battery-powered, had to be replaced regularly at a cost of $800 million a year. Each load of bombs destroyed the sensors in the target area. To fool the acoustic sensors, the Vietnamese used tape-recordings of lorries to make the planes bomb non-existent targets. The seismic sensors to detect lorry movements were apparently never very successful: the 'sniffers' intended to detect humans were easily fooled with leaking bags of buffalo urine hung from trees!

The data from the sensors was relayed by drone aircraft circling the trail to the computer of the Infiltration Surveillance Center based hundreds of miles away at Nakhon Phanom in Thailand (it was the biggest building in Asia). When sensor readings passed a programmed 'threshold' point a target automatically appeared on the technician's television screen, and from then on the operation was like a forerunner of an Atari computer game. The TV screen already had the trail drawn on it, and as the sensors picked up the presence of lorries their position would show up as an illuminated string of lights, called the 'worm', moving slowly across the screen. When it entered a 'box', computerized instructions radioed to bombers and helicopters automatically navigated the planes to their targets and released their bombs; the aircrews were little more than passengers.

At the Center they would listen to the engines of the bombers over a loudspeaker, hear the bombs explode, and watch the lights go out on the screen. Technology must have triumphed! The lorries must have been destroyed! And the sensors? They were replaced the next day. By 1971 the air force was claiming that thirty thousand lorries a year were being destroyed. But there was one problem – the remains of the bombed lorries could not be found. Junior officers came up with an explanation – they had been gobbled up during the night by the Great Jungle Lorry Eater!

I asked Lieutenant General Tiep which of the schemes used to fool the sensors was the most effective. He explained that the American system was set up by Western minds who thought along scientific lines. The Vietnamese, he insisted, were inherently unpredictable. The computers would plot the average speed of a convoy and bomb accordingly, without taking into account some drivers' frequent stops for meals and to repair the overworked lorries. Other drivers would simply drive as fast as possible without a break, which equally confused the computer.

Before leaving the Truong Son division I was shown, with some pride, a strange-looking vehicle that looked a bit like a tank sporting a large hat. It was heavily armoured and contained a generator which powered the 'hat', which turned out to be a huge electro-magnet. It was used to detonate magnetic bombs – these were designed to explode as a lorry passed nearby. The vehicle triggered them 100 yards away, and at this distance the occupants were safe from the blast. A driver admitted he had lost his hearing when some went off much closer, but his main complaint was that after being exposed to the strong magnetic field year after year he had been rendered sterile.

The main lesson I learned from the men at the division was just how inaccessible most of the trail was. It was built deliberately to pass through some of the most rugged terrain in the world. The journey to Nam Bo, as the south is called, originally took six months. Later it was cut down to two, and towards the end of the war it took only a week on a trail with a vastly improved crushed stone surface. But the constant effort needed to keep the trail open (seventy-five thousand men worked on it during the war) ended fifteen years ago. For most of its length nature has taken over and the roadway has disappeared. However, armed with a compass and old US air force topographical maps left over from the bombing days, we set off on our adventure.

Like many before us, we said goodbye to our friends in Hanoi and finally started our journey south. A goodly portion of Vietnamese poetry is taken up with this event – the heartbreaking farewells of wives and husbands and mothers and sons as the menfolk set off on a journey from which many never returned.

We sped along route 1 in our large Russian jeep. Soon the vehicular traffic near Hanoi gave way to bicycles and carts pulled by buffaloes, and quite often by people. A driver in Vietnam is expected to perform a multitude of tasks – one being to drive over sheaves of rice placed on the road by farmers in order to separate the husks, and another being to manoeuvre the wheels over pieces of corrugated iron to flatten them out.

Near the towns the fields contained crops of sweet potatoes, peanuts and vegetables, but after a mile or two the traditional Vietnamese countryside reappeared, awash with paddy fields. As we travelled further south the fields of rice got yellower as the season became more advanced with the increasingly warmer weather. Standing

Preparing a rice paddy for planting outside Hanoi.

Dawn on the Perfume River in Hue, Vietnam's old Imperial capital.

out against the green of the fields were frequent mileage markers, which often gave the distance, not to the next large town, but to a small town hundreds of miles away. I assume this must be an effort to instill some sort of geographical unity up and down the length of the narrow country.

The first major river crossing was at the Phu Ly bridge, which is actually a floating pontoon (of British design). On the river there were many boats propelled by oarsmen lying on their backs and rowing with their feet. I know of no other place in Vietnam where this technique is used.

Further on we passed the Ham Rong bridge, which proved an elusive target to the American air force during the war. It has hills on either side, and these had very effective anti-aircraft guns mounted on them that prevented accurate bombing and resulted in many planes being shot down. It was not until the Americans started using laser-guided bombs that the bridge was destroyed. The lorries then passed over submerged structures that the engineers built about a foot under the surface of the water so that they didn't show up on aerial reconnaissance pictures, as the bombed bridge did, thereby fooling the pilots into thinking the road was cut.

We set off inland from the town of Ha Tinh towards the official start of the trail – the bridge at Khe Veh. The trail had many beginnings, but the one that starts at Khe Veh is the most northerly one. The road led through paddy fields full of bomb craters, many in the straight-line pattern of a B52 'carpet-bombing' raid.

Soon we were in the mountains and I caught sight of my first Montagnard – a member of one of the thirty tribes who inhabit the Truong Son mountains. Entirely different from the Vietnamese, with their own language, dress and manners, they are a delightfully friendly people and their pleasant, trusting demeanour make them an easy target for missionaries hell bent on destroying their culture. At one time the saying was, 'When the missionaries first came they fell on their knees, then on the aborigines.'

The Vietnamese are never really happy growing rice at elevations higher than about 10 feet above sea level, but the population pressure on the limited land of the coastal plain has caused a demographic shift to the highlands. As we ascended the mountain roads the paddy fields grew smaller.

In front of one house a mother sat on a pile of metal pipes, which I recognized as the ones used to build the petrol pipeline which ran along the trail all the way to within 75 miles of Saigon. She explained that they had been collected to bring water from a stream above the village to a new medical dispensary that was being built.

A little further on I noticed the two halves of a 'cluster bomb unit' being used as gateposts for a farmer's house. These horrifying weapons were much used over the trail. The 'mother bomb' was a 6-foot-long canister set to open at a low altitude and spewing out dozens of 'baby bombs'. These had grooves on the outside to make them spin out over a large area with the characteristic noise of a swarm of bees. It was the last sound many people heard, for when the bombs exploded they shot out thousands of steel 'fleshettes', small darts that shredded human bodies.

Khe Veh itself turned out to be a narrow gorge, with the remains of what had once been a substantial bridge over the river that runs through it. Our jeep crossed a ford at the base of one of the remaining stone pillars. I was undoubtedly the first Westerner to look *up* at the remains of the bridge – many looked *down* on them from the cockpits of their bombers. Later, as the road continued higher, we crossed another river near a bridge that had been bombed to smithereens. Sitting nearby in the water were four men with hacksaws, cutting up the metal remains into portable pieces. As I was to discover, collecting scrap metal is a thriving industry along the trail.

At nightfall we reached Y Leng village, where I was welcomed by Mr Ho, the secretary of the district administration and a member of the Khuo tribe that accounts for about two-thirds of the population. The trail ran right through the middle of the village. 'Where the lorry cannot pass we cannot keep our house,' was the saying at the time. Homes had to be torn down and the people relocated to make way for the traffic, which often numbered over a hundred lorries a day. The population of the village hid in caves in the mountains at night (the trail was bombed mostly after dark) and came down to tend their fields during the day. By this means casualties were kept very low – only eleven villagers died during the war. However, Mr Ho told me that the same number had died since the end of the war from unexploded bombs. Six were children, who had been killed the previous year while trying to remove the explosive from a bomb to use it for fishing. Detonated underwater, the explosive stuns fish which can then be easily scooped up from the surface.

He explained that before the war the valley teemed with wildlife – in fact it was dangerous to walk anywhere alone because of the tigers that roamed the hills. 'Ol' Stripey', as tigers were called by all GIs who fought in the mountains of Vietnam, struck fear in American hearts: many stories were told of men who had braved bullets only to be dragged off in their sleep. Up to now few animals have returned, and the forest was strangely silent apart from the sound of one bird with a distinctive call. It sounds – to Vietnamese men, at least – like 'Bat Co Troi Cot', which to their delight means 'Capture a lady and tie her to a pillar.'

Nowadays, to make a living, the villagers go out hunting for scrap metal. At the village store, where we spent the night sleeping in the store room, a man arrived from a nearby town to collect the pieces of bombs and mines that the villagers had stockpiled there since his last trip. As he weighed their harvest I noticed that some of the women had water carriers on their backs made from aluminium flare canisters. These were dropped over the valley by parachute to illuminate the trail, and are particularly valued because they do not rust. The scrap eventually makes its way to a port, from where it is shipped to Japan. There it is made into steel which is in turn exported to America for use by the motor car industry. The Confucian mind delights in the concept of circular connections, and the knowledge that the pilots who dropped bombs over Vietnam could now be driving around in cars made from the very same bombs sustains their philosophy.

As we continued towards Cong Troi (Sky Gate) the road was littered with the remains of perhaps a dozen lorries and bulldozers, and we often found ourselves steering around unexploded bombs that had been left in the middle of the trail. The 'Sky Gate', a rock formation in the shape of an upturned U, was one of those freaks of nature that was famous within Vietnam. The trail went right through it, but in

Top: One of Hue's abandoned temples.

Above: Stone figure in caves near Da Nang.

Left: Gateway to the Imperial Palace in Hue.

1969 the lorries started carrying loads of artillery pieces and missiles that would not fit through its opening. So with great sadness the top was dynamited off to allow them to pass.

We had lunch at the border post at Cha Lo, where this part of the trail crossed over into Laos through the Mu Gia pass. Under the watchful gaze from an alabaster bust of Bac Ho we ate our rice and fish caught from the local river. Above us hung an open parachute that had once belonged to a shot-down American pilot. The Mu Gia, a 'choke-point' on the trail, was the site of some of the heaviest bombing and also one of the heaviest concentrations of anti-aircraft fire. Many Americans died in this remote pass; others were lucky enough to parachute to safety before being taken to the 'Hanoi Hilton'.

Interestingly enough, the longer a pilot remained in captivity, the greater his longevity. Medical tests on pilots released in 1973 revealed a much higher standard of health than those in a control group who had not been captured. They had been on a 'balanced' American diet, whereas their colleagues had been fed the wartime Vietnamese rice and vegetable 'health-farm' diet.

A mile down the trail was what must be the sleepiest border post in the world. Nothing crosses here between Vietnam and Laos. The last vehicle was logged through in 1978 before a typhoon destroyed whatever remained of the road after years of American bombing. The commander confirmed I was the first Westerner to visit the pass since before the war. 'At least by jeep,' he said smilingly. 'I'm not including those who arrived by parachute when we shot their planes down.' I was asked to desist from photographing the guards – but, as it turned out, only until they found their uniforms. This took some time, as they hadn't been worn for many years. Like everyone else, they supplemented their meagre wages by collecting scrap, of which a large pile sat rusting near the crossing – this isolated spot was rarely visited by the roving scrap-collecting lorry.

On the way south to the Sung Sung ferry, the trail passed through a sea of bomb craters; yet it seemed to have been hit hardly at all, and when it comes to bombing roads a miss is as good as a mile. At the only direct hit I saw, the trail skirted around the 5-yard-wide crater which the Vietnamese, with typical ingenuity, had filled with mud and planted with rice. At the ferry I sat in a small thatched-roof café drinking from a coconut. A mother stood holding a fat baby that kept crying. She reached up to the roof and removed a dead leaf and gave it to the baby to chew on; the crying stopped at once.

During the war the lorries were ferried a few miles upstream to the Phong Nha caves where they were protected against the bombs. The caves were a major staging area, where loads were stockpiled and lorries got ready for the next leg of the journey.

As we journeyed south through the 'pan-handle of North Vietnam', as the Americans called it, we were never out of sight of the mountains to our west. Finally we reached the Ben Hai River that runs along the old demarcation line, where the country was divided in 1954 when the French left. The 5-mile-wide buffer zone at the neck of the hourglass-shaped country was only 55 miles long. American technology deemed this a reasonable distance to close off with an 'electronic fence' that was duly built to prevent 'infiltration' from North to South. It was not very successful, mostly because the soldiers went around the end of it in neighbouring Laos.

Today the south-eastern part of the buffer zone is the Doc Mieu State Farm, with many of the agricultural workers supplementing their incomes, as ever, by collecting scrap metal. I talked to one middle-man pushing a cart full of old bomb-casings with his wife and son. He explained that he bought the scrap from the farmers for the equivalent of half a penny per pound and sold it to the man with the lorry for an extra 10 per cent. This yielded a profit equivalent to £15 a year on the average daily haul of 100 pounds – a 'useful' sum of money, he declared. As the Americans dropped the equivalent of half a ton of bombs for every man, woman and child in Vietnam, their extra source of income is assured for generations.

Here, on the south bank of the river, the government has established the Truong Son cemetery dedicated to those who died on the trail. Over ten thousand bodies lie buried in this quiet spot that lies in what was once the world's most militarized demilitarized zone. The graves are arranged according to the home province of the deceased, and each tombstone gives three dates: birth, enrolment in the army and the day killed. I spoke with one father who was making his first visit to the cemetery. Nguyen Van Tuc came to pay tribute to his son, Hung, killed in 1972 at the age of twenty-two. There had been a ceremony to mourn his son in their village, and years later he was sent a map of the cemetery with the location of his son's resting place. 'It could not be sent earlier,' explained Madame Tuc. 'Not until his bones could be sent here to live.' The father placed a bowl of fruit on the grave, lit some incense sticks and wept quietly as the birds sang nearby.

Just south of the Ben Hai River lies road number 9. It runs east to west, crossing over the border to the town of Tchepone in Laos. It had long been the dream of the American commander, General Westmoreland, to push his forces along route 9 over the border, thereby conclusively cutting the trail. In 1971 he got his wish, when Operation Lamson 719 was launched by his successor General Abrams using South Vietnamese troops. By this time the trail was well defended, especially by very effective anti-aircraft guns, and Westmoreland's dream became a nightmare. Half the invading troops were killed or wounded, and many of the others made dramatic retreats into South Vietnam hanging from the underside of fleeing helicopters. Almost a thousand helicopters were lost and it was here, over the trail, that I lost two good friends. Larry Burrows, the British photographer working for *Life* magazine, and Keisaburo Shimamoto, a Japanese photographer on assignment for *Newsweek*, were killed in 1971 when their helicopter crashed in flames after being hit by anti-aircraft fire.

As early as October 1966 Westmoreland had activated the old base at Khe Sanh, just off route 9, as a jumping-off point for the invasion of Laos to cut the trail. He had six thousand American Marines stationed there by the end of 1967, waiting for the go-ahead from President Johnson. In the meantime the Communist troops were planning the Tet Offensive, the attack on the cities in the lowlands, for the end of January 1968. To keep the Marines tucked safely out of their way in Khe Sanh, they

Boat crossing the Perfume River, scene of heavy fighting during the month-long Tet Offensive in 1968.

Left: Coastal fishing village, just south of the old demilitarized zone.

attacked the base. Here, finally, was something Americans understood – something as familiar as Indians circling the covered wagons of the early settlers. Every American television viewer became obsessed with the outcome – would Khe Sanh fall? Suitably distracted, the Americans failed to detect the build-up along the coastal plain that ensured the successful attack on the cities.

It is only fair to point out that this view of events is not shared by the 'new academia' presently busy at work in American universities rewriting the history of the war. Such a task is normally undertaken by the winning side in any conflict, but the Vietnam War is the one exception because its history is being written by the losers. Almost every Vietnamese victory is being reclassified as a defeat, and even those who admit that Vietnam won the war hasten to add that it 'lost the peace'. I suppose Goliath's family got up to the same sort of tricks – Goliath never lost a fight when both sides were equally armed with clubs, and anyway David was the real loser because he sprained his shoulder.

Today, Khe Sanh is a pleasant highland village with the local Montagnard population somewhat outnumbered by new Vietnamese settlers. We made our way to the old base along streets lined with neat houses complete with flowered hedgerows. The runway was still there, but the metal sheeting that covered it had long since been removed: it can be seen in use for miles around as fencing, walls of houses, bridges and the like. Women were still milling around looking for scrap, and considerable digging had taken place in the search for buried metal. My 'find' was a half-used tube of Colgate toothpaste said to contain some miracle ingredient long since forgotten. Nearby some boys showed me the remains of a tank that now sat half buried beneath rows of newly planted trees.

As we continued southwards the trail passed through mountainous country that had seen some of the fiercest fighting of the war. We passed old American firebases named after wives, sweethearts and occasionally the first man to die. LZs (Landing Zones) Anne, Robin, Pedro, Mike, Smith and Suzie had long since returned to virgin forest. The trail basically followed a river near which many Montagnards have built their villages. Rivers were useful during the war – rice and guns, suitably wrapped, could be floated down stream with minimum effort.

During the war the ordinary Vietnamese had great difficulty understanding exactly why America had invaded their country. Never short of a plausible theory, the most popular one was that they had come to try to find the legendary mountain of gold that the French had sought for so long. The evidence was overwhelming – the Americans were strangely attracted to hilltops, and the first thing the soldiers did when they got there was to dig trenches and foxholes – obviously to check for gold. When attacked, they fought furiously to retain their position and quickened the pace of their digging. Today, in the very area where some of the fiercest fighting took place (Hamburger Hill was close by), gold has been found. In the river that winds through the old battle sites groups of people can be seen panning for gold, using contraptions like small Ferris wheels to direct water into the sluicing boxes. They earn about £2 a day – a small fortune by Vietnamese standards.

The River Da Krong runs south to the A Luoi valley, which in turn leads to the A Shau valley, the site of my wartime visit. The trail itself had hardly changed at all in the intervening twenty-one years. A modern tarmac road was built parallel to it in 1974, leaving the trail untouched, and I had no difficulty finding the stream where we found the first lorries of the war. Quynh Tren, the district chief, belonging to the minority Katu tribe, showed us with pride the advances made in the valley. I saw an old Chinese lorry that had been used on the trail now carrying young trees for transplanting. A major reforestation programme was well under way to counter the massive defoliation of the valley – the lunar landscape I saw in 1968 was slowly disappearing. Bits of the old pipeline brought water for irrigation and for fish-breeding ponds. These are plentiful in Vietnam, especially near bridges – thanks to the US air force, whose 1000-pound bombs did the original earth-moving.

For the people of the valley the war was more than just a memory. A few months earlier a man and his wife had lit a fire in the forest to cook their lunch; the heat caused an old bomb to explode, killing them both. 'Actually,' explained Quynh Tren, 'the woman survived long enough to get down to the road, but she'd lost so much blood she didn't make it to the hospital.'

Another macabre souvenir is the genetic time bomb that ticks away all over Vietnam. The Americans defoliated large areas of the countryside under a programme called Operation Ranch Hand – whose motto, naturally enough, was 'Only we can prevent forests!' The most infamous herbicide, Agent Orange, contained dioxin, one of the most toxic substances known to man. Apart from the immediate horrible effects, dioxin causes serious genetic damage that is passed on from generation to generation. Although it may not always be possible to link a specific case to exposure to Agent Orange, the incidence of birth defects in Vietnam is much higher than in any other Asian country. The more extreme examples, such as babies born without brains or with internal organs on the outside of their bodies, usually die shortly after birth. Others may be normal in every way except for a limb malformation, like two knees on a leg or two elbows on an arm.

At the local hospital, lying in the shadow of 'Hamburger Hill', the doctor showed me photographs of malformed children born there since the end of the war. He took me to visit eleven-year-old Quynh Lan, the eldest of five children, living with her family in the valley. Lan's brothers and sisters are normal, but she was born with only one arm; her left arm simply isn't there. Her father was sprayed many times as he worked on the trail, and enough clinical research has been carried out by doctors from Hanoi to establish conclusively the connection with dioxin. The father and daughter seemed close – he was house-bound, as the blast from a bomb had collapsed his lungs.

We left the valley travelling along the old French road number 547 towards Hue. Once again I was the first foreigner to pass this way – the road had only been opened a few days earlier for the first time since the end of the war. Route 547 served as a branch of the trail, and it was through these hills that the troops passed who attacked Hue during the Tet Offensive. The road descended sharply, and before long the humid air of the lowlands enveloped us.

Even before reaching the city there were indications that Hue was somehow

A soldier resting during an exercise on the Ho Chi Minh Trail in the
Central Highlands, an area populated by Montagnard hill people.

Left: Drinking home-brewed alcohol in a Montagnard home and a
Montagnard boy.

special: we passed the ancient tombs of past emperors, some set in acres of neat grassland surrounded by a high wall. Nowhere else in Vietnam are there such buildings, for Hue is the old imperial capital where mandarins lived and emperors ruled. One result is the existence of substantial structures in the city – the centre, the Citadel, is surrounded by miles of massive walls, moats and canals – which made Hue the only defensible town or city in Vietnam. It took the Americans one month to dislodge the defending troops from the city in 1968, and in the process they largely destroyed the one place most revered by all Vietnamese. In their desperation they used napalm, 1000-pound bombs and inaccurate naval gunfire to suppress Viet Cong snipers.

Today, Hue has hidden most of the scars of war, but a programme to repair the war-torn Citadel is way behind schedule, and the only man familiar with the technique of restoring the ornate rooftops is now very old. Students from all over Vietnam come to study at the university, and the number of English speakers is the highest in Vietnam. I asked one, not very seriously, how *glasnost* had affected his life. He replied, 'I think I can safely say we can see a faint light at the end of the tunnel,' and went on to give a lengthy criticism of the government.

Before following the trail southwards into the Central Highlands, we stopped in Da Nang to pick up one of the three men who had been commissioned to set up the trail thirty years before. Colonel Lang had the sort of face that used to strike terror into the hearts of young American soldiers. He was the 'Viet Cong' of their nightmares – thin-lipped, and not an ounce of fat on his body. I asked him some questions, which he ignored until he had finished telling me his life story from beginning to end, with no interruptions allowed. A young 'apparatchik' from the People's Committee Headquarters sat in and chided Madame Tuc for allowing the old man to 'babble on'. She took him to one side and tongue-lashed him into oblivion (I could make out 'We owe our independence to people like Comrade Lang, you ignorant boy!')

The interview was held in the foyer of Da Nang's poshest hotel, and as Colonel Lang was finishing his second Coke ('I got a liking for it during the war,' he confessed) I noticed a crowd of children peering through the plate-glass window. Alas, they were not admiring the National Hero decorated personally by Ho Chi Minh, but ogling a French woman at the bar wearing a low-cut evening dress. Her companion, who could easily have passed for Maurice Chevalier, was entertaining two business-men. Later I asked the doorman who they were. 'They've come from a French gold-mining company. They want to start digging for gold in the mountains. There's gold in the mountains of Vietnam, you know!'

Colonel Lang had been responsible for setting up the section of the trail that passed through the Central Highlands. He had spent most of his life in the area and spoke many of the Montagnard languages, making him the best possible guide for the next part of my journey. We sped through rich, fertile lands planted with everything from rubber trees to pineapples. The main part of the trail followed the border but, as the colonel pointed out, the whole high plateau was criss-crossed with minor trails. Both sides had realized that control of this area was crucial to the winning of the war, and indeed the final offensive that ended the conflict in 1975 had begun there. We visited a number of army units well known to Colonel Lang, and discovered that many of the old techniques used during the war are still taught. The Vietnamese soldier is expected to be self-reliant, to be able to live off the land and to operate indefinitely deep in the forest.

I had not been back to the town of Ban Me Thuot for twenty-two years. In 1967 the Italian priest-cum-coffee planter was playing Mussolini's speeches at full volume on a wind-up gramophone. Nearby, some American missionaries boasted, 'When we first came here these people had no sense of shame. Now, I'm proud to say, I've seen a Montagnard blush!'

When I was here during the war I had heard that men from a Special Forces camp at the village of Ban Don near the Cambodian border were setting off to reconnoitre the trail on elephant-back. This seemed particularly photogenic, so I spent a week with them lumbering around looking for 'Charlie'. The elephants were indeed ideal, as they were practically silent and there seemed a real possibility that we would actually stumble across the enemy – everyone seemed very relieved when we didn't. As all elephants were considered 'Viet Cong' by American pilots, they were liable to be shot on sight. As a precaution the mahouts brought along large American flags, and at the sound of a plane or helicopter the Stars and Stripes was quickly hung around the elephant's posterior, like a giant towel wrapped around a fat and patriotic sunbather suddenly overcome with modesty on some Californian beach.

In the village I found the traditional Montagnard house where I had stayed whilst the elephants were being prepared for the trip. I well remembered the American CIA man who had arrived to donate a sacrificial buffalo to the village to 'promote village anti-Communist unity'. A feast had been prepared in his honour and we all sat around eating from a cauldron of simmering stew. 'Damn fine meat, Phil,' he enthused, and asked his interpreter to ask the village chief what kind of meat we were eating.

The reply came, 'Duck, boss, duck!'

His next spoonful revealed a 5-inch long bone. 'Gee, this is pretty big for a duck, Phil,' he said, sounding worried. He turned to his interpreter, saying, 'Ask the chief again – is he sure this is duck?'

The impatient reply came, 'Sure, boss, sure. Duck! Duck! Bow-wow, bow-wow-wow!'

Seconds later, the field-grade officer – Langley's best – knelt as if in prayer on the riverbank with his fingers down his throat.

Colonel Lang had an excellent rapport with the local people. He confirmed that the villagers were loyal to the Viet Cong side during the war and that many had helped the troops on the trail – at the same time that the Americans were supplying sacrificial buffaloes. One unhappy legacy of the Americans' largesse was the many tin-roofed buildings in the village. They turn homes into ovens, and as soon as it rains the noise drowns out all voices, as indeed happened during an interview in the People's Committee Headquarters.

Ban Don has sadly lost some of its Montagnard flavour because of an influx of

*Saigon, renamed Ho Chi Minh City, has retained some of
its Americanized atmosphere, with Western goods and fashion still
much in evidence.*

Lao, Cambodian and lowland people. Vietnamese has become the *lingua franca* of the village, and I caught sight of many Montagnards wearing their traditional clothing topped off with a Vietnamese conical hat.

The trail continued southwards, weaving in and out of Cambodia, until its official end at the town of Chon Thanh, 45 miles north of Ho Chi Minh City, as Saigon is now called. The petrol pipeline ended near Loc Ninh, the captured town that became the capital of the provisional revolutionary government in 1972. Nearby, buried in the forest and covered with trees, were old petrol tanks that were used to store the fuel that had flowed 1000 miles down the pipeline. Lam Khanh, a member of a Khmer minority tribe living in the area, was my guide. He had helped to set up the trail in the area and had been responsible for looking after the welders sent from Hanoi to construct the tanks. 'We dug the hole first,' he explained. 'The pieces came down on lorries and they were joined together underground.'

We happened to be in Loc Ninh on 19 May, the thirtieth anniversary of the setting up of the trail. A modest celebration was held with a garlanded lorry, a handful of veterans and the village Pioneer Youth Group, who sang patriotic songs while outside lorries thundered past. Some were the same lorries that had been used on the trail, but now they were loaded down with logs for export. The bombed and defoliated trees that gave shelter to the fighting men are being cut down and sold to the Japanese for sorely needed foreign currency. The price is not high, because almost every log contains bits of shrapnel that crack the blades of saw mills; in many parts of Vietnam every tree contains shrapnel.

The Loc Ninh area was the terminus for the trail. Scattered throughout the nearby forest were the sites of supply depots, training camps, hospitals, a radio station and the legendary COSVN (Central Office for South Vietnam), the Liberation Front's military headquarters. Capturing COSVN became an obsession with the American military – they saw it as a Communist Xanadu. Many operations were conducted to capture what was in reality no more than a bunch of thatched huts. During one of them, near Loc Ninh in 1970, an American infantry captain explained to me what he thought was the nature of the prize. 'It's their nerve centre for running the whole war. The air force can't damage it. It's hundreds of feet underground, air-conditioned and protected by 3-foot-thick sliding steel doors!'

The sweeps, the shelling and bombing had minimal success, for it was from this area that the final thrust into Saigon came in 1975. As we left behind the last of the trail and travelled south on route 13 the road improved, and we were soon passing through prosperous villages on our way to Ho Chi Minh City, the former Saigon. At the point where the road intersects route 1, just north of the city, we met our first traffic lights since leaving Hanoi and our first traffic jam. Fourteen years after the tanks that had made the arduous journey down the trail, trundled along the main boulevard and through the gates of the Presidential Palace to end the war, the question that is still asked is, 'To what extent does Ho Chi Minh City remain Saigon?'

During the war the Americans turned most of the countryside into a 'free-fire zone', where anything that moved was annihilated. The population of what was once an agricultural society was herded into urban enclaves where the people were 're-programmed' to become good consumers. As a US embassy official explained at the time, 'To make progress it is necessary to level everything. The inhabitants must go back to zero, lose their traditional culture, for it blocks everything.' The message was, 'Forget about staring at the backside of a buffalo in the ricefield all day and writing all those boring poems. Make money! Service us Americans! Cash in on our wealth! And the light at the end of your tunnel will be a spotlight illuminating a shining brand-new Honda motorcycle!'

In 1975 the bubble burst. The black-marketeers, pimps, prostitutes and the rest of the 'entrepreneurs' who were so abruptly denied their livelihood promptly left Vietnam on old fishing boats for greener pastures abroad. But enough remain to give Ho Chi Minh City some of that raucous flavour of old Saigon.

In the street where I lived during the war the Mimi Bar was still open. I entered, and a girl cautiously sat next to me. I asked her if she'd like a 'Saigon tea', a coloured liquid that GIs bought bar girls at a dollar a shot. This was the link with the past that confirmed I wasn't Russian. The girl relaxed. I explained I was from London. 'Oh! You Anh [British], same same BBC!' She absent-mindedly stroked my arm, felt the hairs, and with tears in her eyes blurted out, 'Oh, you remind me of the good old days!' Her criticism of Communism centred around the observation that 'When we have beer, no ice! When we have ice, no beer!' With great disdain she told me that now the bar had to close at 10 o'clock, as if this contravened some law of nature. I asked her if she was a Communist. She looked at me as if I'd just arrived from Mars. 'You don't know? We *all* VC now!'

Finally, at the end of our journey, with time to contemplate the magnitude of our travels – the awesome terrain, the stoical drivers, the heroic support workers, the lucky survivors with their gripping stories – it was like a rerun of a bad movie to be meeting Wayne, an American, who sought to 'put me right about the trail!' He was visiting Ho Chi Minh City in the hope of getting a timber exporting franchise which would, he hoped, make him 'a very large amount of money'. Although far too young to have served in Vietnam, he was nevertheless a self-proclaimed expert on the war.

'The Ho Chi Minh Trail didn't exist,' he announced. 'It was all made up by the press – the press liked the idea, so it caught on. The trail couldn't have gone through those mountains. They're too steep – no men, let alone trucks, could ever cross them!'

'What about the bombing of the trail?' I asked.

'It was never bombed!' he declared, 'The planes just pretended – they really dropped all their bombs on an uninhabited island off the coast.'

By this time Madame Tuc was having some difficulty in keeping a straight face.

'You've got it all wrong,' he continued. 'All the supplies came from Thailand via a tunnel built through a mountain. I've forgotten its name. It had a four-lane highway running right through the middle of it!'

And then came the familiar refrain, like an echo from the distant past, 'It was protected by 2-foot-thick sliding steel doors!'

Cholon, Ho Chi Minh City's China Town, built along a tributary to the Saigon River.

Right: A man peddles some ducks to market.

Page 282: A naked child walks into grand French-built legal buildings in Ho Chi Minh City.

INDEX

ACKNOWLEDGEMENTS

My most important acknowledgement and thanks must go to Sheila Ableman at BBC Books without whose persistence and vision this book would never have come to fruition. Many thanks also to Linda Blakemore and Martha Caute at BBC Books.

A special thank you is due to David Wallace and Anthony Geffen who first suggested that a photographer should accompany each of the crews and who helped get the project started. I am also extremely grateful to all the directors, PAs, crews and presenters with whom I worked, many of whom went to *considerable* trouble to help me; many thanks especially to David Wallace, Annie Miller, Derek Towers, Alex Branson, Peter Dale and Charlie MacCormack, and to David South for the use of his photograph of Colin Thubron in 'The Silk Road', as well as to all the local fixers, and others, who did so much to assist us while on location.

In Britain my special thanks to Ian Dickens at Olympus Cameras for servicing all my equipment and for the magnificent OM4 Ti which remarkably held up completely unscathed after the battering I gave it on the Great Journeys. Thanks also to Mark Thackara, Christine Gunn and Sunil Patel at Olympus; to Paul Gates at Kodak for his advice and for supplying my Kodachrome 64; and to the staff at The Image Bank in London, New York and Hong Kong.

Lastly a huge thank you to my wife Katie Hickman, who accompanied me on three of the Great Journeys, for her incalculable support and assistance; and also to Beatrice and James Hollond and Christie Gavin.

Sunset behind a solitary Moai on Easter Island.